'An incredible record of the baptism of fire that is parenting a toddler'

DAD.info

'A must-read for all parents'

Projectfather

'Just when you think you've got to grips with raising a baby – along comes a toddler'

MANtenatal

'Terrific tales of tantrums and tyrannical toddlerhood'

(not so) Secret Dads Business

'Brilliantly captures the humour and everyday torment of parenting a toddler'

The Diary of Dad

'Honest, heartfelt & hilarious!'

Mamatoto

'A heartwarming, insightful, witty, and amusing memoir about "dadding"'

Reedsy Discovery

TODDLER INC.

TOM KREFFER

Charlie Cat Books
Kemp House, 160 City Road
London, EC1V 2NX

First published in Great Britain in 2022 by Charlie Cat Books

Copyright © 2022 Tom Kreffer
All rights reserved.
www.tomkreffer.com

Tom Kreffer has asserted his right to be identified as the author of this Work in accordance with the Copyright, Designs and Patents Act 1988.

No parts of this publication may be reproduced, stored in a retrieval system, or transmitted in any form or by any means, electronic, mechanical, photocopying, recording, or otherwise, without the prior written permission of the copyright owner.

This book is sold subject to the condition that it shall not, by way of trade or otherwise, be lent, resold, hired out, or otherwise circulated without the publisher's prior consent in any form of binding or cover other than that in which it is published and without a similar condition including this condition being imposed on the subsequent purchaser. Under no circumstances may any part of this book be photocopied for resale.

Some names and identifying details have been changed to protect the privacy of individuals.

Cover Design and layout by MiblArt
Illustrations and cover artwork by Chandana Wanasekara
© Can Stock Photo Inc. / indomercy
A CIP catalogue record for this book is available from the British Library

ISBN 978-1-7395902-1-5

To Charlene
Together, we made something beautiful

Also by Tom Kreffer

Adventures in Dadding

DEAR DORY: JOURNAL OF A SOON-TO-BE FIRST-TIME DAD

DEAR ARLO: ADVENTURES IN DADDING

TODDLER INC.: THE SEARCH FOR SANITY

Table of Contents

Before we get started 8
Toddler Inc.: Mr Jacobs 10
November. 13
December. 33
January 65
February 101
March. 121
April 153
Toddler Inc.: Half-Year Assessment 179
May 185
June. 219
July 243
August 267
September 303
October. 317
November (again) 335
Toddler Inc.: A Look To The Future. 359
Acknowledgements 361
A Note From The Author 363
About Tom Kreffer 364
Want Free Stuff? 365

Before we get started ...

This is Book Three in the *Adventures in Dadding* series. By now you should all know what to expect, but here's a reminder just in case: I'm not an expert parent – I'm barely a competent one. And even if I claimed to know what I was doing, what works for one child might not work for another. You may not agree with some of my actions or choices. That's fine – you're entitled to your opinions, and I respect that. These memoirs are an invitation for the reader to explore parenthood with me from my point of view as I experience it. I haven't written a *Parenting 101* textbook that's revised and republished each year with the latest dos and don'ts dictated by cutting-edge research and well-funded in-depth studies. Nothing here is written retrospectively save for this introduction, so if it seems like I'm winging it as a dad, making mistakes left, right and centre and generally learning on the job, it's because I am!

I also swear in my books. A lot. If that offends your sensibilities, please regift this copy.

If I thought my parenthood journey thus far had been interesting, it was nothing compared with watching a baby grow and develop into a toddler. Toddlers are remarkable beings transitioning through an emotionally tough stage of life, and as with all the other phases that have come before, including my partner's pregnancy, it's an honour to be involved. To shepherd another human being as he or she discovers the world is a priceless, sacred privilege. And I love every second of it ... OK, perhaps not every second, especially when I'm woken up at 5 a.m. and screamed at, but you get the picture.

Enjoy.

'Enjoy the cute noises, endless naps and minimal movements — toddlers are fucking savages!'

Samantha, a friend from work

(Offering me some advice a few weeks before I became a father)

Toddler Inc.: Mr Jacobs

'The world does not belong to men or to women or to those in power; it belongs to toddlers.'

Mr Jacobs

Mr Jacobs cut an impressive figure for a man in his late fifties. He was over six feet tall with broad, solid shoulders and a head of shiny grey hair cut in military style that shone like misted silver even in a low light. Every day, he shaved using his grandfather's cut-throat razor, polished his jet-black steel-toecap boots and ate for breakfast a whole box of Weetabix – that's the large family pack containing forty-eight of the bastards; not the pitiable, piddling, paltry regular pack containing the meagre sum of twenty-four. Mr Jacobs believed that to start the day any other way was a criminal offence.

For over thirty years he had been running Toddler Inc., and he showed no signs of slowing down. How could he? Not when he boasted such a long list of impressive achievements. That is unless you believe a 100 per cent success rate isn't impressive. No, Mr Jacobs was still the man for the job. And what a job he had: ensuring that every single one of the planet's population of one-year-olds transitioned from baby to toddler and then through the various toddler phases, right up to their third birthday when they would graduate to become preschoolers.

I'm still needed, thought Mr Jacobs.

He was.

His first appointment of the day was with a young man named Arlo. It was Arlo's first birthday, and Mr Jacobs needed to walk him through the plan for the next six months, ensuring Arlo understood exactly what was required of him.

Tap tap.

Arlo, a tall boy for his age, tottered in. He had beautiful sapphire-shaded eyes with a hint of emerald green, along with an unkempt mop of sandy-blond hair that was in desperate need of a trim. Oh, and he wore baby-boy blue glasses that he'd had since he was three months old.

'Ah, Arlo, there you are, my boy. Please come in and take a seat. Would you like some milk?'

'Yeah,' Arlo said.

'Very well, my assistant will bring you a bottle.'

Mr Jacobs relayed the order for milk through his intercom system, and then, from a nearby pile on his desk, pulled a stack of files towards him.

'I won't keep you for long. I know you've got some birthday celebrations to enjoy, and God knows, you've earned them. It's been a tough year for babies with this nasty pandemic business, and it's showing no signs of ending. But pandemic or no pandemic, you're about to become a toddler, and it's important you understand what that entails.'

Mr Jacobs' assistant, Michelle, entered the room, gave Arlo his milk and left without saying a word.

'Now, Arlo, as you know, your parents have developed some pretty sickening feelings of love and affection towards you. I see it all the time. Parents ignore the fact that they haven't slept all year or that they've given up many of life's freedoms, all so they can stay at home and spend ninety-nine per cent of their lives taking pictures of their baby, talking to their baby, talking about their baby, cuddling their baby, staring at their baby or some other bullshit to do with their baby. The remaining one per cent is reserved for parents to think about their baby. Quite remarkable when you consider childcare's gone down the fucking pan. Excuse my language ...'

Arlo nodded, or perhaps he was draining the last dregs of his bottle.

Mr Jacobs continued: 'If only they realised how much of a shock they're in for.'

Arlo put the empty bottle down just as Mr Jacobs placed the file back on his desk. Then Mr Jacobs walked round to Arlo and crouched, so that they were on the same level, and he placed his hand on Arlo's shoulder, like a kindly grandparent who's about to impart the wisest of words.

'Arlo, my lad. You know what you need to do.'

'Yeah.'

'Excellent. Then give Mummy and Daddy hell. Give them unbearable, self-immolating, grief-stricken hell. You want something, scream for it. If Mummy takes longer than a microsecond to fulfil your demands, shout at her. Do the same for Daddy. You see those things that hang either side of your head? They're called ears, and you're only to use them when *you* want, not when *they* want. OK? And finally, make sure you've had your first official tantrum by around the eighteen-month mark. Do you understand?'

'Yeah.'

'In that case, I'll check back in with you later in the year. I wish you the best of luck on the next stage of your journey. It will be tough, but I know you can do it.'

'Ta,' Arlo said. He got up and tottered back towards the exit.

'One more thing, Arlo.'

'Yeah?'

'Happy birthday, young man.'

November

'My daughter is seven months old. I feel like I've got past the worst bit, but every parent I know loves to remind me that babies are easy and that toddlers are ruthless little bastards who will test me in ways I cannot yet fathom.'

Mark J, an old uni mate

Happy First Birthday
Thursday, 19 November 2020

Today is your first birthday. You'll never remember it, but your parents will, and I don't care what anyone else says – that's important. It's a big day for us too. We've completed the first year of parenting and you didn't die! I'll admit it was touch-and-go at times, like that incident where Mummy dropped you out of a trolley and onto your head. Or what about that time when you had an allergic reaction to eggs that resulted in your first ride in an ambulance? I say we sweep those under the rug – along with the regular trips to A & E and the multiple calls to the NHS 111 phone line. If we bury all those near misses and pretend they never happened, then I believe we can go ahead, grab a megaphone, turn the volume dial to max and announce to the world that we're wonderful parents who know exactly what we're doing, right?

OK, maybe not. But do any parents know what they're doing? After a year on the job, I'm almost certain they don't.

For your birthday celebrations, Mummy has caused the living room to undergo a rainbow-themed transformation. If you show no interest in the balloons and the coloured streamers, Mummy will be gutted. Come to think of it, so will I, which is something I never would have expected, but if there's one thing I've learnt about parenting, it is that we surprise ourselves every day about what matters and doesn't matter so far as our children are concerned. Right now, what's important to us is your approval of your birthday decorations.

Your mummy is thirty-six. We've been together for nearly six years, and she is about as phenomenal a parent as you could ever wish for. She's patient, tender and affectionate. The three of us are lying in bed having cuddles while you devour a bottle of milk.

Usually, we affix an eyepatch onto your right eye for a few hours each morning to help rehabilitate your left eye, which suffered a congenital abnormality affecting the cornea. You also wear glasses. The patching treatment is working well, in part because we ensure you *almost* never miss a day of wearing it. However, we've decided today will be one of those rare instances you'll traverse the morning without one. Mummy says it's for you, but I know for a fact it's for her. She wants to take some nice, memorable family pictures and it would seem that colourful eyepatches clash with her artistic vision.

You drain the last drop from your bottle, which means it's now time for the big birthday reveal. I scoop you up in my arms and the three of us shuffle downstairs so that you can pass judgement on Mummy's production design. The first test involves the streamers that hang down the side of the stairs from the first-floor landing – a frozen fruit-juice waterfall. It took Mummy and me ten minutes to arrange them last night, but it takes less than three seconds for you to begin vandalising the display, an action you perform while squealing. We take this to mean that, so far, you approve.

Next, we walk into the living room, and your face lights up like the New York skyline.

Thank God.

There is colour everywhere. It's as if someone decorated a Christmas tree and then stuck a grenade in the middle of it. Your gaze darts from the balloon arch to the loose balloons scattered on the floor to the tassels that hang round the back of your high chair, and then back around to the curtain of coloured streamers that are draped behind us – the ones you've just attacked, maimed and killed.

We got you a climbing … thing. I still don't know what it is exactly, but I'm calling it a climbing gym. It's a rocking horse, a slide, a climbing arch and some other things that Mummy told me, which I've since forgotten. Whatever it is, you approve of it, particularly the slide element. You also approve of the cake. I know this because you sneezed all over it as soon as Mummy presented it to you, and sneezing means you like something, right?

We open more presents. One of them is a wooden train that carries ducks on it. You love the train, but you don't love it when you swing it around and one of the carriages smacks you in the face, welcoming in the first mishap of Year Two – one that is quickly followed by tears. You don't normally favour one parent over the other (which we both love), but if you're hurt or upset, it's usually Mummy you go to.

After the tears stop falling, we return to presents. You get more toys, clothes and lots of books. When opening your cards, I do something I've not done in a long time, and that's hold them upside down to see if any money falls out. It doesn't. *Tight bastards.*

Because of Covid-19, we can't invite anyone over to the house. The UK is midway through its second national lockdown of the year. But there is hope. Two recently developed vaccines show promise, and early results boast an effective protection rate of around 94 per cent. Fingers crossed that it works! I miss our friends, and I miss going to the cinema.

Even though we're in lockdown, we're using a couple of loopholes to our advantage. First, we're going to see Granny Smurf, my mummy, for brunch. We named her Granny Smurf because she *had* Smurf-shaded blue hair. She was devastated to learn later that Smurfs don't have blue hair and that only their skin is blue, so now, almost as a protest, she's revamped her look and gone for grey dreadlocks. She resembles an albino African warlord, and she somehow pulls it off. Despite the wardrobe shake-up, we'll continue to call her Granny Smurf although I for one think the name 'Granny Warlord' is badass.

The reason we can see her legitimately is that she lives alone, and she is your carer for one day a week, so we've been able to form a 'bubble', which means we won't go to prison for taking you over to see her for an hour while we're in a nationwide mandatory lockdown.

For your birthday, Granny Smurf has bought you a height chart and some craft bits, and she has contributed to your climbing gym. As a show of thanks, you retrieve a ball of wool from a nearby basket and unspool it for her. The front room looks like one of those spider diagrams you see in a crime procedural, with red string linking photos of victims to locations. Granny doesn't mind – she loves watching you explore.

Later in the day, we drive up and visit Granny Feeder and Grandad Tools, Mummy's Irish parents who moved to Northampton before she was born. The reason we can

November

see them is, and I don't believe I've told you this before in previous books, that the four of us (Mummy, Daddy, Granny and Grandad) own a modest property company[1]. It's hardly an empire, just a few single lets, but we have some items to discuss and paperwork to sign, so we're having a meeting to talk about said business and sign papers, and obviously we've timed it purposely to coincide with your birthday.

Our business meeting features the tearing of yet more wrapping paper and a lot of smartphone activity. Granny Feeder gets her name from boasting burgeoning food cupboards and from the fact that no guest has ever left her house hungry. Grandad Tools is Grandad Tools because he owns about a billion tools, and he's able to use every single one of them masterfully.

Witnessing your first year come to a close has been difficult for me to endure, particularly yesterday, while we were preparing your birthday decorations. Understand, Arlo, that for me, my dadding adventure has so far been almost note-perfect, and because of that it's passed by in rapid fashion. And I don't like that.

Nonetheless, it has been an unforgettable time watching you arrive into the world and begin your new life and your journey into the unknown, with me and Mummy by your side as we all guide each other one step at a time. It has been, and will always be, the greatest tale I'll ever have the honour of being a part of. But it's a tale I only get to experience once, and the first chapter is at an end. I can't run around and queue up for the ride again, I can't rewind and rewatch it, and I can't attend a weekend matinee to catch a repeat

---

[1] This is true; it's not a fabrication, unlike a lot of Westminster stories – especially those concerning former Prime Minister Boris Johnson and his rationale for attending the now-infamous 2020 Christmas party in Downing Street during lockdown.

performance. There is simply no way for me to relive the adventure.

I guess that makes it all the more sacred.

And anyway, that's not entirely true. I can remember and revisit it by rereading the words that I write to you or by looking at the endless pictures and videos we have that document your development. And I can take moments out of my day to remember the firsts. Like cradling you in my arms, hearing you cry, seeing you smile, listening to you saying 'Daddy' and watching you take your first steps.

Besides, while yesterday was a miserable day for me, today has been very special. And I go to sleep excited about the year ahead. What new tales will we tell, what adventures will we have, and what memories will we build in the next chapter?

I can't wait to see your personality continue on its journey. Your communication and language skills will develop. Your stability on your feet will improve, equipping you with enhanced explorative capabilities. I'm told by people who know about such things that your play and imagination are advanced for your age. You can play a basic form of hide-and-seek that will become more sophisticated as time goes on. I can't wait to see that unfold. Mummy says we should expect this thing called a dirty protest. I have no idea what that could possibly be, Arlo, but I can't wait for the experience.

Last year, I told you to get some rest because you would need it. I dispense the same advice to you now. Get some rest. You have an energy-taxing year of growing, learning and developing ahead of you, but once again, Mummy and Daddy will be here to help guide you, and we will do the best we can.

Happy birthday, my boy. Sleep well.

Know Where Your Bread Is Buttered
Saturday, 21 November 2020

It's bedtime. I've changed your nappy and dressed you in your pyjamas. It's now time to think about selecting a story before we turn the lights out. Mummy enters the room and holds her arms out to you, waiting for you to mirror her action so that you guys can have a cuddle while I choose a book.

But not only do your arms stay where they are, you turn your face away from Mummy and start nestling in the crook of my neck, an action that serves as a big symbolic 'Fuck you, Mum, I want Dad' message to the woman who gave birth to you.

It's great to be wanted, but this is unlike you. Covid-19 has meant I've been working from home all year, so you've seen a lot more of me than you would if I was back in the office, which I believe is why you've yet to settle on a preferred parent.

Is this the start? I don't know.

What I do know is that Mummy has taken this rejection to heart. I can tell.

'Fine, don't come and give me a cuddle then,' Mummy says, pretending to be hurt and upset, but really being hurt and upset.

Quick lesson: grown-ups get upset over this stuff. They might laugh it off on the outside, but on the inside dwells a mirror that reveals the truth.

I need to nip this in the bud, quickly. With deft reflex actions that involve both my left arm and my vocal cords, I snatch *That's Not My Train* from your bookshelf and say, 'Yay. Story time. Who wants a story?' I then sit you down on the floor in front of me while turning to the first page. 'That's not my tr—'

'That's not my mummy, the house is too messy,' says an apparently still upset and pissed-off Matriarch. 'That's not my mummy, my clothes haven't been washed, and my meals haven't been cooked.'

Christ, I didn't realise you'd pissed her off this much. Arlo, mate, we need to chat, man to man.

Are you listening?

You never fuck with the Matriarch. Because the Matriarch does *evvvverything* around the house, for all of its inhabitants. And that includes you and me. If you go ahead and upset her like that, then she'll land herself in bed depressed, refusing any type of company apart from a hoard of empty Kleenex-tissue boxes. She'll think you don't love her any more, and so you and I won't get fed, and we won't have clean clothes.

Understand that your surroundings have been crafted to foster your growth and development, and while I do everything I can to be a good dad to you, I'm only as good at my job as I am because of how much of an asset Mummy is to both of us. She does a lot of the heavy lifting, which enables me to enjoy dadding more. If you go and piss her off, I won't have that, and you'll have to rely on Daddy's cooking, and not only can Daddy not cook, but he especially can't cook and look after you at the same time. Which means you'll be depressed, and I'll be right behind you. Then, the three of us will all be in bed crying, and the only ones who won't be crying will be the shareholders of the Kleenex-tissue company.

Can you see how easy it is to destabilise the established order of our household? Our once-happy family unit is no longer; instead, what we have is waterlogged carpets, evil aromas and … famine. So do me a favour. Even if you think your mother is a grade-one dickhead, which I'm not disputing she is at times, can you find it within yourself to suck it up and hold your fucking arms out to her?

You give me a look that says, 'That's a bit rich, Dad. You piss her off all the time, sometimes just for fun.'

You're right, I do, but the difference between me and you is that she likes you more than me, so she cares more about your actions. Get it?

You seem to have got the message, because after story time, you reach your arms out to Mummy, who's now arrived back on the scene with a pile of clean clothes for you.

'See? Arlo loves his Mummy,' I say. I pull Mummy in close, close enough that she can't see you, so that we're having a lovely family cuddle with you nestled nicely in the middle. I ignore the fact that your arm is still outstretched, because it's not Mummy you want, and it never was: you want another book from your bookshelf.

So Many Toys
Sunday, 22 November 2020

Now that your birthday is over, our house resembles a freshly stocked toyshop. I like looking at your toys because it's as much a reflection of my identity as it is of yours. It also brings back memories of a time when life was simpler (not that I realised it at that age), when my priorities were acquiring toys, watching Disney films (still a priority), staying up late and eating sweets. The memories are soothing, and knowing that it won't be long before you'll begin pursuing similar priorities is nostalgically comforting. I might never be a child again, at least physically, but I can, through your activities, remember snippets from my childhood, and it's enough to trigger a smile.

Come to think of it, I always look back on my life, even my early thirties, and think to myself: *Those were simpler times.* I guess there is a lesson there because, assuming I continue on the current trajectory, I'm likely one day to feel the exact same way about my life now.

Makes you think, doesn't it?

Therapeutic?
Monday, 23 November 2020

It's evening, we've got you down for bed, and it's time to reclaim our living room, which currently resembles a post-fight battlefield, as if all the characters from *Toy Story* have had a run-in with a group of Predators – I'm talking about the badass alien hunter Predators, and not a pack of wolves or any other earthbound carnivores.

The floor is strewn with toys. Many are injured. They should live to fight another day, but only if someone can get to them quickly. I step forward, volunteering my services to resurrect as many of your fallen comrades as I can.

'I think organising his toys is quite therapeutic, don't you?' Mummy says.

No. No, I don't.

There's nothing therapeutic about having to dislocate my shoulder so that I can reach far enough under the sofa to reclaim drool-stained wooden blocks, dented cars and balls that insist on slowly, almost mockingly, shifting away from my fingertips.

Sticking with the sofa, while also returning to the *Toy Story* analogy, the space under ours looks like Sid's bedroom: a forbidding, dusty darkness; its residents banished there by your hand or arriving of their own free will, like asylum seekers, deeming the unilluminated isolation a preferable existence to being eaten, bashed, thrown and stamped on.

Sometimes, once the tidying is done, I sit down with a cup of tea, ready to begin unwinding for the evening, only for a rendition of 'Old MacDonald Had a Farm' to stop me in my tracks. I release a loud and unnaturally long exhalation of air because I know at least eight of your toys are capable of playing 'Old MacDonald Had a Farm', and all of them are buried in your toy box. I now need to go online, quickly qualify for my archaeology degree and begin the process of excavating the pit of toys until I find the one I forgot to switch off.

I complete tonight's clean-up operation and sit down with an unrelaxed posture, just in case I have to get up again. Fortunately, I don't; there's not one single musical note dancing through the airwaves. *And relax.* Except I can't, because Mummy is squirming and fidgeting in her seat, a bit like you do, Arlo, when you have a dirty nappy. 'What's wrong?' I say, even though I know the answer.

'Oh, nothing ... well, almost nothing ... it's just, you see his duck train? Well, you've done a lovely job of putting it together, but you've stacked the flower underneath the leaf, and, well ... it should be the other way round.'

'I'm certain Arlo won't mind, nor will any of our friends, who, if you didn't know, can't come over to the house at the moment because we're in lockdown.'

Mummy says nothing, which means ...

'But ... Arlo's mummy will know,' I continue, 'and that's why you can't relax, isn't it? No matter. I will correct the problem quickly and immediately.'

'Oh no, don't be silly, you've done loads. I'll do it while you sit and drink your tea.'

Do we need to hire a translator for that one, Arlo? No, we don't. What Mummy meant to say is this: 'Don't you dare go near that fucking train set. You'll only fuck it up more. I fed back on the flower stacking, but I've got a list of twenty other areas where you've not done it properly. The train isn't even facing the right way!'

So no, Arlo, tidying your toys away is not therapeutic.

The Life Expectancy Of A Book In A One-Year-Old's Hands And/Or Mouth
Tuesday, 24 November 2020

You're becoming overzealous with how you pull back the flaps on your pop-up books. Poor *Spot the Dog*; only last week it stood proudly on the bookshelf, like a newly qualified Roman centurion, shinier than a rare polished gemstone, the escutcheons on its armour gleaming like golden sunlight. Now it looks like it's had polio and rubella for breakfast and anthrax for lunch. Come dinner time, it has the appearance of a scrunched-up twenty-pound note. We no longer need to say to you, 'I wonder what's in the box?' because the box lid was ripped off yesterday, and we know there are three penguins in there.

Where's Mrs Snail? fares better. Its flaps are made of felt so it can weather more of your heavy-handedness, and *Dear Zoo* is somehow limping along without any tears, despite being creased to fuck.

I don't mind. It's all part of your book journey. So long as you keep your marauding little hands away from my Matthew Reilly collection!

This Year's Parent Worries
Wednesday, 25 November 2020

Last year, my primary focus was on keeping you alive, a priority that you'll be thrilled to learn has made it onto my list of Year Two parenting objectives. But now we've traversed the newborn stage, I have others priorities, ones that are better described as concerns.

The first one is money. It's a big one, and it can be divided into several subcategories that are all linked to not having enough of it. Mummy doesn't work. Well, she does: she looks after you and me, but she doesn't get paid a salary for it. With my income, we have just enough to cover our outgoings, but not a penny more. We have no savings, no personal budget, no family-day-out funds and no other anything-else funds. I've even had to cut down on buying books.

I don't like our family being wholly reliant on one source of income. So many people have taken a whopping financial kick in the nuts because of this blasted virus. Entire businesses have gone under, and many people have lost their jobs. These scenes are a stark reminder that I need to take out an insurance policy for us to ensure household economic stability. For now, my job is secure, but I can't assume that will be the case forever.

So, what have I been doing about it, you may ask. Well, we have our modest family property business that's slowly growing. But it's not large enough for us to take any money from yet. We use the income received to save up for the next investment, and we are looking at years of work to acquire enough properties to start drawing financial support from the business. Also, our family business is – wait for it – family-run, and if funds are needed to support livelihoods, then Granny Feeder and Grandad Tools are at the front of the queue. Grandad Tools is coming to the end of his working life; I am not.

What about books? As I write this, *Dear Dory* has been on sale for a few weeks now, and I'm on track to release the follow-up, *Dear Arlo*[2], at some point next year. Problem solved, right? No. I might now be a published author, but *Dear Dory* isn't exactly flying off the shelves yet. I need to sell thousands

---

2 *Dear Arlo: Adventures in Dadding* (Book Two in the series) is now available from all good bookshops, and it makes a particularly robust coffee coaster. Well, that's true of the print editions at least.

of copies just to break even and make back what I spent on launching it. This will take time, hard work and a lot of luck. I don't have, and have never had, a budget for marketing costs. I'm relying on free PR and word of mouth – a strategy that's working, but at the pace of a one-legged sloth. Additionally, not to mention surprisingly, I'm not getting any responses to all my unsolicited attempts at contacting celebrities to see if they would like to read my witty descriptions of your mother's pregnancy flatulence. Go figure.

Moving away from making money, we come to the opposite topic: spending it. Thanks to Covid-19 and the periods of national lockdown, we've not had to pay for a lot of stuff we would have done otherwise, like baby classes and family days out. But with optimism for a viable vaccine growing with each set of published test results, the world stands a strong chance of reopening its doors next year, which means family adventures are once again up for grabs, and we want to grab 'em – but many of the ones we want aren't free.

Then there are nursery fees. Since your cousin Haylee started going a few months ago, nursery has been transformative. Her vocabulary, social skills and confidence have rocketed. Naturally, I want you to climb aboard the nursery train so you can enjoy those same benefits for yourself. But it's not cheap.

We get government support, but that's not until you turn three (I think), and I don't want to wait that long. I want you to start going as soon as a vaccine programme begins rolling out across the country. My reason for this is that you're not great in groups of more than a few people. You get anxious and upset, and while this is something we've potentially fabricated in our minds, Mummy and I see it as social collateral damage from the lockdown measures that have impacted much of your short life.

Of course, this could be your personality and nothing to do with Covid-19, but we have no way of knowing that, so the narrative we've opted to believe in is that the virus is to blame and that we now have a parental duty to course-correct, nursery attendance being our strategy for doing so. If Daddy can find the pennies.

That wraps up money worries for Year Two. But it's not my only concern. I'm unsure how to approach the next phase of parenthood in general. I joked that our Year One priority was to keep you alive, but that was true. Now you're more aware of your surroundings, we need to pay closer attention to how you're exposed to the world. This morning, for instance: we rarely have the television on, and yet you swiped up the remote from the bed, pointed it towards the TV and started pressing buttons. It's the same with phones: we try not to have our phones out around you, but you have a lot of interaction with them when video-calling other members of the family like Haylee, whom you speak to almost every morning. Well, she speaks; you just babble and say 'car' a lot.

These early signs of intelligence on your part come to make me realise that I don't have a clue about the next stage of your development. I've got nappy changing, feeding, clothing, bath time, cuddling and playing down, but looking back, that was the easy part. How do I prepare for the next stage of psychological development, one that involves nuances that I simply cannot research?

To be continued.

Bowling Ball Or Human Head?
Thursday, 26 November 2020

It's 4.30 a.m., and I'm delighted to report that you're awake. Our go-to blueprint for making you not awake – at least, between the hours of 7 p.m. and 7 a.m. – is to reunite you with your dummy; place Louie, your soft toy chimpanzee (and BFF) in your arms; and then, finally, switch on Ewan, your white-noise-generating sheep.

You doze off a few minutes later, so it's back to bed for me and Mummy. *Yay!*

But now it's 5.15 a.m., and once again, you're awake. As before, we repeat the steps, but this time, they don't work. No idea why, but I'm too tired to conduct an investigation. 'Let's just bring him in with us,' I say, yawning and slurring my words.

This decision is a coin toss. If the coin lands with the heads side facing up, then we're in for one of the most enjoyable experiences that we can have as your parents: you snuggling up to one of us while you drift off to sleep and we have a blissful slumber, followed by cuddles and conversation in bed.

But on the other side of the coin, the darker side, lurks an injunction not to sleep any more, because you won't settle, and you sure as hell won't allow your parents to do so either.

Heads it's bliss, tails it's hell.

And it's too late to back out because the coin has been flipped.

It's rising, rising – at its peak – and now it's falling, falling ...

Mummy gets back into bed with you in her arms. She lies you down in the middle and puts her arm over you just as the coin lands.

What is it, I wonder?

It's tails.

FUCK!

And so it begins.

First, you scratch my face, then you slap my face, then you go back to scratching my face.

I swat your arm away.

A few moments later, you shove your index finger up my right nostril and your middle finger up my left nostril, and your thumb slides into my mouth and clamps the top of my lip against my top teeth. I then receive feedback from both nostrils that your nails need cutting.

I'm not a fucking bowling ball, Arlo!

Mummy comes to my rescue, but her heroics are rewarded with similar treatment.

It gets to 6.30 a.m. We know that none of us are going back to sleep, and so we stop trying.

You stand up. I muster as much energy as I can, and without looking, using only one arm, I release the poppers on your sleeping bag so that it falls away, giving your legs freedom to move.

And what's the first thing you do with that freedom? I'll tell you. You stand on my head, slip, fall, and land with your piss-scented crotch smashing me in the face like I've been shot in the nose by a beanbag gun – one where the ammo has been soaked in ammonia. Of course, you find this all incredibly funny and accompany your fall with some baby giggles.

Head or tails. Some you win, some you lose.

Scandalous!
Saturday, 28 November 2020

Mummy has booked us in to take you to a soft-play park (for when *after* lockdown ends). You've been before and you loved it though, admittedly, it has been a while. But there must be a problem with the booking system, or perhaps they've been hacked. Last time, it cost us £3 for your ticket, but now we're being charged £9.50. The computer informs us this is because you're now one year old. I inform the computer that it can go and digitally fuck itself. A £6.50 increase is a bit steep, isn't it?

Something tells me I had better get comfortable with this type of computer malfunction.

Terrific. More financial worries to add to the list!

Booorrrriiinngggg!
Sunday, 29 November 2020

The Matriarch is overseeing your introduction to the world of thank-you cards – an activity I recall from my childhood with great revulsion. I remember thinking life was cruel, rewarding me with a load of cool presents only for Granny Smurf to drag me away from them to make a bunch of shit cards that were nothing more than lip-service announcements to others that Granny Smurf appeared, at least, to be raising a polite, delightfully beholden son, and not a spoilt, unappreciative little arsehole. I mean, I was thankful for what I got, and that's the point. I wanted to spend time playing with my new toys, not fucking around with glitter and glue. I'd be like, 'Snore off, Mum, you dick!'

Given the current technological landscape, I believed you had escaped such tortures. I figured you could smash out all your thank yous within a few minutes using GIFs and video messages. I mean, who doesn't love a video message from a cute kid? But alas, old traditions die hard, and the Matriarch believes the 'proper' way to say thank you is with a thank-you card.

Don't worry, son. At your age, you have yet to develop the revulsion I had. Today, you've enjoyed the activity, though not as much as Mummy. So for now, it looks like you can live life outside the boredom zone. But mark my words, it will get boring, perhaps when you turn ... shit, I don't know ... shall we say when you're around three? That gives us a couple of years to plan and execute a solution. Fuck it,

I'll do them for you; my handwriting gets mistaken for that of a child all the time.

Segueing from thank-you cards to works of art produced by children, Mummy presented me with 'Arlo's first painting'. Your inaugural contribution to art comprises red and blue handprints that range from 'this looks nothing like a hand, barely a finger' to 'this looks kinda like a hand, if you turn it upside down and shoot some brown into your veins'. But what struck me was how I immediately formed a strong emotional attachment to it. I couldn't believe it. Mummy went to hang it up, and I felt compelled to intervene to stop her from ruining your masterpiece. I said, 'That needs to be laminated first before you start molesting it with White Tack, otherwise you'll damage it!'

A combination of age and becoming a father has meant I've been blindsided by sentimentality in a surprising way. I can't imagine how many works of art you'll return from nursery with that I will value and prize beyond anything else.

Right, I'm heading into town. I need to buy a laminator!

December

'My daughter lets me know she's finished her food by throwing the leftovers up the wall and sometimes on me. At least she's communicating effectively, I guess.'

Matty S, an old uni mate

Light At The End Of The Tunnel
Wednesday, 2 December 2020

A Covid-19 vaccine has been approved. The news is an early Christmas present for the world. Mass distribution will take time, but it's there.

Another early Christmas present is that the second mandatory nationwide lockdown is at an end. The UK has returned to a 'tiered' system, which is the government's attempt to balance reducing the number of Covid-19 cases with allowing life to return to 'normal'. This was enforced before the second lockdown, but it's now being reintroduced, with tighter restrictions. Tier one sees the most relaxed rules, permitting shops to stay open, among other freedoms. Tier three is the most restrictive of the lot (all non-essential shops must close) and is reserved for those areas in the UK where the virus is at its most prevalent. For now, Northampton is in tier two, which allows for some limited flexibility. For example, shops can remain open so long as social distancing is maintained.

I hope this is the beginning of the end.

Don't Be Such A See-You-Next-Tuesday
Thursday, 3 December 2020

Ring ring. It's Mummy.

'Watcha, fat tits, what's up?'

'Some stupid woman took the last family parking space, and I had to park in one of the normal bays, and they're super tight, and I struggled to get Arlo out without scratching the door of the car next to me.'

'That sounds—'

'And then, I see the bitch walking to the lift without any fucking children. I said, "Excuse me. You don't have any children, do you?" She said, "No, I don't. Do you want me to move the car?"'

'Tell me you dropped her with a double thunder-dragon kick.'

'There was no fucking point. I'd already got Arlo out. But she was definitely a massive twat.'

'I don't doubt that for a second.'

Do you know, Arlo, I never realised how precious family car-parking bays are until I had you. Having that extra space to open the door and export the baby, the buggy and the nappy bag can make all the difference between a stressful trip to the shops and a 'nice-to-get-out-of-the-house-and-do-something' trip to the shops.

If by chance you're reading this and you're a non-parent who has broken the sacred rule of parking without children in a family bay, please don't do it again. It's really fucking annoying.

And if you're a parent reading this and you know of any perpetrators, you tell 'em from me, Arlo, and Arlo's mummy – next time, don't be such a cunt.

Snip Snip Cry
Friday, 4 December 2020

We've taken you to the barber's to have your first-ever haircut. The establishment specialises in a particular demographic: children. The seats inside are less seat-like and more in the soft-top sports car range, with plenty of buttons to bash – you know how much you love bashing. They even have seat belts.

Mummy and I strap you in. You're a bit uncertain of your surroundings and, initially, you don't even fancy bashing, but you soon relax and turn your attention to repositioning the wing mirrors. The barber (barberess?), Emma, introduces herself and gets acquainted with her next customer. 'And what's Arlo having done today?' she asks, after we tell her your name.

Mummy and I look at each other, stunned – we don't know.

'Is this his first haircut?' Emma asks.

'It is,' we both say.

Emma stands patiently, waiting for either one of us to attempt to enter some sort of decision matrix, and for us to actually do so before she retires. I look down at my shoes, which means Mummy's in play.

'Er ... well ... we definitely need to lose his mullet ... and then ... tidy up the sides ... and I guess ... maybe take some off the top. Sorry, I'm not used to boy haircuts.'

I wouldn't fare much better; I've had grade four back and sides for as long as I can remember.

Emma smiles and nods, which in turn makes us smile because hopefully it means she's not about to ask us any more questions that we don't know the answers to. You've since become energetically engaged, changing your mind about the position of the wing mirrors, adjusting them often while bashing buttons quicker than a potential gold medallist at the Button-Bashing World Championship.

Emma begins by giving your hair a brush, which you react to with a smile. Next, she reaches for the clippers. 'If he's going to kick off, chances are it will be now when I turn these on.' You don't kick off, but neither do you keep your head still. Instead, you turn from left to right, pursuing the source of this new buzzing disharmony. Mummy distracts you by giving you her keys. 'Look, Arlo, what are these?'

Bingo!

Emma finishes with the clippers and reaches for a spray bottle, an item which serves to distract you from the thing that was distracting you from the previous thing. The bottle is shiny and you want it. You drop the keys and thrust both arms out towards Emma, who, after wetting your hair, turns the spray nozzle off and presents it to you. I think you want to marry Emma; she's instantly become your best pal. You shake the bottle and bash it on the dashboard, before launching it into the footwell of the car for safekeeping. Just make sure it doesn't roll under any of the pedals.

Next, Emma moves in with the scissors. Honestly, watching her work is impressive. She gracefully dances around you, reacting with ease to your every sudden movement, snipping your hair as she sways, in the zone, absorbed in her craft. I take a look at her hands, and I'm surprised there aren't any scars visible. How is she doing this? It's like watching Jedi reflexes. In fact, if I were going to make a film about a Jedi who retired from the order and became a hairdresser, I'd cast Emma as the lead, as the studio would save a fair amount of money from not having to hire a stunt double.

You behave beautifully throughout.

After Emma's finished, she presents us with a grown-up little boy with a 'my first haircut' certificate, and a lock of your hair – something Granny Smurf insisted upon.

Your new grown-up look is, as with all of your milestones, a story of two halves: one is pride in watching you grow and develop; the other is sadness, as you've once again left a stage of your life that you can never return to. And neither can your parents.

As soon as we all get back in the car, Mummy turns to me and starts crying.

A Day In The Life Of Arlo: Mornings
Saturday, 5 December 2020

Yawn.

Morning, world. What have you got in store for me today? No point lying in bed; I might as well get to it. My first order of business is to announce to my handlers that I'm awake. If I get to my feet then I can improve my lung capacity - an important metric because it's imperative I shout as loud as I can. I don't know why, but I've always intuitively known that's the case.

For fuck- Why do my handlers insist on putting me in these stupid sleeping bags? It makes movement very difficult.

Finally, freedom. Now, stand up, grip the bars on the cot, and- Hang on, where's

Louie ...? Oh, here he is. Come on, Louie, come to Papa.

Right, now to alert them. 'Mummy, Daddy, Mummy, Daddy, MUMMY, DADDY!' Why do they take forever long every fucking morning? 'DADDY!'

'All right, buddy. Daddy's on his way.'

Oh-my-God-oh-my-God-oh-my-God, that's totally my daddy's voice. And there he is, my daddy, wearing that big soppy grin on his face. 'Dad, how the heck are you? Did you sleep OK?'

'Good morning, Mr Arlo. Shall Daddy get you out?'

Obviously get me out, you silly bean. What do you think I'm shouting at you for? Honestly, such a dickhead sometimes.

Ah, that's nice. My daddy gives good cuddles. Not as good as Mummy, but still good— Dad, geroff me with those kisses, your stupid stubble hurts my face!

'Shall we change your nappy?'

'WHHHAAAAAA.' Daddy, I don't want that! I've been on my back for twelve hours, I want to roam around and fly, not lie back down on that stupid changing station, which, by the way, is getting too small for me, so you might wanna look into that, you tightwad.

Wait. What's that rustling? I know that sound ... Oh crap, it's those stupid eyepatches.

'Lie still, buddy.'

What, so you can deprive me of 50 per cent of my sight like you do every morning?

'Arrrgh, me hearties.'

For God's sake. I get it, I've got an eyepatch therefore I'm a pirate, and you're doing a pirate impression ... the same one you do every day. Truth be told, you sound more like a frog who's had his throat cut.

'Come on then. Up we get.'

Oh, I love this part. OK, Dad, don't rush this ... that's it ... stop for a second so I can touch the lampshade. Good. Done. Right, now take me to my books so I can touch them as well. Also done.

'Do you want to walk?'

I'd rather not, but if you insist.

I march - all right, stumble - down the hallway, which is totally the size of three football fields, and into my handlers' bedroom.

Wait, where's my mummy? Dad, Mummy needs to be here because she's got the you-know-what. 'Mummy! MUMMY! WHHHAAAAAA!'

'Arlo, calm down. Mummy will be here in a sec, mate.'

Fuck off, Daddy, I will not calm down. I will not have my emotions toyed with in this manner. You know I don't like to be kept waiting for my—

'Arlo.'

Mummy! Yay. What's in your hand? Wait, I can't see what's in your hand because you've got it behind your back. Why is your hand behind your back? And why are you smiling at me like that?

'Is this what you want?'

BOTTLE! Yes, that is exactly what I want. Dad, get out of my way. Wait, Dad, don't get out of my way. Pick me up. 'Daddy, Dad, DADDY!'

'Up you come then.'

Fuck me, you're slower than a stone-dead pig.

'Do you want your botbot?'

Obviously, I want my fucking botbot. Now gimme. Gimme gimme gimme. 'Daddy?'

'Wait one sec, I just need to get comfort—'

'Whhaaaa.'

'For fuck's sake. Here you go, Arlo.'

Yes, milk, glorious milk. Yummy, yummy, yummy.

'I don't understand why you get so impatient.'

Because shut up talking and tilt the bottle up higher. Thank you. Love you.

The Big Slide
Sunday, 6 December 2020

We're at a soft-play adventure park called The Hub, with our NCT[3] parent friends and their kids. We've met for a Secret Santa gift exchange, along with a general catch-up and a play. Current Covid-19 guidelines require us to socially distance, but luckily, we've secured a group of tables together. I've not seen some of the NCT babies since this time last year. They're not even babies any more; they're part way through their transition into toddlers. It's quite a sight, and it's a reminder that there are others on their parenthood journeys.

---

3 NCT stands for National Childbirth Trust. They're a charity – the UK's largest parent charity. I attended NCT classes with Arlo's mother when she was pregnant, and we made friends with other soon-to-be parents. We've maintained those friendships ever since.

Your Secret Santa gift is a pair of *Star Wars* trainers. Mummy rolls her eyes when I display more excitement than you do. Once we're done with presents, it's playtime.

You've not been here in a while, but my God, it's like watching a different small human. Last time, you were curious but timid, nervously shuffling forward a few paces at a time before reaching for Mummy or me to pick you up.

Today, you've come equipped with confidence, and it's incredibly satisfying to observe. You're climbing over walls and up 45-degree ladders. I took you down the small slide on my lap the first time, but when we return to the top, you push past me as if to say, 'Don't worry, Dad. I've got this' – the action a declaration of your intent to take on the slippery obstacle alone.

I'm anxious at first, but it's unwarranted. You approach the slide and peer down before backing up, spinning around and descending feet first and on your tummy – reverse-Superman style.

You are nailing life right now.

Led by your self-assurance, Mummy and I decide to take you into the bigger boys' section. It's a colourful fortress: four storeys of slides, ropes, climbing nets, ball pits and soft objects that swing. The place seems big to me, and I'm an adult. To you, it must seem ginormous.

We approach the entrance. You squeal with delight and approval and then commence your ascent from the ground up, tackling the climb one step at a time, falling back to crawling when it takes your fancy. Mummy and I patrol the route, keeping one eye on you so we can enjoy the experience; the other is reserved for threat-watch, because in a place like this there are a lot of threats. We shield you from stampeding children and obstacles that are too advanced. This is a team pursuit, Arlo, and everyone is having fun – tremendous, unforgettable, joyous, unadulterated fun.

I always knew soft-play adventures would be a significant part of our lives, but I didn't think we'd be tackling the bigger boys' section until you were around the three-year-old mark.

What a bloody great day.

I'm Not Convinced
Monday, 7 December 2020

Here's something that I don't buy into: high job satisfaction among children's TV presenters.

Since you turned one, we've relaxed the no-television rule in the mornings, because ... well, let's just say you're a lot more enthusiastic about starting the day than we are at times, and – incoming judgement from the world – having CBeebies on does help keep the Arlo tempo down to manageable levels. Plus, the theme tune to *Go Jetters* is awesome as shit.

Back to presenters. The new rule has allowed me to spend some quality time with a few of the faces of children's television, and my theory is that they are deeply unhappy individuals.

Right now, for instance, I'm watching two young ladies perform a dance routine. Their moves are so wooden that I could instead be looking at a log cabin in the middle of the forest. After they finish, they look straight into the camera, smiling, and declare: 'That was so much fun.'

Unless 'so much fun' is code for 'kill me now', they're lying. They may have been smiling the whole time, but the sides of their mouths look like they were pinned into place against their wishes. The muscles in their faces are twitching and convulsing, desperate to let gravity reveal the truth, as their eyes silently scream out to be melted with acid.

It's the complete lack of motivation, masked with false enthusiasm, that gives the game away. The two do not hold up under scrutiny. I've seen more believable acting from an adult performer[4] when she says she can't wait for the three generously endowed men to come and enter her behind all at once.

Anyway, what's the next show?

Great! It's that annoying prick *Bing*.

I Did Not Consent
Tuesday, 8 December 2020

It's morning. I've showered, and now I'm towelling myself in our bedroom while thinking about my day. I finish drying my torso, reposition the towel and start working on my back, leaving the front of my dad bod exposed.

You're nearby, performing your usual routine of destroying everything in sight. The next thing you've targeted to smash is the blinds. You've begun tottering towards them with violent purpose in your eyes.

As you walk past me, you allow yourself to be momentarily distracted from vandalism as you look up, and, before I know it, grab my willy and give it a yank.

Mummy is on the floor howling with laughter.

I'm in shock, and trying to process the fact that my one-year-old son has violated me. Please don't ever do that again, Arlo. Only Mummy and I are allowed to fool around in that area.

Fuck knows where I stand from a legal viewpoint. Can you imagine the conversation? 'So, you're saying you were minding your own business when your one-year-old son sexually assaulted you?' says the judge.

Never – I repeat, NEVER – did I ever foresee this scenario when Mummy was pregnant with you. But alas, once again, parenthood is here to educate me.

---

[4] I want it on record that any references I make to viewing adult performers concern events that took place before I met Arlo's mother.

I'm going to make the assumption that this sort of thing must happen a lot. I bet mummies get their tits slapped, and daddies' balls no doubt get similar treatment. Unless, as in my case, the daddies get a single non-consensual yank to the penis.

Bedtime
Wednesday, 9 December 2020

It's no secret that you've traditionally been a good sleeper, going down for bed without any fuss or furore. Sadly, that's no longer the case. Let me give you the rundown of what a typical bedtime routine looks like at the moment.

At 6 p.m. you're handed your bedtime bottle. You like me to give you the first half, before signalling with a shove that you want to go and see Mummy for the second half. So far so good.

Then, I carry you upstairs to the bathroom to clean your teeth. My priority is scrubbing the six teeth that have cut through. I also like to try and get in a quick, glancing scrub of your gums. This is not without difficulty, though, because you like to mount an offensive, sucking the toothpaste off the brush before I've had a chance to begin, and then clamping both your jaws together, preventing any and all movement of the toothbrush. I often have to call Mummy in for support. She performs a silly dance that makes you laugh, which in turn loosens your jaws so that my job moves from impossible to a more tepid classification in the still-hard-but-not-impossible category.

Next, we change your nappy, enfold you in your sleeping bag and read you a story. We lay you down in your cot, switch Ewan the sheep on and ensure Louie is by your side. Finally, we say goodnight and leave the room.

And then the fun begins.

And by fun, I mean you stirring up some mischief that seeks to delay us from winding down for the evening.

The confines of your sleeping bag limit movement but do not prevent it. And so, you slowly shuffle to the bottom of your cot, stand up and begin shaking it like a wrongly imprisoned man who's desperate to protest his innocence to a merciless justice system. Your camera is attached to your cot, so it experiences the full effects of your shuddering. Watching this on the monitor reminds me of an earthquake captured on CCTV.

Mummy and I ignore this behaviour.

Thud.

That noise confirms that Louie has been launched unceremoniously overboard – a victim of a one-year-old's campaign to capture the attention of his parents.

Again, we ignore this.

But you still have one last card to play, and so you spit your dummy out, and then you begin crying. Actually, it's more like screaming.

It's usually at this point that I resign myself to going upstairs.

As soon as I enter your room, you smile. Your cot continues trembling, but this time, it's due not to frustration on your part but to excitement, because you assume I've come to get you out to play.

I haven't.

I don't say a word, and I don't make eye contact. Instead, I search for your dummy. But of course I can't find it, because your dummies seem to be imbued with the same stuff they made flubber out of, and it somehow always ends up hidden *under* something, like your cot. Even Captain America's shield doesn't mock physics that far.

Once it's eventually located, I stuff it back in your mouth, lay you down, reunite you with Louie, who, it should be said, is a rather forgiving primate, and then I leave. The cycle comes to an end.

How long until it resets? Sometimes it's minutes; often it's seconds. All I know is that I can't remember the last time you abandoned these bedtime theatrics altogether.

How Fucking Dare She?
Friday, 11 December 2020

'Yes!' exclaims Mummy, fist-pumping the air.

'I know, I know – a new episode of *The Mandalorian* is out. We can watch it together,' I say. It's nice to finally see Mummy coming around to accepting how special and important *Star Wars* is.

'I don't give a shit about stupid *Star Wars*.'

'Oh ...'

'I'm excited because I've finally got it working.'

I suppose I should bite. 'What have you got working?'

'I've linked his baby-monitor sensor to your phone app. This means your phone will automatically go on when he stirs.'

'Err ... yay?'

'Right! It's a massive win, baby. Now, we won't have to manually open the app when we want to check on him.'

Mummy must use a different dictionary than I do, Arlo. If I look up 'linking the baby sensor to my phone' in my copy, I don't find 'massive win' in the definition. I find 'that's a stupid thing to do. Reverse the action immediately.'

We don't need an electronic sensor to alert us to you being awake. We've got our trusty biological ones. They're called ears!

Also, *STAR WARS* ISN'T STUPID!

Mealtime Dejection
Sunday, 13 December 2020

It's frustrating when you refuse to eat a meal that you've had countless times before. Especially when you select and coordinate different methods of rejecting said meal, so that my levels of frustration compound and amplify themselves.

Let me explain.

It starts with you allowing me to insert a spoonful of food into your mouth. You begin chewing, but then you stop chewing and spit it out. Next, you up the ante by not even opening your mouth. You keep your lips locked while I unsuccessfully attempt to tease open an entry point. Naturally, you maintain eye contact with me the whole time. You don't even blink.

I try again, but inspiration takes you, and you swing an arm, knocking the spoon away from your face and splashing its contents into my right eye. You follow this with a glare, one that says, 'Dad, *you* fucking eat it if it's "num-nums".'

Before I can rethink my strategy, you turn your body through 180 degrees like you're some sort of owl, refusing to acknowledge my existence until I present you with a more appetising dish.

I cave.

I stomp to the kitchen and return presently as a beaten man, but one with a banana. Your body language transforms: you're no longer an owl with locked lips – or a beak – and you're finally eager to receive sustenance. I peel the banana and give it to you to hold.

But alas …

Your behaviour once again Optimus Primes it, and I watch you purposely drop your banana on the floor not once, not twice but three times. I'm now refusing to let you hold it. Instead, I feed you one piece at a time, except of course I can't, because you're an owl again, and I'm trying to feed the back of your head!

Transitioning
Monday, 14 December 2020

In case it's not clear that you've transitioned into a toddler, from the last twenty-four hours alone, I can report the following: I caught you placing the Sky remote in the freezer; you launched your bath sponge into the toilet and then kicked off when I wouldn't let you get it back out again; you climbed an entire flight of stairs without any supervision (Mummy's back was turned for a few moments and I was downstairs working); and every time we've said the word 'no', you've laughed, and then done the thing that we've told you not to do. Yesterday, you barged past me to get to the freezer, opened it up, helped yourself to an ice lolly, shut the door and then barged back past me while going to town on said ice lolly. Does any of that seem like the behaviour of a baby? Also, we have a couple of extra decorations on the Christmas tree: two size-4G Mickey Mouse shoes. You put them there.

And What Would Arlo Like For Christmas?
Friday, 18 December 2020

With the UK still observing a tiered-system approach to combatting Covid-19, it was touch-and-go whether a trip to see Santa was on the cards at all this year.

Northampton remains in tier two, but there was a review yesterday and there were rumours of us moving into tier three. This would have meant the North Pole becoming off limits to humans.

Fortunately, we've remained in tier two, which means … Santa baby, here we come!

I've been preparing you all week for this moment. Grandad Tools bought you a Santa figure that is almost as tall as you are. We've had it on display since our Christmas tree was erected. You're obsessed with it. If I say to you, 'Arlo, where's Santa?' you totter straight over and grab it. You can say 'Santa' as well. Side note: a one-year-old saying Santa is adorable.

We arrive at the North Pole, which is actually our favourite soft-play park, The Hub. The owners have gone all out on set-dressing it for Christmas. It looks spectacular. We've been given a particular time slot, and when it arrives, we make our way to the part of the building that's temporarily housing Santa's grotto.

We enter.

SANTA!

You can't sit on Santa's knee, because we still have to socially distance, but the organisers have adapted well. There's a short wall that's made out of presents, positioned two metres in front of where the famous toymaker is sitting.

'And whom do we have here?' Santa warmly enquires.

I make the introductions.

'And what would Arlo like for Christmas?'

I answer on your behalf. 'For Christmas, Santa, Arlo would like anything to do with *Star Wars.*'

'*Star Wars*? What an excellent choice. I'll speak with my elves, and we'll see what can be done about it. How does that sound?'

Sounds delightful. Isn't Santa the best, Arlo?

Next, it's time for our photo. We sit facing forward on the makeshift wall of presents, ready for the photographer to capture our second family photo with Santa in the background.

'Ready, three, two—'

'Whhaaaa.'

Oh no.

'Arlo, it's OK. Mummy and Daddy are here. Shhh, shhh, shhh. There, there,' Mummy whispers, her voice laced with desperation.

'WHHHAAAAAA! WHHHAAAAAA!'
Even Santa tries. 'Oh dear, Arlo, why don't—'
'WHHHAAAAAA!'
And so it continues. The photographer does the best he can, but you have decided you are not a fan of the North Pole today. We have no choice but to leave.

The most clichéd family photo ever is a Christmas snapshot where one member of the family is utterly distraught.

We now have that photo, Arlo.

December Monthly Review
Saturday, 19 December 2020

I'll tell you something great about the second year of parenthood. There's none of this 'How many weeks old is your baby?' crap. This year, you're either one, just over one, one and a half, almost two, or two. You're not three days old, two weeks old, nine months old, or even nine months, two weeks, three days, four hours and twenty-seven minutes old. We can reduce the number of age categories from a thousand to five. I will, however, continue with your monthly reviews, as they're as good a time as any to report on your latest developments. As usual, there's a lot to cover[5].

---

5 Test readers fed back that Arlo was perhaps quite advanced in several areas of his development. Truthfully, I had no idea at the time of writing *Toddler Inc*. I only have one child and I never really knew if he was behind, on track or ahead. Of course, I looked stuff up online, and Arlo's mother is very knowledgeable. But one can't escape the fact that all of us are individuals journeying through life in different directions and figuring it out at varying tempos. The moral of the story is this: don't get hung up on reading these monthly development chapters and worry that your child isn't doing what others are. You will, of course, because you're a parent, but at least I can say I've done my bit to dissuade you.

Yesterday, you stood up from a seated position without the aid of anything animate or inanimate; it was core strength all the way, baby! You performed this several times, so it's definitely a case of 'skill acquired'. Your footsteps, once shaky and unsure of themselves, are now stable and confident.

I mentioned the other day that you can now say 'Santa'. But you can also say 'buh-bye', 'finish', 'chair' and 'baba' – your cousin Haylee calls you Baba Arlo. But even the addition of new words to your vocabulary fails to illustrate how far your language has come on. You attempt to copy everything we say. Speech was the one aspect of child development that I was most curious about. I could wrap my head around a baby learning to sit up, crawl and walk, but learning to say words, words that they understand the meaning of? I could never picture it. Until now.

Another word you can say is 'tea'. Every morning, you take your dummy out of your mouth, hold it up to Mummy and say 'Tea'. Mummy then takes your dummy, dunks it in her mug and hands it back to you for consumption.

You understand more commands. You understand that 'Arlo do it' means 'copy me'. And you understand what to do when we say 'shut the drawer'. Actually, you believe 'shut the drawer' means shut it, then open it, then pull all the contents out and set-dress the kitchen floor with them. We can say 'come here', 'bedtime', 'other arm', 'shall we put your shoes on' and many more.

My favourite new command is, 'Arlo, can you put your glasses on, please?' Admittedly, you've not mastered putting them on, and one of us has to be nearby to stop any punctured-eyeball injuries, but you're almost there. It's incredible.

Playtime keeps getting better and better. You hide in the utility room, pulling the sliding door shut, while Mummy and I 'look' for you. After a few seconds pass, you slide the door open again, 'surprising' us with a mighty reveal, followed by laughter and clapping. You hide objects and then shrug both shoulders as if to say, 'Where is it?' before performing a similar reveal.

Playtime, to me, is such a special and sacred thing. I remember watching *Monsters, Inc.*, thinking it was a clever little twist to capture the sound of children laughing, instead of screaming, to power the city. I guarantee the writers of that film were all parents, and I now understand the metaphor in a whole other light. When I hear your laughter, my body is saturated with a serotonin-like substance, repelling any negative thoughts and generally making me feel wonderful. And alive.

There's still a lot of waking in the night. And sometimes it's difficult to settle you back down. If it's after 4 a.m., and it's me that gets to you first, I'll almost certainly return to bed with you in my arms, knowing I risk *the coin* landing unfavourably.

Covid-19 is still a huge factor in our lives. The UK has begun to roll out the vaccine, but a mutated strain of the virus has caused the rate of infections to rocket. It was announced that the social-distancing rules would be relaxed over Christmas for a five-day period. That's no longer the case. We can now only see family on Christmas Day.

It's shit, but it could be shitter. As far as we know, none of us have caught the virus, and I can still work. Christmas is a time of celebration, but many experience loneliness. Not us, though.

On the subject of Christmas and gratitude, did I tell you Mummy found a *Street Fighter* Christmas jumper in a charity job the other day? Don't get jealous. You've got a *Spider-Man* one.

We're now well into our Year-Two journey, and I remain, as ever, smitten by you and everything you do.

My Next Book
Sunday, 20 December 2020

Mummy has suggested the title of my next book. She thinks I should call it *Journal of a Single Dad*. She says that I should describe the pick-up and drop-off arrangements, how paying maintenance works and what it's like for a dad to go to court to fight a custody battle. I can't remember what I did to piss her off prior to this conversation, but I assume I did piss her off. Come to think of it, this isn't the first time she's encouraged me to write *Journal of a Single Dad* ...

Controlled Crying, Part 1
Monday, 21 December 2020

Bedtime dramas continue, so we've decided to take action. Effective immediately, neither Mummy nor I will react to any efforts you summon up to seize our attention once we've said goodnight. Our rationale for the rule-book shake-up is that it's not fair to keep going into your room, because it encourages you to associate that behaviour (us coming in) with the performance of a particular action or set of actions on your part, like throwing Louie on the floor and spitting your dummy out and crying.

There's a term for what we're doing: it's called controlled crying. The approach is to let you cry it out until you realise that no one is coming. Hopefully, you'll then lie down and put yourself back to bed. By trialling this method, we accept that we're in for a couple of rough nights while we allow for an embedding period as we install this new change.

We're not forcing you to go cold turkey, though. Once you start crying, we'll set a timer for two minutes. If you're still crying at the end of that period, one of us will go in, hand Louie and your dummy to you, lie you back down and leave – all without talking or making eye contact.

Let's see how we do.

'Whhaaaa.'

Let the countdown begin.

2:00, 1:59, 1:58 …

The mechanics of time have aways fascinated me, more so since you were born. How is it that when you're happy and playful, minutes can dissolve into what feels like seconds? But when you're not happy, like right now, seconds feel like minutes: slow, agonising minutes that drag their feet with the weight of a cargo ship's freight stacked perilously on their shoulders.

'Whhaaaa.'

… 0:58, 0:57, 0:56 …

This is excruciating.

You've always been such a breezy and upbeat little boy, and it upsets me when I hear you cry. It's that quivering bottom lip of yours, it kills me. That, combined with the softer pitch of your cry and the rarity of it happening, means my default move is to want to comfort you, though I'm sure that will be tested when you're lying on the floor of a public place, kicking off because I won't buy you a toy. The bottom lip might not cut it then.

But we're not there yet.

'Whhaaaa.'

… 0:03, 0:02, 0:01, 0:00.

Mummy enters your room to carry out the agreed routine and then leaves.

A few minutes later … 'Whhaaaa.'

Once again: 2:00, 1:59, 1:58 …

I'm sorry, buddy, but some tough love is needed.

Controlled Crying, Part 2
Tuesday, 22 December 2020

It's evening again. Mummy has gone food shopping, leaving me to brave night two of controlled crying. The good news is that we made progress last night, so I am going to increase the countdown from two minutes to five.

'Whhhaaaaaa.'

You know the drill.

5:00, 4:59, 4:58 …

We barely get past the four-minute mark when the most remarkable thing happens.

'Whhaa—'

The crying stops. I check the monitor. You're lying down, without a dummy and without Louie. *What the fuck?* You *never* go to sleep without them.

A few minutes later, the crying starts back up. I check the monitor again and this time, you're in your default position, standing at the foot of the cot shaking it. I start the timer again, but the same thing happens. About a minute in, you stop crying and lie back down. And now you're asleep.

What? How? Why? Are you OK? Surely this hasn't worked already!

Controlled Crying, Part 3
Wednesday, 23 December 2020

Tonight, you went to bed without complaint. The countdown timer wasn't required, and for once, Louie and your dummy remained by your side – you didn't send them overboard.

Wow!

Super-fucking-proud-dad moment right here.

Santa Was Hungry (And Thirsty); Rudolph Wasn't
Thursday, 24 December 2020

Like last year, I couldn't help but indulge myself and leave a Baileys and a few mince pies out for Santa and a carrot for Rudolph. And, once again, Santa drank the Baileys and ate the mince pies, but Rudolph didn't touch the carrot. I'm not surprised. It was the most wretched, sorry carrot you could ever lay eyes upon – a mouldy, spray-tan-gone-wrong witch's nose that had every strain of every existing sexually transmitted disease known to man[6]. It also had white patches of I-don't-know-what, a couple of orangey-yellow hairlike growths and a collection of foul-smelling, brown-tinged, moisture-laden crevices. It was gnarled, crooked and withered – its best carrot years out of sight in every direction other than in the rear-view mirror.

In short, it didn't look very appetising. No wonder Rudolph avoided it.

Merry Christmas
Friday, 25 December 2020

The alarm goes off at 6 a.m. It's the actual alarm, not the Arlo-talking-or-screaming alarm. 'Merry Christmas, baby!' shriek-whispers Mummy. 'Come-on-we-need-to-get-up. No. Wait. Let-me-ring-Lisa-and-make-sure-they're-up. And-then-I'll-call-and-wake-up-Mrs-Claus-and-then-we'll-wake-Arlo-up-get-in-the-car-and-leave. Oh-my-God-there's-so-much-to-do. Yikes-I-can't-believe-it's-Christmas. Merry-Christmas!'

I haven't even turned the alarm off yet. By the way, in case it isn't obvious, Mrs Claus is Granny Feeder (for the day, at least).

---

[6] I received this comment back from my editor: 'Good God, man, what were you doing with the carrot for this to happen?'

'How long have you been up?'

'Oh my God, so, I woke up at twelve thirty, then two thirty, and I've been up since twenty past five waiting for your stupid alarm to go off. But I didn't wake you up, which means I was a good girl, right?'

'Right.'

'Eeek. Merry Christmas!'

And they say Christmas is only for children.

You're naturally jubilant at being woken up, snatched from your cot and then flung into your car seat. All in under thirty seconds. Sorry, bud, you know what Christmas does to your mother, and I have no say in today's proceedings or, apparently, the timetable.

We park up at Mrs Claus and Grandad Tools' house. Mummy bounds through the front door like a dog returning to its owner with its favourite saliva-coated ball. Auntie Lisa, Uncle Matt and Haylee arrive a few minutes later, ready for Mrs Claus to reveal the presents under the tree.

Ta-da ...

My God! I thought last year was insane. I believe I described the scene as an 'ocean of colour'. This year, it's like looking at a multicoloured mountain range: bright, neatly wrapped peaks jut out, competing for our attention, each of them displaying an impressive array of shades and hues.

Wow.

There aren't presents under the tree, there are just presents, with a tiny potted flower that's allegedly quartered in the middle somewhere.

When I was a child, I remember having to wait until after lunch to open the majority of my presents. Is that not the worst? Don't worry, son, we will not be adhering to that when you're older, or today, in fact. The sight of six adults spiritedly ripping paper apart, taking pictures and videos, directing you and Haylee on what gift to open next while also cueing you both to look up at the camera at intervals is overwhelming. But somehow, you're not freaking out. Not yet. You're sort of taking it moment by moment.

All of your Christmas presents are second-hand wooden toys that we purchased through Facebook Marketplace. First, you receive a camera – a special moment for me and Mummy as it's the first-ever Christmas present that you've unwrapped by yourself. I say yourself; you had assistance from Grandad, but that only added to the scene. Your presents interest you, but you much prefer it when I hand you something for Mummy and ask you to deliver it to her, which you do while wearing a smile bejewelled with pride.

At some point, Mrs Claus excuses herself to check on the status of the kitchen. From the brief glimpse I get when she opens the door, I can report a controlled flurry of activity, as she effortlessly prepares the traditional feast. Mummy was clearly waiting for this moment, because she immediately grabs a nearby present and hands it to Grandad Tools.

'Dad, that's from you to Mum. It's a necklace that's engraved with the kids' initials.'

Grandad Tools nods, confirming he's fully understood, but I don't believe he has understood, because he's started unwrapping it for himself.

'No, Dad. That's not *for* you. That's for Mum *from* you!'

'Oh, I see,' he says, shaking his head while chuckling.

Mrs Claus returns and is handed a small gift-wrapped box. 'Here. Merry Christmas. Don't mind the wrapping, Arlo's already torn into it.'

Mrs Claus removes the paper. The first thing she pulls out is a key ring. Without even acknowledging that Grandad Tools is in the room, she looks at Mummy and says, 'I presume this was thrown in for free when you bought it?'

'Yes,' responds Mummy. 'I mean, when Dad bought it …'

'Of course. When your father bought it, that's what I meant.'

Grandad isn't listening to this exchange. He's eagerly waiting to see what else is in the box.

Brilliant!

After we're done with presents, we think about getting you down for a nap. I envelop you in seven layers of fabric, place you in the buggy and then take you out for a walk. I've had a lovely morning, but I too have found all the excitement a little overpowering even though, like yourself, I got a bunch of cool shit, which includes half a ton of new books!

But of all the gifts I received, of all that generosity, my favourite present is you, here with me right now in this moment as we amble down a path hidden under foliage and into an empty park that's guarded by trees, all with impeccable postures. It's calm and peaceful. There's no one here but us, Arlo, enjoying the moment, father and son. After all, that's all any of us have – this moment. Our lives and our very existence are made up of these moments. When one passes, it's gone, and dwelling on that serves us not. Happy Christmas, son; may we share many more meaningful moments.

Boxing Day
Saturday, 26 December 2020

Our living room looks like the toy section of an Amazon warehouse. *How do we even begin to think about organising all this stuff?* Let's see if you can hazard a guess at what toys you've played with the most today. I shit you not, your favourites were these: a soft-toy ball that you got given when you were a newborn, which you haven't shown an interest in for the last six months; another toy that vibrates around the floor when you drop it, which was also not one of your Christmas presents; and finally, an empty two-pint milk carton that you've found to be an excellent bashing implement.

And that is why all your presents were second-hand purchases!

Christmas Lessons
Sunday, 27 December 2020

Christmas is over for another year, and one thing that's apparent, now that we are a family, is that we need to rethink our approach to it. Mummy and I spent an hour sifting through the lessons that Christmas Day taught us, and we've arrived at a few resolutions.

Next year, we'll open presents at home, just the three of us. There were too many people in the room, too many voices competing for airtime, and you found it all a bit confusing and overpowering. I know I did. As I said, you didn't freak out, but you were definitely quieter and more reserved than normal.

Your cousin Haylee is two. She understands about Santa, and that he brings presents to children who behave themselves. And even though she was *clearly* a very good girl this year, she still got jealous of some of your gifts, which resulted in a minor dust-up over a hammer. Not her fault, as she's only two, but I think where toddlers are concerned it's better to opt for a calmer, less populated environment.

Something Mummy acknowledged was that she got you too many presents. She purposely tried not to go mad, but she had no blueprint to work from. Last year doesn't count, as you were a newborn. You were given nine gifts from us, which, because of the countless other presents you received from other members of the family, was eight too many. But Mummy said she got hit with the mum-guilt because all your presents from us were second-hand. She felt that this meant she needed to buy more, which she later admitted was a crazy approach to take.

You were noticeably subdued and relaxed on Boxing Day when we were back home, but you still struggled to sit and play with one thing for more than a few seconds without reaching for something else, such was the vast selection of toys on display. So what we've decided to do is box up the majority of them and store them away. Our approach, something Mummy picked up from working in childcare, will be to have fewer toys on display, but for us to rotate them every week or so. This will hopefully lower the sensory overload. It's an 'out of sight, out of mind' type of thing.

One of the highlights from this year was seeing how excited Haylee got when unwrapping presents, which tells me next year will be magical. You'll be older, more clued up about the whole Santa thing, plus you may have developed a taste for a particular brand – please let it be *Star Wars* or Marvel.

Just remember: when it comes to lightsabres, make sure you ask for two!

Toy Story
Wednesday, 30 December 2020

Before today, if you had asked me my thoughts on *Toy Story*, I would have said something like, 'It's an all-time classic, and I would watch it any time.' But that was before today. Now, if you asked me, I'd stand by only one of those sentiments: it *is* an all-time classic, but it's not a film I could watch any time. Why? Because it's 1 a.m., and guess what film I've just put on to calm a screaming one-year-old?

This is what happened. A little before 7 p.m., we tried putting you to bed, but we failed miserably! You weren't upset; you were enraged. So, Mummy scooped you up, took you into our room and then spent the next ninety minutes getting you off to sleep. Yes, she does deserve a medal, though she has so many already that I've no idea where we would put it. At 9.30 p.m., I crept in, more silent than silence itself, like a deft ninja of the night wearing sound-absorbent ninja trainers. I slid into bed without a single ripple fanning out across the bed covers.

But alas ... your eyelids snapped open.

You were like, 'Fuck, it's Dad. Hello, Dad. What's going on? Why am I in your bed? And – oh, wow – are we playing?'

No, we're not. Go back to sleep.

You tried sitting up but Mummy halted your action by gently lowering you back down. Your response? Crying, then screaming and then raging.

Mummy looked drained and exhausted. 'He wants you to play with him,' she said.

'Fine. I'll go and sleep in the loft.'

Conflict accompanied me as I stomped upstairs. Part of me was thankful that I wasn't the one charged with settling you back down and that I could go bed. But another part of me spared more than a few thoughts for Mummy. The trouble is, if you're upset, it's her you always want. I'm just a distraction. You see me as a playmate and a climbing frame, and neither of those identities lends itself to the task of persuading you to go back to sleep.

But for the first time ever, Mummy could not calm you down. I could hear you crying, and your ferocity was only increasing. I messaged her.

Do you want me to tag in?

She responded, saying she had tried everything. She'd given you Calpol, she'd rocked you, she'd even put you back in your cot to let you cry it out. You resisted everything. So I abandoned the notion of rest and returned to our bedroom to see if I could help. I found Mummy standing up, swaying from side to side with you in her arms, but once again, it was no use.

The three of us went back to bed. You would not lie still. You kicked me in the head, face, chest and bollocks on several occasions.

But then … finally … you stopped crying and thrashing.

At long last! It had been a tough—

'Dadda?'

Damn!

The crying started up again … and then the screaming … and then the raging.

'Fuck it, let's whack the TV on,' I said, as Mummy, having had the exact same thought at the exact same time, reached for the remote.

On went Disney+, and on went *Toy Story*.

Your change in temperament happened instantly. The TV hijacked your attention like a master hypnotist, and even though your eyes were squinting as they adjusted their focus to the unexpected light, you altered your position and got comfy for movie time.

All sympathy you had amassed from me has been confiscated, and your next three birthdays have been postponed indefinitely. Now you're smiling – fucking smiling? – at Woody and the gang. There's nothing wrong with you: you're not in pain, distress or any sort of discomfort; you've just decided to behave like a bastard!

January

*'I live with two toddlers. One is an actual toddler.
The other is his father.'*

Arlo's mother

Fireworks
Friday, 1 January 2021

I used to love fireworks. I believed them to be the stuff of magic and wonder. What else could soar up into the sky, float motionless for a heartbeat and then explode in perfect symmetry in such a beautiful array of light, colour and vibrancy, the explosions seemingly timed and choreographed by the gods themselves? It was all such trance-inducing stuff, Arlo.

But those were the beliefs of a non-parent.

Beliefs that are no longer held.

Because now, I hate fireworks.

Seriously, what is the fucking point? 'Oh, I've got an idea. Let's collectively set off a fuck-ton of explosives while all the babies are asleep.'

What a great idea that isn't.

Obviously, we all woke up.

At least Mummy and I got to see the New Year in. That was nice … I guess.

Happy New Year, son.

Forwee
Monday, 4 January 2021

You keep pointing to everything and saying 'forwee'. It sounds like 'three', but that makes no sense. You point to Mummy's cup of tea: 'forwee'; to Daddy's phone: 'forwee'; to the coffee and tea jars: 'forwee'.

This goes on for hours with books, toys, clothes and pens – 'forwee'.

What is it, buddy? What are you saying?

And then Mummy solves it. 'I think he's saying "for me". Arlo, are you saying "for me"?'

You point to the breakfast cereal that she's eating and say 'for me'.

Aha! I toast the moment by pointing at Mummy's boobies and saying 'forwee?'

A Tasty Snack
Tuesday, 5 January 2021

I'm in the shower when you come ram-raiding your way into the bathroom wearing a stupid grin and with a cotton bud hanging out of your mouth. It takes me a moment to realise the cotton bud is of the used variety ... You must have fished it out of the bin in our bedroom.

And I'm not sure if you need to know this level of detail, but I don't really use cotton buds, so you can be assured that it's Mummy's earwax you're munching on.

A Nice Cuppa
Wednesday, 6 January 2021

You're standing in the doorway of the kitchen, and you are one angry little man. You're having a proper Hulk-out: balling your fists and shaking your body while screaming. Except it's less of a scream and more of an internalised rage because you've got your dummy in your mouth, and it's blocking most of the sound.

'Arlo, spit your dummy out!' Mummy says.

Thud.

'Right. Now use your words. What is it you would like?'

The rage evaporates and is replaced by an expression of longing. Your formerly incensed eyes have transformed into two glistening spears of sapphire-shaded hope, as you gently murmur the word, 'Tea?'

The instantaneous change in your disposition has caught me and Mummy well and truly off guard. I'm almost crying with laughter.

'OK, buddy, pick your dummy up, and go and see Mummy.'

You do as instructed, strutting over to your mother with purpose and a smile, proffering an outstretched hand with your dummy in it, waiting for Mummy to dunk it in her tea.

I'm not sure if it's frowned upon to give a one-year-old caffeine, but I presume it's not a two-thumbs-up recommendation from the NHS. I should probably read up on it, but I daren't, as it might be a bad thing to do, and then we'll have to wean you off it. Can you imagine the faff? Best keep this between us[7].

---

[7] For anyone already dialling the number for children's services, this is a joke. The most Arlo would consume would be a couple of drops of tea when he dunked his dummy in.

The Road To No
Thursday, 7 January 2021

'You have to let him do it before we tell him no, otherwise he won't understand,' Mummy says.

'OK, just so I'm clear, in order for us to teach him not to eat his book, we have to first let him eat his book?'

'Exactly, yes.'

'Even if it fucks the book up and he gets ink poisoning.'

'Correctamondo.'

Right on cue, you open your jaws and chomp down on the corner of the book you're holding.

'No, Arlo, we don't bite books,' I say.

But you translate the phrase to mean: 'Try the other corner, son, it's much tastier.'

The Good Samaritan
Friday, 8 January 2021

The UK is in its third mandatory lockdown, but essential shops can remain open. This is helpful because I'm walking back from Tesco, having just procured a bottle of Calpol. Evidently, I was getting a bit of a strut on because the bottle came flying out the base of the box and smashed on the pavement. The plastic syringe that comes with it also made its way to the ground.

I'm midway through a deep, exaggerated shrug of the shoulders when a young chap walking by stops, notices the syringe and then enquires, 'Hey man, you wanna get hooked up with some weed?'

I decide right there and then that I like this man.

Why?

Well, his decision to procure my custom was based solely on the observation of a syringe that I had dropped. This means he's either zeroed in on a newly presented business opportunity and acted on that opportunity (a life skill that I would encourage anyone to learn), or he felt bad for me, and he's following up on section 4b of God's T&Cs which says something to the effect of 'play nicely with others', in which case he's also deserving of my positive appraisal of his character.

Ultimately, I decline the sale because I need the money to buy another bottle of Calpol, but I leave the encounter feeling warm and fuzzy inside. I then wonder if this chap is legally allowed to work at the moment, given that we're in lockdown. Evidently, the government sees him as a key worker.

Biting, Part 1
Saturday, 9 January 2021

It's evening, and we're winding down for bed. You've finished your bottle, and you're having five minutes of playtime before we take you upstairs, brush your teeth and read you a story.

You wander over to where I'm sitting and, without warning, sink your sharp little gnashers into my leg.

Ouch!

Mustering all my inner strength, I refrain from reacting in a dramatic way. Instead, I calmly turn to you and say, several octaves above my normal speaking voice, 'We don't bite, Arlo.'

Which you translate as, 'Bite Daddy again, but harder, and also while laughing.'

OUCH! My inner strength has gone AWOL.

'No, Arlo!' I say, this time with a raised voice.

Once again, you ignore my command. Instead, you begin winding up for a third bite.

Pulling my leg away as you strike, I try something else. I say, 'Arlo, I said no!' and then I turn you around so that you're facing the other way.

The message must have registered in some way because you don't pivot back around for another nibble. Instead, you stand still for a few moments before walking away and into the kitchen, where you sit yourself down in front of the fridge and lower your head to the floor. Watching you do this causes my heart to wrench itself horizontally and vertically apart.

I feel awful – not just guilty, but dismayed.

It's not the first time in my parenting journey when a single defining moment has served as a crystal ball of sorts, providing the answers to questions: I now understand how hard saying no to our children is and why it's so easy to default to yes, and through that same crystal ball the cloudy mist dissipates revealing a brief insight into the future: I now understand how difficult it will be for me to discipline you.

To be clear, I don't believe my action was bad in itself. You absolutely need to learn not to bite and not to see biting as a game. But it was your reaction to a choice I consciously made that I wasn't expecting. It's caught me unawares, and the emotional weight has crushed me. A few seconds later, I scoop you up and hold you tight, not wanting to relinquish you from my grasp – *ever*.

Once you go down for bed, I go online and research books on parenting toddlers. If this is something I need to get used to dealing with, then I want to be as certain as I can of the right way to do it.

Today is one of those days where Santa isn't real[8].

The Card
Sunday, 10 January 2021

Before you were born, Mummy and I agreed that we wouldn't be those parents who insisted the other go about the day as

---

[8] A term I use to describe the moment you learn a disappointing truth about life – such as the fact that it isn't always fair.

normal if they'd had a drink the night before. We established rules: if both of us were hung-over, then we'd try and rope one of the grannies in to look after you for a few hours in the morning. Failing that, we'd double-team it as best we could, promising not to hate ourselves if we employed the TV to share the parenting duties.

But if only one parent is hung-over, then they can lay the too-hung-over-to-parent card, which permits them to remain in bed while the other soldiers on alone. Yes, it's more work for one of us, but it's worth it, because a) parenting on a hangover is so horrifically tortuous that I'd rather get trunk-fucked by the General Sherman tree without any lube (yes, even spit), and b) it's quid pro quo, which means when the other parent is hung-over, they too will have the luxury of a hall pass.

This works because the too-hung-over-to-parent card is rarely laid (we don't drink much) and when it is, it's evenly split, so it's fair.

Today, Mummy has laid the too-hung-over-to-parent-card. This was prearranged. Last night, she participated in a virtual baby shower, where she had 'one or two' cans of mummy juice. It's just you and me, and I'm feeling the effects of looking after a one-year-old who is stress-testing my physical capabilities. You've been running me ragged all morning, never sitting still for longer than a handful of seconds, so I've thrown you in the buggy and taken you to the park to feed the ducks.

It's now 2 p.m., the ducks are full up, and I think about taking us home. I plan the route carefully because I want to bypass the swings and the slide. I'm sorry, buddy, Daddy is too tired. I feel guilty, but my guilt is unwarranted because—

'There,' you say, pointing ... somewhere in the distance.

What are you— Oh fuck. You can see the slide. And now you're staring at me as if to say, 'I'm going down that slide, right?'

Sigh.

Of course you are, buddy. Daddy just wanted to take the scenic route.

We move closer and I free you from the confines of your buggy. You trundle over to the slide with an inverted-rainbow-shaped smile and a large pair of vibrant, coruscating eyes. I lift you up and place you at the top of the slide. You clap while I do this. I then hold your hand, and you slide down.

Once you arrive at the bottom, you quickly alight and point to the top, which obviously means, 'Again, again!'

Again, again it is.

And also again.

Oh, and it's again, again, again, again and another again.

My arms and shoulders are burning, and my back is threatening to collapse like a poorly erected tower of cards.

I steer you *around* the slide, and towards the swings, but you sidestep me and attempt to climb the steps to the slide yourself.

Eventually, we make it to the swings, an item of park apparatus that's a lot less labour-intensive.

After the swings, I manage to coerce you into your buggy and take you home.

I've zeroed in on the park but the whole day has been non-stop.

It's now 5 p.m. I find myself looking at my watch, counting down the minutes before your bedtime. Please don't misunderstand me; you have been tons of fun, and you've behaved beautifully. I've enjoyed our time together (as I always do), but I'll admit that despite you being a fraction of my size, you've physically outgunned me today, and I'm shattered.

It's times like this when I spare a thought, not just for Granny Smurf, but for anyone out there who is a single parent with a limited support network to lean on. If they look at the cards they've been dealt, they won't find a too-hung-over-to-parent card, a too-ill-to-parent card or even a can-I-have-five-minutes-to-drink-a-cup-of-tea card. I look at my hand, and I'm spoilt for choice at the cards I can lay down, Arlo.

Now, go to sleep and don't wake up until 7 a.m.

The Return Of The Arlo Demolition Squad
Tuesday, 12 January 2021

You've been in the business of wrecking your plastic stacking cups for months now. I like to refer to your destructive capabilities as the ADS – the Arlo Demolition Squad.

But the ADS must have recently undergone a training course. In it, they learnt how to raise the stakes in both efficiency and aggressiveness every time something *needs* destroying.

Prior to this training, the ADS would make a beeline for any newly erected stacking-cup tower and send it crashing down with one clumsy swing of the arm. Once finished, the ADS would go off in search of something else that it could destroy. That's no longer the case.

For the fifth time in as many minutes, I've erected a tower from your cups. Even if I say so myself, it's an impressive construction. But there's no time to marvel at my skills as both builder and architect, because the ADS approaches, slowly, like a hunter stalking its prey on the savannah. It curls the sides of its mouth up, forming a grin that is 100 per cent gleeful malevolence. Then it circles the tower, ignoring me as I command it not to come anywhere near my masterpiece.

It strikes!

Unlike before, it takes its time, first removing the top layer and dropping it, then doing the same to the second layer, and the third, before clobbering its way through the bottom levels.

The fragments of a once-magnificent edifice are distributed around the surrounding area, grouped together as fractured, uneven piles of debris. Several pieces lie under the sofa, waiting for UNESCO to come and slap a World Heritage Site sticker on them. And yet, despite all that destruction, the ADS isn't finished. It slides forward among the wreckage and starts kicking, trying to further vandalise an already damaged pile of rubble.

You, Arlo, are the ADS, and you're no longer smiling; you're laughing, and in a final stunning move you pick up the pieces that are nearest to you and throw them.

If anyone ever finds himself in the path of the ADS, he is encouraged to abandon all hope, for he is about to come to a violent and grisly end.

Bananas

Wednesday, 13 January 2021

'Forwee?'

'No, buddy, you've had enough now.'

'Forwee?'

'Arlo, you've already eaten nearly two whole bananas. You cannot possibly need a third.'

'Forwee?'

You're pointing at a bunch of bananas that is two participants shyer than it was twenty minutes ago. To help increase the odds of procuring the coveted third banana, you give me the puppy-dog eyes.

'You can have some more banana later.'

'Forwee!'

I sense a tantrum.

The thing is, these bananas are considerable in size. Their height and girth rival a rolled-up magazine, so although you've polished off the best part of two of these beasts, you've probably had the equivalent of three standard-sized bananas. I'm surprised you haven't died of potassium poisoning.

And now, the cute puppy-dog eyes have left your face, making way for a stern frown with slanted eyebrows and ruby-coloured blotches on your face.

'FORWEE!'

Oh, fuck, you're about to blow.

Reacting quickly, I snatch you off the kitchen worktop, transport you into the hallway and hastily throw on your hat, gloves and coat so that we can go for a walk, the change of scenery hopefully ensuring you forget about bananas.

We make it thirty metres down the road when a middle-aged man gets out of his newly parked car, sees you in your glasses and smiles. This is a reaction we see regularly, because, personal bias aside, you are an extremely cute little boy, and when you add on a pair of glasses, it often causes strangers to stop in their tracks and stare at you while making some sort of high-pitched 'awww' comment, which is exactly what has happened now, though the pitch isn't as high as usual, because the owner of the voice is male and his testicles dropped decades ago.

'How old is your son?' the man asks, wearing a warm, grandfatherly smile.

'He's fourteen— I mean, he's just over a year old.'

'He's a very cute little boy.'

'Thank you for saying that.' I make to continue on our walk when—

'Oh, before you go, let me do something nice for him.'

He leans into the back seat of his car and busies himself for a few moments, before extracting himself, and presenting to you – of all the treasures and trinkets on the planet – a goddamn fucking banana.

My bottom jaw has shattered on the pavement, and I look upon the scene dumbfounded. You couldn't make this shit up!

Your eyes sparkle in delight, your legs start shaking, and you start clapping. Before I can graciously decline the offer, you fire out an arm with an outstretched hand glued to the end of it. There is no way that I can't allow you to accept this mighty gift.

I should remind you that we're still in lockdown and that we're legally required to remain at least two metres from anyone who isn't in our household. But, if it's a toss-up between contracting a deadly virus that's killed over two million people and telling you that you cannot have your third banana of the day, then I'm obviously gonna roll the dice on death.

A World Of Pure Imagination
Thursday, 14 January 2021

It's 11.30 a.m. I've been up since 5 a.m. stuck in front of a computer screen, and I need to get out of the house for some fresh air. I head upstairs to find you trashing the dining-table chairs. Mummy is in the kitchen.

'I might take Arlo for a walk,' I say to Mummy.

'OK. Buggy is in the car.'

I then look out the window and see that it's raining, and now I'm debating whether to take you with me after all, owing to the amount of faffing that's entailed in assembling the buggy and rain cover, all for a ten-minute walk. Mummy can read my face.

'Why don't you leave the buggy in the car and let him walk?'

Huh. I didn't know that was an option. You have become more stable on your feet of late, so I guess ... there's no reason why I can't.

Aside from being in the park and walking up and down the quiet street Granny Feeder lives on, you've not really been outside to explore on foot. This could be fun, right?

I wrap us both up warm in our rain jackets, and then we go off on a little father-and-son jaunt.

'Car?' you say, pointing.

'We're not going in the car today. We're going to walk instead.'

You accept my statement and permit me to walk with you hand in hand, past the car and down the street.

Puddles are of great interest to you. You purposely bring your feet down hard, smashing into the reflecting surfaces so that the water ripples and splashes. You do this while smiling. Next, we pick up the pace and jog for almost two whole metres, skipping our way *through* the water.

You are loving life right now.

And so am I.

It never occurred to me how much joy you'd obtain just from walking down the street.

But that was nothing.

Next, we come to a small car park that's situated at the bottom of our road. It's completely empty except for one red Vauxhall Corsa.

You take in the scene with a sense of awe, wearing the expression of someone who's been transported into Narnia. You look at me as if to say, 'Is this really happening, Dad?' I let go of your hand and encourage you to go off on your own and explore.

You don't need telling twice. You carve an irregular path forward. Imagine a bird's-eye view of a bumblebee buzzing around in a random pattern.

The parking-bay lines fascinate you. You try and trace them with your feet. Then you stumble upon a parking meter. You're not sure what it is, but you approach for a bashing inspection to test out its durability. Next, you discover a raised section over on the far side. On it sits a modest patch of grass. You gently sway your gloved hand through the foliage, pausing every so often to look at me to ensure I'm watching.

Your curiosity is firing on all cylinders.

This is a delight to witness. *Such a simple activity.* It's not like you haven't been in car parks before, but in those instances, you've always been transported from the car seat to the buggy. My allowing you to wander off on your own two feet and at your leisure has enabled you to access a part of the world in a way you've never experienced before.

When I think about it, this must be a similar feeling to when Mummy and I travel to a new destination, marvelling at the planet's visually breathtaking natural formations or revered works of human ingenuity and creativity.

Is this how you see the car park, like a wonder of the world? Does bashing the parking meter create the same awe-inspiring impression as I felt when I first laid eyes on Victoria Falls?

Fascinating stuff.

Biting, Part 2
Friday, 15 January 2021

Tonight, an intriguing thing happened. You went to bite me on the leg, but then instead you paused and turned your face to look at me, and then you laid your head on my leg and cuddled it instead.

'Oh my God, look what he's doing,' Mummy said.
Huh?

I don't believe you've learnt that biting is wrong yet, but you have learnt that biting results in one response, and being lovely and cuddly results in another. You're not sure why, but you're experimenting.

How remarkable.

I'm already a couple of parenting books down since the other night when I felt terrible for physically turning you around. Apparently, the turning around bit was precisely the right thing to do, but saying no in a stern voice wasn't, because psychologically, you can't yet understand that biting causes us pain.

So our new protocol is to try and avoid the word 'no' and redirect your attention elsewhere, without displaying any rapid change to our body language, such as when your little front gnashers bury themselves in my quads and my neurons scream 'Pain!'

Ducky And The Toothbrush
Sunday, 17 January 2021

Today, I'm of the opinion that your mother is a bit of a dickhead. My position stems from us having our first parental disagreement. At least, it's our first since you started behaving like a toddler. The plot of the argument is contained in two things I did that Mummy thought I shouldn't have done. I guess this is a natural part of our journey as parents, and it's something I should expect to happen more often as your personality develops and the complexity of our decisions increases.

The first choice I made was to let you take Ducky to bed with you for your afternoon nap. Ducky, of course, is your yellow rubber duck who's left quite the impression on you recently. His name also continues the trend, not to mention high standard, that we've set in selecting unique and original names for your soft-toy companions.

Ducky usually inhabits the window ledge in the bathroom, inviting the question of why I let you take Ducky to bed. The answer is simple: you asked for him.

Here's my approach to parenting at the moment. If I can't find a logical and valid reason to say no to something, then I don't. Saying that I can't be bothered doesn't count. This approach is a lot simpler, especially when we're trying to avoid saying the word 'no' altogether. But because I'm something of an overachiever, I say yes to pretty much everything, which Mummy takes to mean that I'm a massive pushover.

'You can't give in to everything he wants,' she says.

But here's the thing – I don't. If you had asked to snuggle up to the bread knife, obviously I would be saying no, regardless of how much you protested. But I've learnt that saying yes to some things and no to others is confusing to a toddler, so my default is to say yes to everything possible, and only use no when it's something that places you or others in harm's way. Until I'm given a valid counterargument that encourages me to rethink my approach, I won't.

Which brings us to my second choice: I let you take your toothbrush in the bath with you. It was the same story. You pointed to something that you wanted, and I couldn't see the harm in giving it to you, so I did.

'Oh, I wouldn't have given that to him.'

'Why not?'

'I just wouldn't have.'

That doesn't answer my question, you coagulated piece of discharge! [9]

---

9 This might seem harsh but it's in italics, which means I only thought it rather than said it, so your opinion of my outstanding character should undoubtedly remain unchanged.

Obviously, I'm referring to Mummy here, buddy. I wouldn't stoop so low as to direct such indecorous phrasing in your direction. I'm simply way too principled for that. Your mother, on the other hand ... she totally deserves it. Here's the thing: I've said all along that she knows more than I will ever know about children of your age, and I still stand by that. We're both extremely lucky to have her. But she is terrible at explaining things to me at times, which is frustrating because knowing that my actions cannot be undone, I regularly think about making the right decisions for you. So if someone tells me I've made the wrong decision about my son, I want to understand why, so I can decide differently next time if necessary. Until then, you can take Ducky to bed, give your teeth a thorough scrub in the bath and tell your mother from me that I'm not a pushover and that she can fuck off.

Ewan's Heart Transplant
Monday, 18 January 2021

I'm downstairs working when I'm summoned by Mummy.

'Can you come up here and read Arlo a story? The batteries in that fucking cunt Ewan have died, and now I need to use one of those stupid fucking screwdrivers to get the old ones out and replace them.'

I don't know about you, Arlo, but I get the feeling that life has been a bit of a struggle for Mummy today.

January Monthly Review
Tuesday, 19 January 2021

Your intelligence and awareness have once again taken a quantum leap forward, and you are a different child to the one you were last month. Not for the first time, I'm astonished by how much children learn and how quickly they develop in such a short space of time.

In the morning, when you feel hungry, you walk from our bedroom to the upstairs stair gate and wait patiently for all of three seconds before shouting, demanding we go down for breakfast. In the evening, when we tell you it's time for bed, you walk over to the downstairs gate, ready to begin your bedtime routine, one that starts with having each of your six teeth cleaned.

You've been waking up earlier, usually between 6 and 6.30 a.m. To compensate, Mummy and I have brought our own bedtime forward, so that you're not greeted by zombies when you courageously endeavour to engage our attention in the predawn hours.

You've learnt to say 'tree', 'there' and 'down'. When we ask you what a cow says, you say 'mooo'. You can also say 'Ducky', 'Duggee' (from *Hey Duggee*) and 'dirty'. Add the word 'daddy' to the mix, and that's a lot of similar-sounding two-syllable words beginning with the letter 'd'.

I mentioned the whole 'forwee' incident the other day, but let me give you another example of verbal frustration on your part. You recently spent a day saying 'ear-ooo', and we didn't know what you meant. This pissed you off because, in your head, your instructions were as clear as polished glass. It wasn't until we took you upstairs for a nappy change, when you started pointing to your bookshelf and yelling 'ear-ooo, ear-ooo!' that we understood. You were saying *'Dear Zoo'* – you wanted us to read it to you.

Despite the frustrations, we're getting by. It's incredible how much we can understand from you pointing. And you're very patient with us, happy to repeat words if we ask you to.

That covers words you *can* say, but you attempt others, though you struggle with the pronunciations – something which is admittedly adorable. For instance, '*Bing*' is 'ing', and 'that' is 'dat'. I'm careful to repeat those words back to you correctly, never mirroring how you say them. This is something I picked up from the parenting books (and your mother, of course).

Today, you returned home from a walk with Mummy, and I helped take your shoes off. Then, without any encouragement from either of your parents, you picked them up, walked over to the shoe rack and placed them on it while saying something that sounded like: 'They go here.' The action stunned us because it's not an activity that we consciously practise with you, but clearly, you've been watching.

You help out with chores. Mummy hands you child-appropriate items from the dishwasher, and you walk over and give them to me to put in their rightful places. You also help make the tea. You're in charge of lifting the milk in and out of the fridge. Watching you lift (but mostly drag) a four-pint carton of milk is hilarious. It's too heavy for you, but you don't give up. It reminds me of a World's Strongest Man competitor performing the loaded-carry event, but with toddler-grunting.

Toasting at mealtimes has become a tradition, and you insist on clinking your royal-blue spaceship sippy cup against our glasses at least three times before we're allowed to begin eating.

We're still in lockdown and will continue to be for the best part of another month, maybe longer. The vaccine roll-out is going well, but we're still months away from the majority of the UK being inoculated. The government programme is targeting the most vulnerable people first and working backwards, meaning we're at the bottom of the list, which is a good thing when you think about it. There are new strains of the virus, each with greater transmissibility than the original. The UK death toll is almost at 90,000 while the global count is over two million.

Lockdown, along with your general development, has meant it's become harder for me to work with you in the house. That's despite me having a closed-off working environment in the basement. You regularly bash on the door while shouting for me, and you always want to come downstairs and explore. Something you've not shown any interest in for a while is my keyboard and mouse. But that interest has returned, and I'm met with heavy resistance in the form of a shriek of disapproval when I refuse to allow your destructive, bashing little hands on either piece of essential work equipment.

As always, thank you for another month of parenting adventures.

Ooofer
Wednesday, 20 January 2021

Another new word you've learnt that I didn't mention yesterday is 'Hoover'.[10] When you say it, you lose the 'h' so it sounds like 'ooofer'. The inflection reminds me of the Pixar character WALL•E saying 'Eva', which he does with a lingering intonation on the letter 'e', so it's like 'Eeeva'. You do the same, but with the 'o' portion of the word – 'ooofer'.

You've not only learnt to *say* the world 'ooofer', you've fallen head over heels in love with our actual Hoover. You

---

10 I have already been reminded that the correct term is 'vacuum cleaner' and that Hoover is a brand that happens to have its own product line of vacuum cleaners (we do not own one, because Arlo's mother insisted we buy a Shark instead). If it bothers you that much, you're welcome to swing by our house and educate Arlo all about it, as long as you also agree to clean him up after dinner time.

demand to spend a considerable amount of your time in its company, and your face lights up when you see it each day. It's like your best friend has come over for a play date, and you guys have concocted a ton of mischief and devilry that you can't wait to unchain and liberate.

As parents, we're trying to ensure that this relationship remains healthy, regardless of whether the recipient of your affections is made of plastic and other non-biological materials. We do this by limiting the time you spend with it though, between you and me, I think this is less about healthy relationships and more about Mummy's concern for the well-being of the Hoover, which is a household appliance she loves more than me. Come to think of it, she might be jealous of you guys.

Anyway, Mummy has tried hiding it in the basement so you forget about it, but you don't – ever! You bash the basement door while yelling 'ooofer!' We tell you that the ooofer is sleeping, and that you can see it later. But you continue banging until I bring you down to see it, or I bring it up to you. I wonder if you believe it's alive. I read somewhere that children of your age can't distinguish between what's real and not real. That said, the passage I read references mythical creatures like dragons and unicorns. Are Hoovers and other inanimate objects included? You certainly respond to the ooofer like it's anthropomorphic. I wonder.

Tell me honestly: do we have a problem here, Arlo?

Last night, Mummy was looking on our trusty go-to resource, Facebook Marketplace, searching for your very own toy ooofer. Turns out she didn't need to, because the postman has this second dropped off a parcel for you, one that contains something red and shaped like the thing you love. It's from Granny Smurf.

'Arlo, what is it?' I ask purely for my enjoyment.

'Ooofer,' you say with smiles and wonder.

Dat
Thursday, 21 January 2021

'Dat,' you say, while pointing to one of your toys.

'You want your till?' I ask.

'Dat,' you repeat, but this time while nodding.

'OK, you can have it, but are you sure you want it?'

'Yeah. Dat.' Still pointing.

'It's just you were sure you wanted to play with the drum that Daddy got down for you, but you swatted it to the side before I could give you your drumsticks.'

'Dat.'

'Or before, when I got your piano out, and you didn't get round to hitting a single note because you then wanted to play with your shapes and then your cars and then your wooden blocks, without then playing with your shapes or your cars or your wooden blocks. Can you understand why there's a small-to-medium degree of suspicion strewn across my face?' *And a large degree of stupidity, no doubt.*

'Dat.'

'OK then, buddy,' I say, while retrieving the blue wooden toy from the shelf. I put it down, and I'm about to go knee-deep in a large order of books when—

'Ooofer?'

Always with the ooofer these days. 'The Hoover is sleeping.'

'Ooofer?'

'Yes, sleeping.'

'Dare?'

'You want to go downstairs. I thought we were playing shops.'

'Ooofer.'

'You want to go downstairs and see the Hoover, who, as I've said, is sleeping. And you know it's rude to wake anyone or anything that is sleeping, especially if they're sleeping in the same house as a rampaging toddler.'

'Dare. Ooofer.'

'Come on then, let's go and wake Hoover up.'

No, Me Neither …
Friday, 22 January 2021

To anyone reading this who's not Arlo, do you ever do that thing where you spit in your hand and rub it on your son's feet so he has increased purchase when gripping his indoor slide as he ascends it?

Oh good, me neither … I was just curious, that's all.

What's Your Story?
Saturday, 23 January 2021

Your interest in books has grown into something of an obsession, one that could possibly rival my own. You've recently developed a fondness for a certain section of floor space by the back door where you like to sit and read. This is a habit you've developed entirely by yourself. We thought it was a coincidence at first, but you keep doing it. You choose a book from under the table in the living room, and then you toddle off over to your little reading spot, plonk yourself on the floor and begin babbling away as you flip through the pages. A request has been submitted to Grandad Tools for him to build additional shelving solutions for both of our book collections. I'm proud that this is a passion we look set to share.

You've also started trying your luck at bedtime, asking for another story once the first is finished. You do this by pointing to your bookshelf and saying 'bur'. Your current favourites are *Spot the Dog*, *That's Not My Badger*, *Where's Mrs Hen?* and *The Very Hungry Caterpillar*.

I've said to you before that Mummy and I are going to be mindful of how many physical things we buy you, but books are an exception. I will always ensure we have money to buy you books.

What many people don't realise is that stories are sewn into the fabric of our DNA. As a species, we see the world and interpret its meaning through storytelling. We are governed, moulded and shaped by narratives. And I'm not just talking about going to the cinema to watch the new Disney film or reading the latest Julia Donaldson book. It's the stories we tell ourselves that forge our identity. And it is here where you can discover the true power of storytelling and leverage its perpetual energy for a better life, for you and for others.

Lose your job – what's your story? Are you a victim who's been side-shunted in favour of a less qualified individual, or has life given you an opportunity to take that coding course that you've been talking about?

Been dumped – what's your story? Have you had your heart crushed, or is now the perfect time to go backpacking for a year and see the world?

Been beaten, trodden on, betrayed, abused, attacked – what's your story?

Oprah Winfrey, Nelson Mandela, Malala Yousafzai, Greta Thunberg, Viktor Frankl. By rights, we shouldn't know anything about them, but we do. Why? Because they made a choice to tell their stories differently from the ones that the probabilities of life no doubt intended. Some of them endured unspeakable acts that no human being should ever have to suffer. Yet they took all of that suffering, all of that pain, all of those unenviable odds, and they transformed them into a force for good. They chose to control how they reacted, and because of that, because of their courage, we know who they are and what their stories say about them, and we are inspired to be better.

Think about that.

Adolf Hitler, Saddam Hussein, Benito Mussolini, Joseph Stalin. They too understood the power of storytelling, but they wielded it in a way that enforced oppression and suffering in order to achieve their own selfish ends.

Arlo, understand and accept that your life, and everyone else's, is a series of narratives and plot beats, and know that you have the power to change the genre of your story by developing the right mindset. Go out into the world and live the stories you want, and help others do the same. Let nothing stand in your way. You can't control everything that happens to you, but you can control how you react to it.

Yes, it starts with you finding a quiet corner to sit down and leaf through *Spot the Dog*, but it ends with the story of your life, and it's one you have more control over than you realise.

So let me ask you this: what's your story?

Let's All Just Heave A Sigh
Sunday, 24 January 2021

Today is the worst. You are refusing to work with me in any way at all. I lift you up; you push me away to get down. I put you down; you scream at me to lift you back up again. I get through no more than one page of every storybook you bring me before you change your mind and select another publication, and then, hurling it into the place of its predecessors, you demand that I read it yesterday.

Next, I build your tower out of stacking cups, but instead of demolishing it as per the rules of the game, you walk over to the stair gate and shake it so vigorously that it has the appearance of blurred, wavy white lines, a bit like that optical-illusion trick you do at school with a pencil. And, of course, when I tell you to stop shaking it, you again scream at me, which I presume means 'NO!'

Then I burn my breakfast.

Then I shut my finger in the drawer. Why? Well, obviously I wasn't looking at what I was doing, because I had you dangling from my leg.

I can't even visualise a cup of coffee, let alone get round to making one.

The Sabbath cometh, and it goeth away ...

Can this day get any worse?

Yes. Yes, it can.

You're sitting on the sofa performing the opposite action of what I've asked you do, which is to sit still so I can pull your socks on. Instead, you rotate your body in such a way that you fall off the sofa and face-plant the floor.

There is a tiny part of me that thinks you deserve it, but I quicky shred that part of me as I inspect the damage. *Oh dear.*

You see, face-planting is an unfortunate thing to occur to any child, but because you wear glasses, it's worse. One of the lenses was dislodged from the frame on impact, and it's left a thin-lined cut below your eyebrow, while the eyebrow itself has already swollen and mutated into the colour of a summer-fruits ice lolly.

You're crying – a lot. You still have your eyepatch on, which means we can be assured of some waterlogging. I'm about to write the day off as terrible for us both, but then I look out of the window.

It's snowing.

Chunky, pale, glistening flakes fall from the sky in a slow, graceful, almost dreamlike arc. The world is a flurry of snowfall: giant-sized white, fluffy quilts blanket the road and all of the street-parked cars in opaque beauty.

You've never seen snow before. You immediately forget the trauma of the fall that happened only moments ago, and instead you allow curiosity and wonder to burgeon as your wide eyes dart from side to side like a metronome, absorbing the sight of this brand-new, stunning environment.

A terrible day has morphed into a special one.

And it cometh back again.

'Arlo, shall we go outside?'

'Yeah.'

Never Deviate
Monday, 25 January 2021

Knock knock.

It's 5.30 p.m., and Granny Smurf has arrived at our house with an unhappy toddler named Arlo. You guys have been hanging out for the day. Granny reports two disturbing pieces of information. One: you only had one nap lasting less than an hour. Two: you woke from that nap at 11.30 a.m.

It's now 5.30 p.m. Which means you've gone without sleeping for six hours.

Granny Smurf has not returned with our son. She's returned with a walking, highly unstable biological weapon of mass destruction.

The signs are evident immediately.

'Dat?'

'You want your books?' I say.

'DAT!'

'OK, OK. Calm down. Here.' I give you a stack of books to leaf through.

'Tower.'

'Tower? I thought you wanted to read a story.'

'TOWER!'

Fine. I'll build a tower. I'm sorry I've not done it already.

And so it continues, but the goal here is less about communication etiquette and more about not setting off the WMD.

'See?'

'Yes, buddy, you can see. Come with me then.'

'See' means that you want to look at your toys that are stored away at the top of the basement stairs. We walk over, but you beat me to the door. 'Let Daddy go first because it's the top of the stairs.'

'NAOOIIIS!'

'Fine. You open the door then.'

BANG BANG BANG.

'I told you Daddy needs to go first so he can do it.'

Begrudgingly, you slowly back away with your mercurial temperament, not breaking eye contact with me or softening the deep, furrowed brow that rests on your forehead.

'Now, what would you like to see?'

'Dat.' You point to a box of wooden toys.

'Not a problem. Daddy will get that.' I retrieve the box, but you're in my way, and I need to set it down on the floor so you can play with it, but away from the top of the basement stairs. So, using my forearm that's gripping the toys, I slowly nudge you a couple of inches to the side—

KABOOM!

'Whhaaaa, WHHHAAAAAA!'

And this is why you should never skip naptimes or deviate from when said naptimes should occur.

Assault Course
Tuesday, 26 January 2021

Newsflash: *Ducky has been captured and imprisoned.* He is being held in the furthest dungeon of the Armrest Penitentiary, the highest max-level security facility in our living room. His execution is scheduled for thirty seconds from now.

Arlo, you are Ducky's only hope of living beyond today. You have to somehow infiltrate the facility, navigate a series of deadly impediments and locate the furthest dungeon. Then, you must break Ducky out and escape with both your lives. I will assist you where I can, but this is a test of your strength, and it is one you must ultimately face alone.

Are you ready?

Then let's begin.

First, to get onto the compound grounds, you must ascend the Rainbow Arch of Deceit. It is imperative that you should not be misled by its lovely coloured rungs, for they exist only to distract you. One wrong step and your leg will fall through the gap between the rungs, resulting in you crying and Ducky dying.

You timidly approach. Will your resolve hold?

It holds. You outsmart the Rainbow Arch of Deceit by using four limbs instead of two, climbing to its highest point and arriving at the next obstacle, the Plank of Never-Ending Wood.

Its distance is incalculably long – at least one metre. To stare at the plank's horizon is to court death, for the overwhelming feeling that the endless strip of wood instils will hijack your attention long enough for you to stumble over the edge and fall a thousand metres to your doom … that is, if we use the toddler-metric.

You advance. As Grandad Tools would say, you need to take things 'nice and steady'.

And you do.

You continue shuffling forward, regularly surveying how close you are to the sides, repositioning your feet when necessary and never looking beyond your next footstep.

After what feels like a lifetime, you reach the end.

Ducky has fifteen seconds left until his execution.

The next trial is the toughest yet. You need to leave the firm ground of the Plank of Never-Ending Wood and walk upon the grey shifting sands of – *insert a fuck-ton of suspense music* – The Sofa Base, where stability is minus one kabillion and where good toddlers fall ... and get upset ... and reach their arms out for their daddy. You stare at the terrain, unsure and unsettled. Yet you conjure up enough courage to dip your toe into the coarse, grain-filled lake.

The sands shimmer and ripple, broadcasting a hypnotic warning: do not come any closer.

You retract the toe and in doing so cause some of last night's biscuit crumbs to bounce into the air.

You seek my support, but I don't give it, at least, not in the way you are expecting. Instead, I urge you on vocally: 'Come on, buddy, you can do this.'

Ducky has ten seconds left to live.

You breathe, calming your fears, finding conviction, becoming a statue of solidarity. Once again, you dip one toe in ... but then you dip another, and another ... until one foot is planted ... then another foot is plant—

You stumble, shake and almost fall.

But you don't.

Instead, you overcome the trial's odds and remain standing.

Ducky has eight seconds left to live.

The penultimate challenge is to navigate the Infinite Maze of Possibility. Don't be fooled by its appearance. It may look like a corner sofa, but in reality, it's ... well, actually it's a corner sofa.

You sprint the length of one side, using the cushions at the end to bounce you into position so that you're facing the final straight.

Four seconds to go ...

You dance across the last section, arriving at the final test: The Ledge of the Heavens, or the furthest dungeon of the Armrest Penitentiary.

Three seconds to go ...

You look up at Ducky. He's scared, he's sweaty, and his feathers, despite him not having any because he's made of rubber, are ruffled.

Two seconds to go ...

You reach out with both arms.

One second to go ...

You've got him. Ducky is saved! Well done, Arlo, you did it! I'm so bloody proud of you.

Thunderous applause stampedes all around you. Ducky's parents, Mr and Mrs Quackson, have written you into their will, and Disney have called offering you the part of Indiana Baby. The PM has declared this date as National Arlo Saves Ducky Day.

'Gain?' you say.

'Again, really? After all that drama and suspense?'

'Yeah.'

OK then, buddy.

I take Ducky from you, place him in another secure location, and begin the narrative again.

Newsflash: *Ducky has been captured and imprisoned ...*

A Day In The Life Of Arlo: Chairs And Tea
Friday, 29 January 2021

I need to move this chair out and then move this other chair across and then move this one back again, and then I need to—

'Arlo, what are you doing?'

I'm building an atom portal so I can go back in time and get the last three seconds of my life back. Honestly, woman, why do you bother asking me those questions when you can't understand me yet? Now, back to business. I need to pull the bench out ...

Knock, thud.

Damn it, why won't it move?

'Arlo, I think it's probably a good idea if you don't trash the furniture.'

Oh, do you now? Well, I think that if my behaviour causes you some anxiety, it's probably a good idea to start asking Daddy to wear a condom ... twenty-two months ago! Oh wait, you can't, because it's too late for that, isn't it? Well, guess what? Touché!

What did she expect - that I'd spend my early years sitting still in the corner crocheting? I think not. I've got business to attend to, and a large proportion of my business involves trashing. Speaking of which—

Crash!

'What was …? Arlo … we don't open the drawers, do we? Can you shut that, please?'

Sorry, Mummy, I'd love to follow your instruction, except I'm too busy doing the thing you asked me not to do. Now, be a good girl and fetch my cup; all this trashing business has left me feeling rather parched.

'Dat?'

'What is it? Do you want a drink of water?'

'Yeah.'

'Here you go.'

Thud.

'Oh, does that mean you're finished with your cup?'

O-b-v-i-o-u-s-l-y.

'I give up. I'm sitting down to drink my tea.'

Tea! Did Mummy say tea? Tea? Mummy,

tea? Mummy? Look, I'm sorry for trashing, now can I please have some tea?
   'You want some of Mummy's tea?'
   Oh my fucking God— 'Yeah. Tea.'
   'Go and get your dummy then.'
   Hmmm. You drive a hard bargain, but I will do as you ask … but just so we're clear, I'm not planning on making this a habit.

Ooofer Returns
Saturday, 30 January 2021

It's bath time, and you're having fun splashing, and I'm having fun watching you splash. You've not long been in, perhaps a couple of minutes. Suddenly, and without warning or prelude, you get angry. There's significant double-handed fist shaking on display, accompanied by some upper-back hunching and a side of growling.
   'Arlo, use your words. What's the matter?'
   You immediately drop all signs of anger. You look at me and, as calmly and politely as if you were a contestant on Countdown asking for another consonant, say: 'Ooofer?'
   'The Hoover is sleeping, he's[11] had a busy day.'
   That of course is a fucking lie. The Hoover hasn't been called into active service since the beginning of the month.
   'Ooofer?'

---

[11] For all you gender politicians reading this, the Hoover has the pronoun 'he' because Arlo's mother refers to it him as such.

'I told you that the Hoover is sleeping. You can see the Hoover tomorrow.'

'Whhaaaa.' The anger doesn't return – just disappointment, sadness and a longing for a non-biological thing. 'Ooofer, ooofer?' you beg.

I have to choose my words carefully. If I say no, then I need to stick to it, which makes negotiating problematic. I've also got a passage from The Whole-Brain Child flickering away at my attention. It basically says some tantrums are for effect, and you should dismiss them as such, while others, for whatever reason, are an authentic bout of sadness, which is what I believe is going on here.

I don't understand it. It's possible that you've grown more attached to the Hoover than to Louie. Real tears are falling from your eyes – you're genuinely distraught.

'Ooofer?'

'Listen to me, Arlo,' I say.

Your attention is piqued.

'If we go downstairs and see the Hoover, you can't wake him up. OK?'

'Yeah. Ooofer.'

I lift you out of the bath, and you're already scrambling to get out of my arms and over to the bathroom door. I wrap you in a towel but forgo bothering to dry you as that's like you asking me to wait a month before watching a new *Star Wars* movie.

We're halfway down the stairs, and it's taking a considerable effort not to drop you because of how far you're craning your head over the side, bending it round so you can glimpse the entrance to the basement, which sits under the very staircase we're descending. It's also where the Hoover lives.

'Ooofer. Ooofer. Ooofer.' You're now excited and bouncing in my arms.

'Remember to be very quiet and not wake the Hoover up.'

You stop shaking and remain as quiet and as still as a rock. I open the basement door to reveal ...

'Ooofer,' you whisper. Your eyes are like starlight, and you have this smile that reminds me of the one I reserve for a close friend whom I've not spent time with for a while – a loving but also mischievous smile, one that contains the many years of friendship, memories, and episodes of behaviour that we don't speak of any more, especially in front of our partners.

That's the same smile you sling at the Hoover.

After a few seconds, I shut the door and we say goodnight – well, I say goodnight; you wave at it.

I'm going to ask you this again. Do we have a problem?

Lad

Sunday, 31 January 2021

I overheard the following sentence from Mummy when she was changing you: 'Arlo, if you don't stop playing with your willy, it won't go down, and I need to put this nappy on you.'

February

'All my toddler did was eat pasta. I don't even like the stuff, and neither does his mother. He was an IVF baby, and I kept wondering if the clinic gave us the wrong embryo.'

Andy M, an NCT mate

The First No
Wednesday, 3 February 2021

I'm on nappy-changing duties. A common activity for you at this point is to rip your glasses off your head, which you duly do.

'Arlo, can you put your glasses on, please?'

'Nah.'

'Err ...' Well, that's the first time that's ever happened.

For context: you regularly ignore instructions, but never have you used dialogue to say no in a direct response to a parent telling you to do something.

All aboard the toddler-train. Next stop Nah-Ville.

A Change In The Wind
Thursday, 4 February 2021

At the beginning of the year, Mummy sat me down and confessed that she would like to go back to work. She loves being the Matriarch. If you ask her, she'll tell you that it's the best job she's ever had. But she's also said that she wants something for herself as well. I can relate to that. I too love my dadding job, but I also appreciate that I get to zone out every day and focus on something else, like writing. I'd go insane if I didn't have that.

When we spoke about it, Mummy said that she would like a part-time job for no more than three days a week and that she would like to go back into childcare and, if possible, time her start date to coincide with you going to nursery. Finally, she said it would be great if you were both at the same one, as that would make drop-offs easier.

That conversation took place at the beginning of January.

Mummy is having another conversation about the subject this morning, only this one isn't with me, it's with a potential new employer – she's at a virtual job interview.

Fast-forward a few hours, and …

'Oh my God, I've got the job!'

Mummy is deservedly ecstatic. She was incredibly nervous going into the interview, but she clearly impressed.

This development ticks a lot of boxes: Mummy has something for herself to focus on outside of being a stay-at-home mum, so her emotional well-being is addressed, and she's bringing money into the house, which we could really do with, not to mention that her new employment comes with a whopping 50 per cent discount for you. Her hours coincide with the availability they have for toddlers, which means you're officially going to nursery for two days a week, and you'll be with one of your grannies for the other day that Mummy works.

I still stand by my position of wanting you to go to nursery sooner rather than later. You'll have a wonderful environment to develop a host of different skills, both physical and emotional. I often think about that African proverb: 'It takes a village to raise a child.' It's something that's always rung true to me. You need to be immersed in different environments and influenced and shaped by many individuals other than your parents, though it's our job to ensure they're the right individuals. At least for now.

Going back to Mummy and her wonderful news: she was excited about her new job, yes, but she was more excited when I said we should have an extra takeaway on Saturday to celebrate.

The Second No
Wednesday, 10 February 2021

'Arlo, shall we go upstairs and brush your teeth?'

It looks like you've elected to ignore me. Instead of tottering over to the stairs, you march valiantly down the harbour gangway (kitchen) and climb aboard your ship (the washing basket): the *HMS Fuck Off, Dad, I've Got Shit To Do*.

'Arlo, shall we go and clean your—'

'Nah – nah – nah – nah.'

The pauses between the 'nahs' are the same, as are your pitch and delivery, which make it seem like the word 'nah' is stuck on a parent-defying loop.

In the end, I have to force a mutiny and physically remove you from the *HMS Fuck Off, Dad, I've Got Shit To Do*, which I've since renamed the *HMS Daddy Doesn't Care*. I know it's bad luck to rename a boat, but I'm happy to roll the dice. You weren't even bothered; you laughed the whole time – further evidence of who's really in control here.

Valentine's Day
Sunday, 14 February 2021

Happy second anniversary since you were created, son.

Here's a Valentine's Day quiz:

1. What time did you wake up?
   a. 5.30 a.m. (aka not an acceptable time to wake up)
   b. 6.30 a.m. (aka not an acceptable time to wake up but better than 5.30 a.m.)
   c. 7.30 a.m. (aka an acceptable time to wake up)

Answer: a

2. How many dirty nappies did Daddy have the honour of changing before 7 a.m.?
   a. None
   b. Two
   c. One

Answer: b

3. True or false? I experienced the following before breakfast: multiple slaps to the face, you stamping on my bollocks, you fish-hooking me and you biting me.

Answer: True

And finally ...

4. Yes or no? Was Daddy's highlight of the day getting a non-weird Valentine's Day card that says *Wanna be my thumb buggy?* featuring a smiling centipede with a body made up of your thumbprints?

Answer: Yes. Yes, it was.

How many points did you get?

By the way, you know if you had stayed in bed, I wouldn't have reminded you that you were made two years ago today. Food for thought for next year, perhaps?

Park
Monday, 15 February 2021

Breaking news concerning the weather: it's warmer and it's lighter, which means we can return to our tradition of an early-evening walk to the park, one of our favourite things to do. Sure, the fifteen-minute tussle to get you ready and out of the house is a little exhausting, and it isn't great that we get only a few metres down the road before I roll the buggy through dog turd, but you make up for it by screaming 'DOGGGYYY' every time you see one, which turns out to be a not uncommon occurrence; it seems every dog owner in Northampton has noticed the favourable change in the weather as well.

We get to the park, and the first thing we do is apparel you in a set of reins. They're essentially a backpack with a dog lead attached to it. Chance dictates we stick to the dog theme, because the next thing we do is meet a lovely four-legged chap – let's call him Gregory – who, with his owner's authorisation, permits a meet-and-greet. Gregory sits down patiently while you stroke him. You're surprisingly gentle, and Gregory likes this. He even feels relaxed enough to let the ball hanging out of his mouth fall to the floor—

'Ber?' (Toddler-speak for ball.)

'That's the doggy's ball,' says Mummy, who clearly didn't get the memo about the doggy's name.

'Ber.'

Gregory no longer holds your interest. You turn your back on him, concocting a plan to acquire Gregory's 'ber' and add it to your collection at home.

But before Gregory can get territorial, Mummy lifts you up and away, a course of action that you're not on board with.

'Whhhaaaaaa! Ber? Ber?' The legs and arms begin to animate themselves and shake like a drunken string puppet dancing on stage. We're moments away from a meltdown. Except we're not, because Mummy's been watching *Hey Duggee*, and she has her Toddler-Bomb Defuser Badge. She points to a bench nearby and asks you if you would like to sit on it. You forget about Gregory and his 'ber'.

'Chair.'

'That's right, Arlo, it is a chair.'

It's a typical park bench, but it might as well be the Iron Throne, given the soppy, awe-inspired grin plastered across your face. You approach and try to climb up, but it's a few inches too high, so Mummy gives you a bunk-up.

A quick glance at the sky on my part reveals it's getting dark. A band of slate-grey cloud has crept over us, and we haven't brought a rain cover for your buggy to protect you should the billowing mass decide to go on the offensive. We need to go home.

'Come on, Arlo, let's go.' Mummy says.

'Chair?'

'Yes, I know, and you've sat on it, and now it's time for us to go.'

'Chair?'

Once again, Mummy calls upon her *Hey Duggee* teachings to distract you. She suggests that you might like to walk the length of the park bench, something you eagerly consent to, and thus the discharging of a chest-birthed jet of rage has been postponed. You stand up and carefully forge ahead while Mummy remains close by. Once you reach the end, she assists you with the dismount before—

'Gain!'

'This way, Arlo.'

'Gain!'

You're fighting to get back to the bench, but Mummy has you by the reins, and she is not letting go. You're using all of your strength – dissident red blotches form on your face, but all your efforts are no match for the Matriarch. Once again, diversionary tactics are deployed.

'Look, Arlo, there's another one up here. Do you want to walk on it?'

It's clear from your body language that you do not; you want to walk on the one you're at right now, and it requires diligent work from Mummy to draw your attention to the bench that's five metres closer to home.

We get there, and the same pattern ensues: you perch on the bench like you're the park's sovereign ruler and the park's visitors are there to do your bidding. Then you stand up, journey to the end and fight with your mother to do it all again.

After the fourth repetition of this scene, I look up and count how many benches we need to pass before we can exit the park. There are nine of the bastards. *I did so enjoy our early-evening walks in the park.*

The rain hasn't made an appearance, but the sky is now black. Enough is enough. I pick you up and jog all the way to the park exit, where we then huddle under a lamp post and strap you back in the buggy. Naturally, you issue whiney, eardrum-assaulting sounds the whole time. I assume what you're saying is toddler-speak for: 'I don't want to go home!'

We end an exhausting twenty-minute jaunt with the discovery of a buggy hack. If we get dog shit on the wheels, all we need to do is head to our local petrol station – one that's conveniently situated on our way home – and take advantage of the free water-hose facilities.

Daddy And The Ooofer
Wednesday, 17 February 2021

It starts like this: you hand me your toy Hoover and indicate by pointing and grunting that you would like me to demonstrate playing with it. I comply because I'd be a monster if I didn't. Your Hoover has inbuilt sound effects, but I'm of the opinion that they're substandard, so I add my own for increased authenticity.

My performance wins your approval, something that means more to me at this stage of your life than it perhaps should. But the story doesn't end there. Instead, you arrive by my side and begin pushing me towards the hallway, while Mummy and I look at each other, bewildered. But curiosity presses me to play along. So, with me still holding on to your toy Hoover, I allow you to steer me into the hallway, where you then back up and shut the door, leaving the two of us alone.

Bang, bang, bang!

I open the door, saying 'boo', but that was wrong because you're not smiling like you would normally. Instead, you've got a heavy-set frown of disappointment strewn across your forehead – a skin-covered inverted pyramid. Whatever it is you want me to do, I'm apparently not doing it.

Once again, you close the door on me.

Bang, bang, bang!

'I think he wants you to play with the Hoover out there,' Mummy says.

'What, on my own?' *Surely not.*

'I think so.'

I run the Hoover up and down a few times, and your reaction is as powerful as it is puzzling. You are pissing yourself laughing, and in hysterics. Usually, you only crease up this much from direct physical contact like tickling, raspberry-blowing or general age-appropriate roughhousing.

Every time I try and come back into the room, you stop laughing, push me back outside and bang on the door until I start hoovering again, at which point the hysterics rev back up.

And let's all take a second to picture the image of a thirty-five-year-old six-foot male, running his one-year-old son's toy Hoover up and down the hallway, alone. After several laps, my back starts to hurt. So now there's another image, this time of a thirty-five-year-old six-foot male sitting cross-legged but still playing with the toy Hoover and still alone.

And do you know what the worst part of the farce is?

I'm still doing my Hoover sound effects ...

Nutter

Thursday, 18 February 2021

Since you were about four months old, Granny Smurf has tried to teach you how to say 'nutter'. It's taken her some time, but she's now succeeded. It's a word that you can recall and utter intrinsically.

'Nutter,' you say, though sometimes you leave the 'n' at home, so it's just 'utter'.

Your mother is less than delighted. She has had to delete several videos of you playing nicely or doing something cute and video-capture-worthy because you've ruined the moment by hurling a random utterance of 'nutter' from your lungs.

It gets worse. Granny used a trigger action to teach you the word, and that action was you shaking your body in an awkward, jerky motion, the appearance of which is not unlike someone having an epileptic fit. Do you see where this is going?

If you plot this behaviour on the political-correctness scale, we're so far down the wrong end that we've fallen off the bottom and landed on a pile of inappropriate behaviours and phrases that you shouldn't use: phrases of racism, sexism and any other -ism that's derogatory to another human being.

As your parents, our job is to teach you that everyone is equal and deserving of the same basic human rights and that we shouldn't be ridiculed for our – or ridicule others for their – race, creed or physical and mental disabilities. Your throwing your head forwards and backwards, convulsing your body and shouting 'nutter' while laughing doesn't exactly scream 'good parents' on our part.

Granny does not give a shit about our concerns. She thinks this is all bloody good fun, and I can hear the glee in her voice when she exclaims, 'I can't wait for him to do this in public,' which, considering Granny works in the mental-health sector, is a cause for concern.

'Arlo, what are you d—'

'Nutter. Nutter. Utter!'

Christ, we have a problem here.

If you think I'm overreacting, then I'll leave you with this scenario to picture. Imagine we're out for dinner and we're sitting down. The table next to us is cleared, ready to seat the already-approaching next-in-line hungry customers, one of whom is a young woman in a wheelchair who has cerebral palsy, a condition that affects movement and coordination. You take one look at the young lady, mirror her movements with a few of your own and then begin laughing at her while screaming, 'Nutter!'

February Monthly Review
Friday, 19 February 2021

You are a sponge. If I ask you what a dinosaur says, you say 'roarrr'. If I ask you what a doggy says, you begin panting. You can point to your eyes, nose, mouth, hair, feet and tummy. You're almost there with your ears. If you see pictures of flowers in your books, you lean in and give them a sniff, and if your food is too hot, you blow on it.

You've learnt to say 'purple', 'blue', 'no', 'more', 'pull', 'in there', 'see', and, of course, 'nutter', along with countless other words that, like last month, neither Mummy nor I have been able to translate. You're also about there with 'one', 'two' and 'three'. It's a routine we've been working on while having splish-splash. You like to place your toys either in the jug or on the side of the bath, and we count along as you place them.

You're more boisterous. You run through small inanimate objects, like toys, and into large animate and inanimate things, like parents and sofas. When you walk in the front door, your first order of business is to charge into the coat rack at the other end of the hallway while squealing. You can almost perform a forward roll. Mummy taught you. She cues you up for the manoeuvre by saying 'head down, bottom up,' before giving you a helping hand to complete the rotation.

You love to climb. You've started dragging items like your small toy box or your toy Hoover to the sofa so you can stand on them and ascend it. You've also been known to tug on my sleeve until I sit down on the floor with my legs out flat so you can use them as a stepping stone to scale whatever obstacle needs scaling – the dining-room bench and your slide being two examples.

Your ability and awareness when playing games have increased. Hide-and-seek now means that you will hide behind the curtain as opposed to putting your hands over your eyes, though there is still a lot of that. You walk outside more. I still take you to the car park at the bottom of our road at weekends for some serious adventuring. It's great.

You remain a phenomenal eater. You've figured out that at dinner time you get dessert, which, even though it's only fruit or a frozen-yoghurt lolly, you ask for before you finish the main course. It's not uncommon to hear Mummy negotiate: 'Arlo, have three more bites for me'. I'm stunned at how you can understand the complexity of negotiation at your age, but it seems that you can.

You now tell us when you've done a 'poo poo'. The other day, Mummy had got out of the shower and she said, 'Arlo, where does Mummy's poo poo come from?' You answered by marching up to her and punching her straight in the vagina.

Your general attention span is barely the length of an atom. You're busier than ever. You move from one toy to the next in seconds. It's exhausting keeping up with you. But sometimes you'll play by yourself for a fairly substantial amount of time. I love watching you play.

Two more teeth have cut through this month.

You've progressed from one to two books a night before bed. You select *On the Farm* without fail because you have a favourite page, one where you can *pull* the stable doors open to see the horses, or 'neigh-neighs'.

Your sleeping habits are still temperamental, and it's a bonus if we get through the night without you waking once, but most of the time, you go back to sleep as soon as Ewan begins doing his thing.

Here's one that none of us can solve: you've stopped saying 'Mamma'. And it's not a recent thing either. Your refusal has been in place for weeks. I don't get it. If we ask you where Mummy is, you point and smile at her. But if we ask you to say 'Mamma', you go shy, laugh because you think it's a game, call her 'Dadda' or ignore us entirely. What gives?

There will be major changes in our lives next month as Mummy starts her new job and you begin attending nursery for two days a week. I'm still convinced it's the right thing to do because of how far you've come in your development, but there is naturally a part of me that's apprehensive. It will be, to date, the biggest change to your routine that you'll have had to adapt to, and it won't be easy on your little mind.

Next week, the UK is expected to learn from the government what the next phase of the Covid-19 recovery looks like. Remember, we're still in our third lockdown. Cases have dropped, and the vaccine roll-out is happening at pace. Granny Smurf has had the first of two jabs. But we daren't get our hopes up that we can start filling the calendar with social events. I speak for everyone on the planet when I say I'm desperate for this moment in history to pass. It's been almost a year since I hugged one of my mates.

Despite Covid-19, I've still had a joyous month with you. As always, thanks for another happy month. I bloody love dadding!

The Sabbath Day
Sunday, 21 February 2021

At 8 a.m., an open pack of Weetabix was taken out of the kitchen cupboard by someone who was told not to go anywhere near it. Ignoring a second directive to return the packet back to the cupboard, the 'someone' slowly, while looking his mother in the eye, tipped the contents upside down and all over the floor.

By 8.15 a.m., the someone had his sippy cup withdrawn from his reach because he was taking large gulps of water and then spitting them onto the floor, once again behaving in a way that ran contrary to how he had been told to behave.

By 9 a.m., the someone had discovered that his bright, shiny colour blocks could be repurposed as *coloured pencils*, so long as he applied enough pressure to them as he scraped them across our off-white-coloured walls. And apply enough pressure he did. One of our walls now looks like the canvas of a Mark Rothko piece with wavy blue lines cementing a well-known and undeniable fact:

Toddlers can be burdensome at times.

We were warned by everyone who has kids. 'The newborn stage is easier,' they said.

I mentioned the eye contact while you were tipping the Weetabix packet upside down, but it's more than that. It's also the sinister half-pipe smile that accompanies it – the smug, sadistic grin of an infant who has 100 per cent confidence that he's in control of the moment. And you know what? I'm not sure the confidence is unwarranted.

The First Lie
Wednesday, 24 February 2021

I've come upstairs from my fortress of solitude to make a coffee. You're standing at the bottom of the next set of stairs, the ones leading to the first floor, pointing towards your nursery.

'Poo poo,' you say.

'You've done a poo poo?' Mummy asks.

'Poo poo.'

'Typical. I've just this second changed him,' Mummy says to me, seemingly a bit stressed.

'I can take him up,' I offer. 'By the way, are you OK?'

'He's had a tantrum because we've come downstairs, and he wanted to stay upstairs with his books.'

Lad.

I walk over to you and carry out a sniff inspection. *Strange – nothing.* I remove your trousers and have a thorough look in from the sides. Again, nothing.

The nappy isn't even wet; it's bone dry. 'Arlo, are you sure you've done a poo poo?'

'Yeah, poo poo,' you say while continuing to point upstairs.

'Oh my God,' says Mummy, who's apparently realised something I haven't.

'What?'

'He's lying! He wants his b-o-o-k-s.'

'No way. Lying at fifteen months?'

Mummy asks, 'Arlo, do you want your books?'

'Bur, bur, bur, bur,' you scream, suddenly becoming more animated than the entire Disney-animation back catalogue. It's as if books were on your mind the whole time, which backs up Mummy's theory that at fifteen months you have probably told your first fib.

At first, I was impressed by your intelligence, but now I'm upset. These are the first signs of you losing some of your childhood innocence, and it has happened already.

But now, I'm back to being impressed and I'm looking forward to this next phase of Arlo versus Mummy and Daddy. I wonder what creative deceptions and falsifications you will offer up. I hope they're inventive. At some point we'll have to teach you why you shouldn't lie, but we're years away from your brain developing enough for that lesson to be learnt. So, for now, leverage resourceful propaganda as a tool for getting out of trouble. But I'll warn you, we will almost certainly know when you are lying. You enter this contest as the underdog.

Not Really Feeling It Today
Saturday, 27 February 2021

No offence, but I do not want to parent today. It's not you. It's me. I don't know what's up – I'm exhausted. I don't feel ill, I didn't stay up late last night, and I didn't drink anything containing alcohol. Yet I can't get it together.

You're in a similar mood – you do not want to toddler. You woke up at 6 a.m. I brought you into bed with us with the expectation that you would go back to sleep. You didn't; you started punching me in the face. Then you tired of that and started crying. Fortunately, the television stuck its hand up in the air and asked if we wanted it to tag in for a shift.

It was a unanimous yes from all of us.

It's now 7.30 a.m., and I suppose we should all think about getting up and heading downstairs for breakfast.

We do. I make drinks, and Mummy makes toast. Once we've finished eating and cleared up, we move on to household chores. You help Mummy by emptying the washing basket containing clean washing that's ready to be hung up. You do this because of course the washing basket isn't a washing basket: it's a boat, and you want to go sailing in it.

You're too young to captain the vessel by yourself, so you've brought me on board to assist with navigating us through a dangerous and narrow stretch of water known as 'the hallway'. Unfortunately, our spur-of-the-moment decision to go boating meant that neither of us bothered to check the weather forecast, and we've ventured out in rough seas. The boat capsizes, hurling you overboard, but not before you collide with the ship's broken mast, aka the spare-bedroom door frame.

If I thought the seas were ferocious, that's nothing compared with the tears of pain from a toddler who's bumped his face. I react quickly to rescue you, but I can already see a purple welt forming on your cheek. The whole thing is my fault. I wrap my arms around you for a much-needed cuddle while Mummy uses a combination of arm flapping, staggered back-and-forth pacing and high-pitched questioning, demanding to know what, why, how and where.

'Do you think you were going a bit too fast?'

Oh, really? I wonder what series of intellectual deductions led you to that conclusion! 'Yes, I suspect I was going too fast.'

So, not only did I start the day not wanting to parent, I've now got our little sailing accident on my conscience, and Mummy really isn't helping me to dispel any of the guilt. Though neither is she deserving of my mentally snapping at her.

I do not want to parent today. Perhaps that will change.

It doesn't.

It doesn't change when you plonk your arm in the toilet, despite clear vocal instructions: 'Arlo, do not do that.' It doesn't change when you climb the stairs on your own without parental support. And it doesn't change when you stick your muddy trainer in your mouth when we're trying to get ready to leave the house.

My mood improves marginally when we get to the park and Mummy hands me a sausage sandwich to eat. But it darkens again when I drop most of it on the floor.

Later, we test out some blackout blinds in your nursery, but you assume we're putting you down for another nap, owing to the room being dark – so you kick off, again. *At least the blinds work.* Oh, and the nap you did have was significantly shorter than I was expecting. You woke up as a *Grumpysaurus rex*, which of course is toddler-speak for 'pissed off to fuck'.

Needless to say, bedtime can't come quick enough, and when it does, I zoom through the entire routine.

Don't take it personally.
And don't wake up early.
Oh, and sorry for the black eye.
Love you.

Everyone Has Shit Days
Sunday, 28 February 2021

I wasn't Superdad yesterday, was I?

Please understand that I structure my life so that I'm in the best possible shape physically, emotionally and spiritually. I do this partly for me because it makes me feel great and enables me to accomplish a lot without feeling overwhelmed and overworked, but I also do this for those I'm committed to.

Including you.

Especially you.

Being parent to a toddler is difficult. You often get up earlier than my body clock wants, and when you do, you're ready to start the day at 100 mph. To you, it's life's natural pace, and it's one you expect me to match so that I can be in the passenger seat next to you, guiding you forward, helping you to metaphorically climb life and to non-metaphorically climb furniture. If I'm not up to that, then you get confused and upset.

To counteract this, I go to bed early, ensuring I'm as well-rested as possible so that when you wake, I'm ready to fulfil your early-morning demands with enthusiasm. But sometimes, for whatever reason, it's not enough. Sometimes I have a shit day and I can't explain why. It's as if the components that make up my physical, emotional and psychological self have broken down. They're trying to repair themselves by siphoning off energy from my reserves, but that action is draining, and my being unable to match your tempo is a side effect of that process.

I can't explain how difficult that is.

The thing with parenthood is you can't wake up and say to yourself, 'I'm not feeling great today. I need a day off to rest,' like you can for work. You sign a waiver forgoing any spontaneous days off when you become a parent. It's one of the more grinding elements of the gig. And no gig is without its pitfalls, of course.

Since I started my public life as an author who writes about dadding, I've had opportunities to give advice to new dads. Something I repeatedly say to them is not to hate yourself if you have a bad day or you feel any in-the-moment negativity or resentment towards your children.

'You're not a piece of shit. Neither are you a failure,' I tell them.

But it's easy to see why they believe that, because it's something I've felt before and will no doubt feel again. Perhaps they've been woken up multiple times in the night, or their little cadet has dropped his apple on the floor and erupted into Armageddon – a scenario that's boxed up and shipped off to Mum or Dad to deal with.

But what do we as parents expect? Try and find one person who looks forward to being woken in the night to soothe a loud, screeching, non-compliant baby. You won't – they don't exist. Yet people queue up for the parenthood gig each day because of the unconditional love they have for their children.

It stands to reason that the most rewarding achievements in life are those you have to work the hardest for. There is nothing more rewarding than parenthood, but you have to work for it. Sometimes you get it right; at other times you don't. And you know what? That's OK. I'm sure even Dwayne Johnson has his off days. I know I do.

I'm writing about this today to tell you that your daddy is not Superman, he's not flawless, and he doesn't always feel his best, and you might feel the effects of that at times. I'm also writing this to practise what I preach when I talk to other dads and tell you that it's OK that I mess up sometimes and that I still deserve to be your daddy.

Learning forgiveness is a fundamental and crucial lesson in casting away negative energy, those feelings that drag you down into a pit of misery. And self-forgiveness is the hardest of them all. But it's possible. And it starts with accepting that you're not perfect. Because I'm not. I'm far from it.

March

'Do you remember when you used to be able to go to the toilet alone? Because I don't.'

Marc M, a mate

Another Good-News-Bad-News Story
Thursday, 4 March 2021

Good news: the thing that makes up the bad news was a thing that I had nothing to do with. Bad news: you fell off your changing table. Yes, it was Mummy's fault. Yes, I'm relieved and glad it's Mummy's fault. Yes, I've reminded her of what happened several times throughout the day, because I'm a supportive partner.

Don't worry, you were fine(ish).

To Whom It May Concern
Friday, 5 March 2021

Hi LG

Would you mind forwarding this email to your washing-machine department? I have feedback about the child-lock safety feature on your F4J6JY2S model that they need to hear. It's critical – I'm talking life and death.

Feedback:

My understanding of a child-lock safety feature is that it is there to prevent the child (in my case a fifteen-month-old headstrong antagonist who ignores me when I ask him to do anything) getting into things they shouldn't – like an electronic device that's midway through its washing cycle.

You guys have got this almost bang on. He can't alter the spin-cycle speed, the type of washing cycle or any of the other million features that, I confess, I don't know by heart. I have watched him type away at the display panel quicker than a journalist on a deadline, and he still can't break through the might of the LG firewall.

Unfortunately, he's found a back door where the child-lock safety feature doesn't work.

And that back door is called the power button.

Do you see my quandary here?

It's all very well coding up the appliance to prevent tampering hands from switching my lights to my darks, but if he can turn the thing off with a glancing sweep of his arm, then confusing lights for darks is the least of my problems because I'll have no clean clothes!

You wouldn't splash out on a roller coaster if the child-lock feature only worked on some of the carts, would you?

March

Nothing induces tears like when you've had to begin an almost-four-hour washing cycle from the start for the third time that day because your darling little mechanic believes he's Doctor Who, and the washing machine is his Tardis.

I know this isn't a fault your end – it's a design choice. I know so because I read the manual and it says: *When the child lock is set, all buttons are locked except the POWER button.*

I'm no engineer, and the only thing I know about washing machines is that they wash clothes and spin really fast (when the power's on, at least), but regardless, believe me when I say you need to take this feedback on board for future product development because when we encounter this little issue at home, the rage that's induced in my partner is of such ferocity that she makes Cruella De Vil seem like the Easter bunny enjoying a joint in a hot bath with candles and Epsom salts. Actually, that doesn't work at all, does it? Can you imagine the sight of a drenched rabbit? It would be horrifying, not to mention uncomfortable for the poor rabbit. And the relaxing scents of the Epsom salts and candles would, of course, be suffused and all but extinguished by the joint smoke. Bad analogy! But I'm sure you get what I was going for.

I've digressed. Allow me to steer us back on track with some suggestions to fix this grave and dicey issue:

- Have it so that you need to press two buttons at the same time to turn the power off.
- Mirror the child-lock setting – you hold the button down for three seconds to turn the feature on and off. Surely

you need only to copy and paste the code over to add to the programming.

- Set a PIN.

I hope my email finds a sympathetic reader. If you're reading this and think it's all one big joke, then I'd assume you don't have children. If that's the case, please forward this to a colleague who does.

Warm regards
A desperate father

PS: I love your TVs, and that's why I wanted to take the time to give you guys this feedback – help give you a leg-up against the competition.

Your First Settling-In Session
Monday, 8 March 2021

Today is massive. You're going to nursery. Well, sort of – it's your first settling-in day. You'll spend an hour with a member of staff (your key worker) in the garden while Mummy and I remain nearby, purposely sitting back out of the way and not interacting with you. This is so that you're encouraged to explore the surrounding environment by yourself, adjusting to the staff and the other toddlers and, as the name of the day implies, settling in.

You have a further two settling-in days scheduled for this week, but for these, you'll be alone with your key worker. We won't even be able to see you from a distance. This is something I think Mummy is apprehensive about. I mean, she brings it up every chance she gets, so I assume it's playing on her mind.

I'm not too worried. Sure, it might take a bit of getting used to, but I believe you'll thrive. Next week, you will officially begin your timetable of two full days at nursery. It's also when Mummy starts her new job here as well, though she'll be in another room. I don't think you'll see her.

For your first day, you are kitted out in a mustard-coloured woollen jumper with smiley faces on it, a pair of navy leggings and white Converse trainers. And, of course, your glasses. The nursery is situated behind the local hospital, which as you know is a short walk from our house.

We arrive, and I form my first impressions of the place where so much of your early-years learning and development will take place. It appears friendly, though I can't say why. Perhaps it's the artwork in the windows, or the bright brickwork, testifying to the building's recent construction. Or maybe it's because of the voices I can hear: small children playing games and having fun. Regardless, it's as I said – friendly. *I think.*

'Nutter!' Nutter! Nuttterrrr!'

'Arlo! Stop saying that,' Mummy barks, but in a whispered bark, the sort where you're trying not to shout but you shout quietly, which is basically an oxymoron.

Naturally, you treat this as a game, one where the objective is to show your mother up in front of her new co-workers. She's about to wrap an arm around your throat when a young woman appears at the door, says hello and invites you and Mummy in.

But not me.

'I'm sorry, we can only allow one parent in because of Covid-19,' she explains.

'I understand.'

I'm gutted – really gutted. I've always considered your birth to have been timed remarkably well, given the whole virus thing. You were born a few months before the situation became a global pandemic so I was allowed into the hospital to comfort Mummy during labour and hold you at your birth. You're obviously not at school yet, so we're parents who escaped homeschooling, which, by all accounts, is a lot less fun than eating pizza at the perfect temperature.

But my luck has run out, and I'm a parent who doesn't get to witness you undertake this particular rite of passage. *Damn.* But there's nothing I can do about it, so I walk home, go back to work and wait for you guys to return and tell me all about it.

'He loved it,' says Mummy an hour later.

'Really?' That's great news and a relief.

'He played with dinosaurs in the sandpits outside. He didn't give me a second look. I think he will be fine next week. He does need to stop saying "nutter" in public, though.'

And right on cue ...

'Nutter?' you say, looking generally inquisitive.

Well done for today, buddy. I'm proud of you.

Your Second Settling-In Session
Wednesday, 10 March 2021

'He didn't even say goodbye to me. He ran off as soon as we walked in,' says Mummy, who sounds happy – but I believe she's also upset.

'Where are you now?'

'Sitting in the car outside, filling out paperwork for when I start work next week.'

I was worried how you would cope being left on your own, especially as Covid-19 has meant no socialising. So it's a relief to hear Mummy's words, even if the evidence suggests we need you more than you need us.

An hour later, and I can hear keys turning in the door. I launch myself upstairs, eager to get the low-down about how your second settling-in session went. But instead of a happy Mummy and Arlo, I'm met by a mummy with an angst-ridden demeanour and a toddler displaying the body language of someone who looks lost, neglected and abandoned. Your eyes are puffy and blotchy.

Oh dear. 'What happened?'

'He realised I wasn't there, and he got *very* upset.'

'Come here, buddy. Come and give Daddy a cuddle.'

You shuffle forward and collapse in my arms. I've never seen you looking this sorry for yourself. 'He was sobbing the entire time. I had to go in and get him early.'

I've always struggled seeing you get upset. And by upset, I mean emotionally distraught, not pissed off because nasty Daddy said you couldn't eat a block of cheese. That might sound like an obvious statement coming from a parent. I'm sure no parent likes to see their children in distress, but hearing you cry disarms me. I'm desperate to halt your tears and rid you of any dismay. It's that bottom lip of yours – it gets me every time.

Your response to being left alone highlights a flaw in our toddler-goes-to-nursery strategy. We had three settling-in sessions planned, and you've now had two of those. Your final one is on Friday, when you're scheduled to spend an interminable *two hours* without a parent. Today, you lasted twenty minutes. And then, next week, you're expected to attend nursery two full days each week. That's a steep embedding period, and today's events tell me that we need to rethink our approach.

In hindsight, we should have pushed Mummy's start date back a couple of weeks, so she could be around for any emotional emergencies that the nursery staff aren't equipped to deal with. But that's no longer an option. So, both grannies have been apprised of the situation, and they are each ready to answer the call of duty, should we need them to. I've also emailed my work to brief them, warning them that I might need some flexibility while we as a family navigate what we now expect to be a stormy patch.

To reinforce how pissed off you are, you snatch an apple out of Mummy's hand and refuse to give it back, even though you have no interest in eating it yourself.

'I think he's punishing me.'

'I think you're right.'

'Can you drop him off at nursery on Friday?'

Early Mornings
Thursday, 11 March 2021

5.20 a.m. 'Whhaaaa.'

I go in, lay you down and walk out.

The crying does not subside.

You waking up early and refusing to settle back down is becoming a common occurrence. We're partly to blame. If you don't go back to sleep after the third cycle of one of us going in, then you usually end up in our bed. Mummy adds that not only is this linked to you adjusting to one nap a day (something you've recently begun transitioning to) but it's also considered normal behaviour in any toddler of your age.

Hip hip hooray!

Regardless of the root cause, it's a pattern of conduct that we hope to break quickly. Because we need you to be able to settle yourself back off to sleep.

Which means a battle.

A battle at a time of day when neither Mummy nor I feel like battling.

It takes considerable effort not to give in. It's hard listening to you in such distress, knowing that we could put an end to it in a flash by reaching into your cot and lifting you out into our arms. But it's still too early in the morning, and if we do that, it sends the wrong message, encouraging an undesirable type of resilience and leading you to have a particular expectation, one you're prepared to battle for vocally.

So, somehow, I again march into your nursery and ignore the face staring back at me, the one that's momentarily full of hope, and longing for human contact. I look away and I lie you back down. I have to look away because I know that to make eye contact is to witness hope drain away from your face as heartache and despair step in to replace it.

It's horrible. I put myself in your shoes and imagine what it must be like for you, believing that your daddy has come to pick you up and take you into his bed for a snuggle. But when that doesn't happen, the frustration erupts. The tears flow, and the sound carries the length of the house and into the place where you want to be.

Mummy starts the timer, like we did almost three months ago when we were battling similar sleep-routine obstacles, but at the other end of the day.

Time slows.

Eventually, the timer counts down from two minutes to zero. The routine is repeated. Mummy and I take turns laying you back down – always without making eye contact and always without speaking.

After the fifth time we cave in. Mummy brings you into bed with us.

You've fought well enough to win this round. Could we have done better? Yes, probably. I mean, there's always room for improvement, but progress is a hard currency to come by when sleep deprivation raids your piggy bank in the predawn light.

Quick side note: it's likely to get confusing with me referring to both your bedroom and your new least-favourite building as 'your nursery', but I'm not about to start referring to either of them as anything different, so you'll need to pay attention.

Also, stop waking up early!

Your Final Settling-In Session
Friday, 12 March 2021

We've made one alteration to our nursery plans today: we're sending you in with Louie. This is not a decision we've made lightly. If you recall the story of Louie's origins[12], which I shared with you last year, you'll remember that he's now about sixteen years old and no longer on sale at any toyshops, gift shops or car boot sales, or on eBay or the dark web. Believe me, we've tried them all. Louie is irreplaceable. After several instances of us *almost* having to file a missing-person report with police, we vowed never to let him leave the house. But the nursery situation is desperate, and desperate times call for desperate measures. Mummy will stress the seriousness of the bond you guys share, along with the fact that Louie is on the endangered-species list. She will repeat this information to staff three times.

For your final settling-in session, you are scheduled to spend two hours with your key worker, Stacey. No parent will be with you. The good news is that the timing of this

---

[12] Read *Dear Arlo: Adventures in Dadding* for the full explanation of how a fifteen-year-old soft toy had remained in my possession long enough to be passed down to my son.

March

particular session means that you will be fed – something that we've found to be an effective pacifying technique.

Despite initially wanting me to drop you off, Mummy has changed her mind. She wants to do it. So, at 1.50 p.m., I kiss you goodbye and wish you the best of luck as you head out the door.

At 2 p.m., Mummy drops you off, leaving you with Stacey. I receive a summary of the handover exchange by text ten minutes later:

> He screamed!!! He clung on to me for dear life, he was so sad going in. I just had to hand him over to Stacey at the door. My heart was in bits!

And after reading that, my heart matches Mummy's. Feelings of abandonment can be excruciating for anyone, let alone a sixteen-month-old. A further update arrives ten minutes later:

> He's stopped crying and he's having a cuddle with Stacey and Louie.

Thank fuck for that.

Further reassurance comes my way. The nursery uses a purpose-built app. Each child has a profile that parents can access. Staff record stats such as what the child ate and how long the child slept for, etc. They also use the app to post pictures throughout the day so we can see what you're up to and how you're getting on. And it's the pictures that have provided me with the extra reassurance. Mummy forwards me a few snaps of you out in the garden. You seem happy enough, though I note that Louie is grasped firmly in your left hand – always a telling sign.

I check my phone regularly, but there are no further updates.

I hear the key turning upstairs a little after 4 p.m. I repeat the same pattern of launching myself upstairs to get an end-of-session summary. Once again, I'm confronted by an upset little boy who's spent the last two hours in the metaphorical trenches, battling feelings and emotions that he's not psychologically equipped to deal with yet. The look on your face is that of a dog walking out of the vet's after it's been neutered.

'Oh, buddy. Did you get upset?'

'He was OK when he was outside, but everything changed when the children sat down for food. He was crying, but he wouldn't eat. He kept pushing his bowl away, so they tried to give him a cracker instead, but he just sat there the whole time holding it, still crying.'

As I hear this, my mind conjures up an accompanying image that runs parallel to the words Mummy speaks, breathing into them nuance and realism and solidifying them into everlasting existence. Unfortunately, this is an image that I cannot and will not forget. It has been incarcerated in one of my long-term memory-bank cells, one that has no concrete walls or prison guards on shift rotation. There will be no periodic review, no good-behaviour benefits and no parole-board meeting – I will never forget.

Hearing this is almost as painful as the time I held you in my arms on the way to the operating theatre for you to have surgery on your eye. The difference here is that I feel responsible for subjecting you to this, whereas the whole eye saga, though it turned out to be almost a false alarm, was driven by the need to fix a physical condition that we had no control over. Sending you to nursery is different because it's our choice. Now I'm questioning whether you're too young and whether Mummy and I told ourselves that it would be

OK because it slotted in nicely with her going back to work. I don't know if we've been selfish or if we've fucked up.

I do know that I can't stand to see you like this. I was excited for you to go to nursery because I believed that you would access experiences and social dynamics that Mummy and I couldn't give you at home.

'What do we do?' I ask Mummy.

'He will be fine, but it will take time for him to get used to it. We just have to accept that it will be difficult for all of us for the next couple of weeks. The good news is he does like Stacey, and she was able to comfort him some of the time. Hopefully they'll become pals.'

The next few hours pass in the same way, with you cuddling a parent while clasping Louie, not once letting him out of your grasp.

I am truly sorry that you're going through this. I know it's hard, believe me. Mummy and I aren't loving it either. I honestly don't know if you're too young to begin nursery or if we were always going to have to get through a pain barrier.

What I do know is that you've been asked to overcome challenges before, ones that I didn't think you were ready to face, and you've vaulted and cleared them every time, and so I'd be remiss to feel anything other than total confidence in you this time round. After all, what is faith if not the belief that others can triumph over adversity?

I believe in you, buddy. *I always do.*

David Attenborough Observes An 'Arlo'
Saturday, 13 March 2021

Sometimes when I watch you eat, I can't help imagining you're the main focus in a David Attenborough documentary. If we stuck cameras all around our house, filmed you during dinner time and then sent the footage to David, I wonder what his commentary on it would sound like.

I imagine it would be a bit like this:

There you see him. That's an Arlo right there. Wandering his home plains looking for food. See how he walks up to his mother and begins hitting her leg. He's telling her that he's hungry and that she's taking too long to feed him. He requires sustenance. And he requires it now. The daddy arrives. The Arlo screams at his parent to pick him up and put him in his chair. You see, an Arlo always associates being placed in his chair with nourishment, so the quicker he's seated, the quicker he assumes he'll get fed. Such an intuitive and clever creature is an Arlo.

Now more screaming, this time accompanied by a lot of banging. Arlos are exceptionally proficient in making unpleasant noises at a surprisingly high volume. He does this to irritate his parents so that they hurry up. Look – it's worked. The daddy has given him some bread to quieten him, allowing himself and the mummy a few precious seconds of silence. But now those seconds have expired and the banging and screaming return. It's always fascinating to see this look of shock on the parents' faces, as if they can't quite believe how a creature as small as an Arlo can consume such large quantities of food so rapidly.

Finally, the mummy serves up tonight's offerings. An Arlo's reaction is often interesting. Sometimes, he'll wolf down the contents in a single mouthful, forgoing any attempt to taste and savour the food. Other times, he suspects foul play – eyeing his bowl with suspicion and comparing the volume of what's in front of him with what's on his parents' plates.

And now the mummy is explaining to the Arlo that what's on his plate is exactly the same as what's on her and the daddy's plates. But he doesn't believe her; that's why the screaming and banging has started again. Success. Here you see extraordinary intelligence at play in the Arlo. He's now engineered it so that both the mummy and the daddy are feeding him from their own plates while the Arlo uses his bare hands to eat from his.

As soon as the Arlo has had his fill, he lifts up his bowl and throws it on the floor and then points to the freezer, demanding a lolly. Remarkable and truly outstanding in every sense of the word: that's the Arlo.

Mother's Day
Sunday, 14 March 2021

'Shall we discuss how today has gone?'
'Nah.'
'Well, I think we should. Let's see. It started with you screaming for us to take you out of your cot at four a.m., didn't it?'
'Nah.'
'I assure you it did because I remember checking my phone while warding off an invisible but deadly auditory assault on my eardrums.'
'Ha.'
'Is that as funny as you slapping me in the face while screaming "Duggee" in my ear at five thirty a.m.?'
'Yeah.'
'Or what about when I tried to put *Hey Duggee* on, but you were pushing me out of my bed while yelling "bottle"?'
'Bottle?'
'No, you've had your bottle.'
'Ooofer?'
'It's interesting that you say that because that's the exact same answer you gave to your mother on Mother's Day when she asked you who you loved.'
'Yeah. Ooofer?'

A Conversation With Louie
Monday, 15 March 2021

It's bedtime, and Mummy is in the bathroom with you cleaning your teeth. I'm in your bedroom waiting. Louie is on the floor nearby, ready to comfort you to sleep. As it's just me and him, I take the opportunity to have a quick word.

'Louie, my old friend, I need a favour. I know I don't need to ask you this as you do it every day, but please look after Arlo at nursery this week. I've underestimated how much of a big deal this is for a young man of his age. But it is. It will be hard for him to adjust to spending long periods of time in a place without anyone he knows. But he will know you. So stay close to him, remind him that his mother and I haven't abandoned him, that things will get easier and that he will come out the other side a better person. Will you do that for me?'

Nursery: The First Day
Tuesday, 16 March 2021

Today more than ever, I could do with you staying in bed until 7 a.m.

5 a.m. 'Whhaaaa.'

I go in, lay you back down, place Louie in your arms and press Ewan's tummy so that he can sing you back off to sleep. *Come on, buddy.*

No dice.

You aren't just unhappy; you are unpacifiable. I set the timer for two minutes. You're still screaming when the two minutes are up, so Mummy goes in and repeats the steps: she lies you down, places Louie in your arms and, if it isn't already there, sticks your dummy back in your mouth.

Two minutes later, and it's my turn.

Another two minutes, and it's Mummy's turn again ... then my turn ... then Mummy's turn ... then my turn ... Eventually, after ninety minutes of almost constant crying, you go back to sleep.

We win this round, but it's not without cost. It's your first full day at nursery and Mummy's first day at work, and now we're behind schedule. Remember, she's starting work at the same nursery as you. She's flustered and a million miles away from reaching a stable enough mental state to begin a new job. 'In what world did I think it was a good idea to go back to work the same day Arlo starts nursery? And why am I working in the same bloody place?!'

Once again, I'm reminded how we've really fucked up your nursery integration. Timing it with Mummy starting her new job was stupid.

I dread going in to wake you at 7.15 a.m., but you stir as soon as I enter the room.

'Bottle?' you say.

Forty-five minutes later, I wish you and Mummy luck, say goodbye and await the drop-off report. It doesn't take long:

> He was so upset. He clung on to me and screamed and screamed. He's not happy at all.

We agree not to make you stay for the whole day. Instead, we enact the contingency protocol that we established last week and call Granny Feeder. She says that she'll collect you after lunch. Mummy sends me a follow-up message an hour later, telling me that you're having a cuddle with one of the staff, and that you've got Louie clenched tight in both hands.

Thank you, Louie.

By the time Mummy finishes her shift, collects you from Granny's house and brings you back, it's almost 6 p.m.

I haven't seen you since this morning, but there's not enough time for us to play. Instead, we have cuddles on the sofa with a bottle and an episode of *In the Night Garden*, before I put you to bed.

I'm not saying it was easy, but you did it. You got through your first day. And so did Mummy. And so did I, I guess.

I am proud of us all.

Nursery: The Second Day
Wednesday, 17 March 2021

Mummy is due to start work at 8 a.m., so we've agreed that I'll drop you off at nursery at 8.30 a.m., leave the car there and walk back home, ready to start my job at 9 a.m. Mummy can then drive home after her shift finishes this evening.

It feels strange to be the one looking after you while Mummy gets ready. I can't remember the last time I was charged with sole parental duties. Nevertheless, it's fun. We watch a bit of television and have breakfast, and I push you around on your bike for ten minutes.

'His eyepatch needs to come off at quarter past nine,' Mummy says. 'If they ask him if he wants them to remove it, he should lie down for them automatically. Remind them that they need to go "low and slow" when peeling it off. Also, don't forget Louie, and remind them of how important and irreplaceable he is. I think you should write all of this down.'

You can tell she's apprehensive. She's not the only one. Still, I'm worried I'll forget something, so I do as Mummy suggests and write down my list of instructions. We then wave her out the door. You and I enjoy some more playtime before I tell you that we need to get ready to leave.

'Car?'
'Yes, we're going in the car. Shall we put your shoes on?'
'Yeah.'

We leave the house without protest on your part. But I believe that's because you're ignorant of where we're going. You've yet to learn the route, but I wager it won't be long. As soon as I park up you recognise the building. Your face transforms into fear. You know what's about to happen.

'Dadda? Whhhaaaa!'

'Buddy, it's OK. I promise you it's OK. Look, we're at your nursery where all your new friends are. There are lots of toys and fun things to do in there. Do you want to play with them?'

'Whhaaaa.'

Mummy wasn't lying when she said this was unpleasant – you are crestfallen and sad. I continue to offer words of comfort and reassurance: a soothing vocal solace to combat the sadness and the emotional instability of a small boy who believes he's once again about to be abandoned. But it's no use. I might as well be speaking a language you don't understand. It's like using a water pistol to battle a woodland blaze.

Because of Covid-19, I can't go into the building. Instead, I walk through a nearby gate that leads me to a side entrance, where I'm greeted by a member of staff who first needs to take your temperature before admitting you for the day. She introduces herself, but her name doesn't register. What does register is how much you don't want to let go of me. All four little limbs are wrapped around me like a latex garment, and I can feel tears splashing on the side of my neck. You're also shaking. Your temperature is fine but there's a part of me that wishes it wasn't.

I take a deep breath and prepare to hand you over, but then I'm asked about your eyepatch – you know, one of the two things on the list that I had to relay, both of which I've already forgotten because I'm having a really hard time right now. I deliver the instructions but with one on-the-spot alteration. I say, 'You may need to remove the eyepatch sooner if he doesn't stop crying. If his tears have nowhere to go, then he's at risk of waterlogging.'

'We'll manage. He will be fine, honestly.'

'And please don't lose his monkey.'

'We won't, I promise.'

I hand you over without making eye contact. This is not for your benefit.

'Dadda … Dadda … Dadda …!'

Jesus Christ.

As I'm leaving, I hear 'Oi!' I turn to find your mother poking her head out of a nearby window. She's got a baby in her arms.

'You look like you're about to cry. Are you OK?'

'I'm fine.'

'Did you bring a dummy with you?'

Fuck, fuck, fuck. She didn't tell me to write that down! 'You didn't tell me to write that down.'

'Wasn't it obvious?'

Obviously it wasn't obvious! Arlo, I don't have a set of weighing scales, but I reckon Mummy has thrown a large cup of salt into the gaping emotional wound that runs from my right shoulder down to my left hip.

'He's in a toddler room in a nursery. They must have a thousand dummies.'

One of Mummy's colleagues steps in to confirm with a smile and a nod that they do.

'There, you see. Right, I'm off.'

I text Granny Feeder to let her know that an early-afternoon collection would be greatly appreciated. Then I use what little physical strength I have left, marshalling my legs to move in a forward direction.

That was one of the hardest bits of dadding I've ever done.

I make it home and have an unproductive morning at work. I still can't shake off the look of rejection on your face. No child should ever be made to feel abandoned like that. What with you starting nursery and regressing with your sleep, you're having a shit month. And it's not likely to improve any time soon.

Conversations On The Toilet
Thursday, 18 March 2021

It's just you and me in the house. Mummy is at work. I'm on the toilet, and you've decided to accompany me to ensure I don't get lonely and to take the opportunity to have a bit of a bathroom sort-out. You start under the sink.

'Dadda?' you say, proffering a brand-new toilet roll that you've found.

'Ta. But there's already one here on the side.'

'Yeah.'

You shuffle away, returning under the sink, where you remove the neatly stacked tower of toilet rolls and begin re-erecting them on the floor.

And now you're biting into one of them.

'Arlo, don't eat that, please. Dirty.'

'Dirty?'

'Yeah.'

You ignore me and continue to treat the toilet roll like it's a stick of candyfloss.

'Arlo. Don't do that.'

'Poo poo.'

'I'm trying to, but it's difficult to focus.'

My meaning registers with you. You stand up and invite yourself over to try and sit on my lap.

'Arlo, I think now's as good a time as any to have a conversation about personal space.'

'Yeah.'

'Excellent. Well first, let me define what personal space is— No, Arlo, that's Daddy's willy. Stop trying to slap it, please. No, this isn't a game.'

Having given up on trying to assault my genitalia, you move on to shaking the glass shower panel before emptying the bin and knocking over the toilet brush. Then you indulge in a second attempt at slapping me in a place where no man welcomes an attack, before finally eating the toilet roll again.

'Have kids,' they said. 'It'll be fun,' they said.

March Monthly Review
Friday, 19 March 2021

It's been one of the toughest months we've had since you were a newborn. That's due to a combination of factors: you continuing to wake up long before any remotely acceptable time; Mummy returning to work; and you starting nursery. There's nothing we can do about it. We need to ride it out and wait for it to pass. Hopefully, it won't be long.

I've spoken to a few other dads about you starting nursery, confessing how hard we've found it as a family. I get the same response every time – words to the effect of: 'It won't be long until he shrugs your hand off and sprints through the doors without saying goodbye.' I take comfort in the consistent response because I'm dreading the next time I'm on drop-off duty.

Tellings-off have begun to ramp up, particularly when you trash *Mummy's* cushions. I did point out that if we both paid for the sofa, then surely they're *our* cushions. But apparently paying an equal share for goods doesn't necessarily mean you have joint ownership of them. That's according to the Matriarch anyway, who as we all know by now only makes statements that are supported by absolute authority, hard facts and more wisdom than the world's collected teachings on philosophy.

Staying on cushions, the subject has caused a bit of friction between your parents. Personally, I'm not affronted if you want to trash them. I find it amusing, and I get a kick out of watching you play in that fashion. Mummy finds it neither amusing nor enjoyable, so you get told off, which then places me in a tricky position because I need to back her up so that we're not broadcasting mixed messages, but as I said, I'm not on board with a bit of cushion roughhousing being a bad thing. I believed I could skirt around the issue by teaching you how to climb up the radiator and use it as a stepping stone to reach the windowsill for a bashing-on-the-glass sesh, which I want on record as being an activity that involves zero mishandling of any fabrics. But Mummy doesn't approve of my physical education programme either. She claims it's dangerous. I claim there's no pleasing some people.

I did have to tell you off myself, though, for tipping the oil diffuser on the bed – an action that was preceded by several repetitions of the warning: 'Arlo, don't do that.'

You've started to say 'Mamma' again. I have no idea why it took a three-month hiatus, but Mummy's delighted to see it return as a regular utterance. What she's not too delighted about is your decision to rip out of her hands any book that she's trying to read from, thrust it into my hands and exclaim 'Dadda'. Apparently, you favour my storytelling voice over hers. She's already suggested to me that you hate her.

You've learnt more words: 'feather', 'park', 'keys', 'apple', 'nana'. We've moved into that phase where we have to spell out certain words like p-a-r-k and w-a-l-k because you erupt in excitement and begin bouncing up and down like a rubber ball, assuming that we plan to action either of those pastimes immediately.

The park has been a great source of fun and vitality for us all this month. The weather has warmed, and your stability and confidence on your feet increase each day. You can now climb the steps to the bigger-boy slide by yourself. You throw oats *at* the ducks, chase pigeons, converse with doggies and are always on the lookout for squirrels.

I'll end by telling you my two favourite developments for March. First, another new phrase that you've learnt to say is 'I did it!' which you exclaim loudly, with pride and joy. Secondly, you have become a lot cuddlier and more affectionate. Often, you'll walk up to us and lay your head down in our lap, and you regularly snuggle in bed or on the sofa, which is sweet.

Your objectives for next month are the following: stay in bed until 7 a.m., and learn that when we drop you off at nursery, it doesn't mean we're gone forever.

Nana and Grandad See-See And Nana Smurf
Saturday, 20 March 2021

Listen, I need you to pay attention because I've got something to explain to you that's confusing. Historically, we named Mummy's parents, your grandparents, Granny Feeder and Grandad Tools. And we named my mum Granny Smurf because, as you know, she *had* blue hair, even though we later realised Smurfs themselves do not (only their skin is blue). They seemed like appropriate enough names, and you were only a ball of cells at the time, so you were unable to cast a vote.

But after you were born, two things happened. First, Covid-19. Second, you started learning to talk.

During lockdown, Mummy would often video-call Granny Feeder as that was our only means of social interaction. It was always Granny who got called, because Grandad barely knows how to operate a toaster, let alone something as complex as a smartphone. As soon as Granny answered the phone you would say, 'See?' which we quickly figured out was your way of asking to see your grandad, and that pattern of you requesting to 'see' him has gradually evolved into his new name, Grandad See-See. It's quite the endearing little story when you think about it. Granny Feeder has also undergone the 'See-See' rebrand, along with another alteration: Granny is now Nana, making her official new title Nana See-See.

Granny Smurf has had the same granny-to-nana overhaul. So, Granny Smurf is now Nana Smurf.

Can you stop doing this, please? Understand that part of our income involves me exploiting our family by writing books about our adventures, and it almost certainly gets confusing when you repeatedly insist on changing the names of central characters. Thank you.

Not Doing The Washing Properly
Sunday, 21 March 2021

I'm downstairs working while you're upstairs in the kitchen eating lunch. Mummy's with you as well, but she's sorting out the washing while also on a video call to Auntie Lisa. I've left the door open, which is fortuitous because I can overhear Mummy stating with absolute clarity how much of an asset I am in our household.

'He's absolutely useless with the washing. He does everything the wrong way. I wish he would do it properly.'

Arlo, I love your mother, and I respect her and value everything she does for me. But if there is one thing that I can't fucking stand, it's when she uses the word 'properly' to highlight my ineptitude. That pushes my buttons harder than an ADHD kid at the arcade.

I mean, for starters, who defines how to *properly* do the washing anyway? Is there a governing body? No, there's not. Perhaps there's a regulator who publishes best practice guidelines on their website. Nope, there's not one of those either. There's no washing dossier, no sanctioned measures to observe and no formal accreditation, and you certainly can't hold a licence in HOW-TO-DO-THE-FUCKING-WASHING!

She's still going on.

'... and he never selects the big items for the radiator. He always chooses something small, like Arlo's clothes.'

If my brain is a limited company, then not only has it undergone a period of intense attrition, but there's a blanket recruitment freeze. It even says so on the company home page: *I'm sorry, but we're not recruiting any more brain cells right now. We're continuing to operate with zero intellectual capacity.*

Arlo, she's still fucking at it.

'He doesn't even bother to fold the washing up before hanging it out ... I mean ...?'

OK, I confess it. Mummy is right. I don't bother to use up fifteen minutes of my life folding up wet washing to then unfold it and hang it on the dryer. I can't be the only inhabitant of the planet who believes that's beyond fucking bonkers, can I?

'... and – *and* – he doesn't even know the right way to hang jeans. Even though I've told him a million times.'

Enough is enough. I walk upstairs and make my presence known. 'You do realise I can hear everything.'

'Yeah,' she says, in a manner that would suggest I've just educated her on the colour of the sky.

'Then why are you slagging off my laundry skills?'

'Oh baby, you silly sausage, you know you don't do it properly.'

ARRRGGGHHHHH!

Mars Vs Venus
Monday, 22 March 2021

'Arlo, what leggings do you want to wear?' says Mummy, who then presents you with three options. You select the mustard-yellow ones.

'Ah. I'm afraid that's incorrect, and Mummy will need to step in and intervene.'

'Why give him the option in the first place?' I say.

'Because sometimes he gets it right, and I like to make him think he's in control, but sometimes he gets it wrong and I need to put a stop to it. I can't have him showing me up in public, can I?'

'Well, when you put it like that.'

'Exactly.'

'We can't afford for our standards to slip, even if we are in a global pandemic and can't get closer than two metres to anyone.'

'Don't start being a prick.'

'What about his top half?'

'Well, first I thought a royal blue would be the order of the day but now I've changed my mind. I want him in an autumnal-brown long-sleeved top.'

'Would you excuse me for a minute?'

'Where are you going?'

'To shoot myself in the face.'

Children's Television
Wednesday, 24 March 2021

You know it's time to burst into tears when you turn on CBeebies only to be rewarded with a bright blue screen displaying a message to viewers telling them that the channel isn't currently broadcasting. Why the tears, you ask? Because if nothing's broadcasting, then it means it's before 6 a.m., and if we're turning on the television before 6 a.m., then it's because we've lost yet another early-morning wake-up battle with you.

But our woes are far from over because when 6 a.m. does eventually arrive, it's *Baby Jake* that kicks off a glamourous session of awful fucking children's programmes. After we slog through *Baby Jake*, we're treated to a double episode of sulky-twat *Bing*.

Next, we're made to endure *Teletubbies*, where the UK's parents-of-toddlers population are still scratching their heads and wondering who is looking after the Tiddlytubbies. Seriously, can we quickly address the issue? Mummy says that there should be a minimum of one member of staff per three babies. There's eight of the dweebs and not a single member of staff in sight. The Teletubbies themselves do fuck all; they just gawp at them from behind a window.

But I digress.

After *Teletubbies* we move on to *Tee and Mo*, a show that presents itself as charming, but I find the character noises unfathomably agonising and the stories dull. A slight reprieve wends its way to us at 6.50 a.m. when *Chuggington* rolls in (pun intended), but I can't tell if *Chuggington* is any good or if it's the best of a bad bunch of shit that airs before 7 a.m.

Of course, when we get to 7 a.m., we've got yet another double episode of that annoying bunny, *Bing*, hopping his way back onto our screens, whining about a broken yellow crayon and the odd number of carrots on his plate.

Eventually, we make it to 7.15 a.m., when good old reliable *Hey Duggee* stops me reaching for a pack of razor blades – thank God for Saint Duggley. After that, you've got *Go Jetters*, which is almost pleasant, mainly because it has an awesome theme tune. Not that we get to enjoy it, mind you, because it's now time for breakfast, and the television has been switched off.

That's our morning. Is that not the saddest, most sorrowful state of affairs ever, or what?

Kill Me Now
Thursday, 25 March 2021

I've read *That's Not My Princess* twelve times in the last fifteen minutes.

The Hungry Arlo Caterpillar
Sunday, 28 March 2021

On Sunday, the hungry Arlo ate through two scoops of brown rice, one scoop of butter chicken curry, two poppadoms, a chunk of naan bread, one whole orange and one small bowl of yoghurt, but he was still hungry. He screamed 'more, more, more' at his Mummy and Daddy, but they decided enough was enough and brought dinner time to a close. Soon afterwards, they wrapped him in a sleeping sack a bit like a cocoon, kissed him goodnight and hoped and prayed that he would stay in there for a minimum of twelve hours, whereafter he would wake in a mood of such jubilance that you'd think he was a newly birthed colourful butterfly.

Fancy Dress
Monday, 29 March 2021

I leave you alone with your sippy cup for all of three seconds, and when I return, you look like you're off to a fancy-dress party dressed as a pond.

Nursery: Update
Wednesday, 31 March 2021

Yesterday was a good day. You didn't cry when we parked up, you didn't cry when we walked to the gate, and you didn't cry while we waited outside for Stacey to come and collect you. Eventually, you did start crying, but this was a softer display of the blues compared with previous handovers. Hopefully, this means we've turned a corner because I'm once again on drop-off duty, and you and I are en route to your nursery this very moment.

But alas, we're not quite there yet. You start crying before I can put the handbrake on: real tears – weighty, free-flowing liquid marbles splashing on your car seat and on your clothes. And, because you woke up late this morning, you still have your eyepatch on, ensuring that once again, your fears of neglect are accompanied by one waterlogged eye.

Does that not paint the most tragic picture?

'Arlo, when you go to school today, are you going to play with the dinosaurs? What noise does a dinosaur make?'

Asking you that question was a mistake because you go ahead and reply, but it's a reply performed through the lens of your current emotional state; you sob out the tiniest 'roar' and your moments-ago clear-as-glass tears turn opaque and cloudy, because it's not only your eyes that are streaming, it's your nose as well.

I get you out of the car and walk over to the drop-off gate. Your head is lowered to the floor. I've got a knot in my chest rotating like a Catherine-wheel, projecting red-hot needles into my surrounding organs, searing and shredding their way through the soft tissue. The only consolation is that when we meet Stacey, you hold your arms out to her. This tells me that the bond you guys share is becoming stronger. And you've also got Louie. Thank God for that monkey. This week, Louie is adorned with an additional fashion accessory: a scarf. Attached to the scarf is a microchip that sounds an alarm if triggered through an app on my phone. It's an insurance policy that's been long overdue. We can now track him if he should go missing anywhere in the world.

I hope your day brightens up, buddy. Again, there's nothing I can say other than what I've said previously: that I'm sorry you're having a tough time of it at the moment, and that I promise you'll come through the other side of this emotionally tricky bedding-in period a happier and more confident little boy. *At least, I hope you will.*

April

'Need to "quickly" pop to the shops with a toddler? Budget at least ninety minutes and you might succeed.'

Martin S, an old uni mate

Wake-Up Call
Thursday, 1 April 2021

In the month of March, there were only four occasions where you woke up after 6 a.m. It should be abundantly obvious what's expected of you for April, young man.

Pick Whatever You Want
Sunday, 4 April 2021

It's Easter Sunday. I approach you with an outstretched hand. In it is a bowl of chocolate and behind the bowl is an orange.

'You can have anything you want,' I say.

Not missing a beat, your hand shoots over the bowl and claims the orange.

Every day I question my decisions as a parent, but not giving you sweets and chocolate since birth is one that I stand firmly behind as being among the best.

Happy Easter, son.

Who Wants To Be A Good Dad?
Tuesday, 6 April 2021

Applause.

'Well, I bet you didn't think you'd get this far, did you?' says a smiling Chris Tarrant.

The applause dies down and the studio audience falls silent. Palpable anticipation ripples through the crowd. The lights reflect off a large sign on the wall: *Who Wants to Be a Good Dad?*

'Chris, I'm as surprised as anyone. No one had any faith in me, and to be honest, I didn't have any faith in myself.'

'OK. Well, look, let's do a recap. You didn't once look at your phone this morning, even – *even* – while Arlo was watching *Tee and Mo*, which, as viewers know, isn't one of your preferred children's television shows.'

'No, it's really not, Chris.' *Stupid Tee and Mo, always bickering every episode.*

'And then, of course, you got through breakfast without making a mess, and you logged some solid playtime involving an assault course, after which you and Arlo chased each other around the house with a broom.'

'I didn't think I'd be able to transition between the two activities quite so naturally, but I did.'

'And then, rounding out a solid performance so far, you managed to brush Arlo's teeth without arguing with him to keep his mouth open.'

'I don't know what to say, I just ... did it.'

'Is there anything you can't do?'

'I don't think I could get away with cheating on my wife for a decade.'

'Oi! You cheeky man! Less of that.'

'Sorry, Chris. Low blow.'

'Well, you've made it to the final. One question remains. Of course, you don't have to play. You can take the prize money right now and leave with a respectable mostly-a-good-dad sum of money.'

'I'm tempted.'

'Or – *or* – you could set your sights on the impossible and become a winner of *Who Wants to Be a Good Dad?*

Gulp.

'Shall we have a look at the question before you decide?'

'OK, yeah. Let's have a look.'

The studio lights dim, engulfing the audience in darkness. Only contestant and host remain visible. A thumping-heartbeat sound effect meshes with edge-of-your-seat-suspenseful music, pressing all sorts of psychological buttons that sit deep within the subconscious. Everything has been designed for one purpose, and one purpose only – to build tension.

'To win *Who Wants to Be a Good Dad?* answer this question: what will you dress Arlo in this morning, knowing, and this is crucial, knowing that he's going to nursery and that his mother's colleagues will see and judge your outfit choice?'

I'm so, so fucked. 'Chris, I ... That's as tough as it gets.'

'Well, it's the final. What did you expect?'

'I know, but outfit choices are subjective. There are countless variables to work with.'

'So, say the word, and the journey ends right now. You walk away as a mostly-a-good-dad runner-up. There's no shame in that.'

'I know ... except ... I can't ... I didn't come this far to settle for second place.'

Thud-thump, thud-thump, thud-thump.

'Chris, I'm gonna play.'

A loud collective intake of breath by the audience reverberates around the studio.

'You're a brave man. I wish you the best of luck. Please begin when you're ready.'

'Thanks, Chris. Well, leggings are a no-brainer, because Arlo will be at nursery. He'll hopefully be walking around a lot, and he's always favoured leggings over jeans. Plus, I know he has a navy-blue pair in his drawer, and navy goes with almost anything.'

'Sound thinking.'

'But his top half is tricky because of the weather. The temperature is three degrees from now until ten a.m., but Arlo's mother is always telling me not to check the temperature but to scroll down on the weather app, and check the "feels like" section because that might be colder than the actual temperature.'

'What does it say?'

'It says it will feel like minus two degrees.'

'Tricky.'

'I think I'll definitely go for a long-sleeved vest and a jumper, obviously. But the middle layer ... I don't know if he needs a short- or a long-sleeved T-shirt ...'

'I'm glad I'm not in your shoes.'

What to do, what to do?

'Remember, you've got one lifeline left. You can phone a friend.'

'Of course. I forgot I had that.'

'You want to use it?'

'Obviously, yes. Let's do it.'

'OK. Who would you like to call?'

'I'm gonna ring Louie the chimpanzee. He's Arlo's best friend.'

'Do you think Louie will know the answer?'

'He has to. He's observed more of Arlo's outfit changes than anyone else, including me.'

'OK. Calling Louie now.'

Ring ring.

'Ooh ah?'

'Hi. Is that Louie the chimpanzee?'

'Ooh.'

'Louie, it's Chris Tarrant here from *Who Wants to Be a Good Dad?* I've got Arlo's father with me. He's managed to reach the final, and he has one parental decision left. He needs your help. Are you ready?'

'Ooh ooh, ah ah.'

'OK. You'll have thirty seconds from the moment I pass you over to Arlo's daddy. Your time starts ... now.'

'Louie buddy, I need to select Arlo's outfit. I've settled on navy leggings, a long-sleeved vest and a navy woollen jumper, but I'm stuck on his T-shirt. Do I select a long-sleeved—'

'Ah ooh ooh.'

'Exactly.'

'Ah ah ooh ooh?'

'Three degrees but feels like minus two.'

'AHHHAAAA!'

'I know, right? If Arlo keeps his jumper on, it will be OK because the jumper and leggings match. But if he overheats and it comes off, then everyone will see what I've gone for. If he gets too hot and the staff realise I've dressed him in three long-sleeved layers, then I'll definitely get labelled a shit dad. But then if I go for short sleeves and they see—'

'Fifteen seconds.'

'Ooh ah ah ooh?'

'No, I only know the outside temperature, but I don't know if they'll let the children outside to play.'

'Ten seconds.'

'Oh oh ah ah ah.'

Yes! Thank God. 'Louie, that is music to my ears. I knew you would know the answer. OK, quick, tell me what to do.'

'Ooh ooh—'

'Time's up. I'm so sorry,' says Chris.

'What? No!'

Pained, sympathetic stares travel in from every single audience member to the centre of the main stage.

'Do you know, I can't remember the last time we had an episode filled with this much drama. If it's any consolation, this will be great for the show's ratings.'

It's not.

'Well, we're at crunch point. What's it gonna be?'

'I'm gonna go with my gut and select a navy and mustard-yellow short-sleeved T-shirt and hope that it remains cold enough that he doesn't take his jumper off.'

'Final parental decision?'

'Final parental decision.'

'OK, that's now locked in. There's no going back from here. You know what to do. Send Arlo's mother the message.'

'OK, Chris. Doing it now.'

It's very important you tell me how well I did with Arlo's outfit selection today. Feel free to ask your colleagues as well.

'And now we wait,' says Chris.

Moments later ... *beep-beep.*

'What does it say?'

'It says, *I think he looks cute. That's one of his best jumpers.* Fuck. I've done it!'

The audience explodes into rapturous applause. Chris and I jump up from our seats and embrace. 'You did it! You've won *Who Wants to Be a Good Dad?*

'I just ... I can't ... I did it!'

The applause becomes louder and more animated; it's joined by a chorus of cheering and even a few wolf whistles. Streamers and balloons fill the air. Fireworks explode safely inside the studio in a symphony of light, colour and coordination; sparks dance together to form the word

Winner in the air. And now, attractive, skimpily clad blondes are strutting into view from the wings, and they're shaking their stuff in a celebratory dance. From above, a section of the roof descends revealing a circular stage, and standing in the middle is Adele, who, in the last few seconds, has managed to write a brand-new song about my journey to winning *Who Wants to Be a Good Dad?* And then, as if things couldn't get any better, Jessica Rabbit sashays up to me carrying a polished silver platter that's topped with Marmite sandwiches. She tells me that I've been given a hall pass from Mummy to spend the night doing anything I want with her.

THIS IS THE BEST DAY EVER!

After shaking the hands of a hundred audience members and rubbing shoulders with some very famous journalists who are desperate to grab a quote, I excuse myself to the side of the studio and respond to Mummy's message:

> I can't believe I got it right, even with the short-sleeved T-shirt over the long-sleeved vest. Is that what Mummy would have done then?

The reply arrives almost instantly:

> What? No. Mummy wouldn't do that at all. Mummy would have done something very different.

The music stops. So do the smiles and the handshakes. The journalists still want a quote, though. Chris Tarrant has his hand to his ear, nodding away in a grave manner, taking on board a hasty set of instructions from the producer.

Adele is nowhere to be seen or heard.

Neither is Jessica Rabbit.

Jessica ...?

The audience retreat back into their seats and wait for Chris Tarrant to speak. Eventually, he looks up.

'Ladies and gentleman, it breaks my heart to say it, but Arlo's daddy hasn't won *Who Wants to Be a Good Dad?*' He looks at me and continues: 'I'm sorry, but you got the decision wrong. I mean, come on, short sleeves over long sleeves! It wasn't that hard, was it?'

You backstabbing bas—

'I'm afraid you leave today with nothing, except the title of Shit Parent. Is there anything you want to say?'

'Fuck you, Chris. Go cheat on your wife again.'

'Well, she left me, so I can't. Anyhow, thanks for playing.' He turns to the nearest camera. 'Join us next time for *Who Wants to Be a Good Dad?* Goodbye.'

An Otherwise Brilliant Plan
Thursday, 8 April 2021

'Dadda, Dadda, Dadda, Dadda.'

'Dadda's right here. What have you got – my jumper?'

'Yeah.'

It's early. I'm still in bed while Mummy is getting ready for work, which means it's my turn to look after you until Nana Smurf collects you at 9 a.m.

'Why have you brought me my jumper?'

'Yeah. Dadda.'

That doesn't answer my question, but OK. I swing my legs out of bed and you sprint away and over to the stair gate.

'Dadda. Dadda. Dadda. DADDA!'

'I'm coming.'

I unlock the gate, throw my jumper over my shoulder and pick you up, and we both head downstairs. As soon as I put you down, you sprint over to the basement door, yelling, 'Key, key, key, key.'

My eyes travel from my jumper, which is now in my hands, to you by the basement door and then to the back door.

You clever little bastard.

Everything now makes sense. Your objective all along has been to go outside. That's why you began your campaign by picking up my jumper and handing it to me because you know I put one on to come outside with you. Except we can't go outside, because the back door is locked, and we keep the back-door key on a shelf at the top of the basement stairs.

You've impressed me. Big time. It's not the level of sequencing, involving several actions that need to happen in order to get you what you want, but it's also the fact that you've remained so focused. Your attention span these days is virtually non-existent, so seeing you this morning progressing through your cognitive process in this way has definitely earned my respect.

But there was one tiny flaw in an otherwise brilliant plan: if you want to go and play outside, don't wake me up at 5.30 a.m.

In Here
Friday, 9 April 2021

'In here, in here, in here, in here, in here, in here, in here, in here, in here, in here, in here, in here in here, in here, in here. Dadda?'

'Yes, Arlo, I understand that you want me to give you the orange so that you can stuff it in your mouth. I also understand that "in here" means your mouth, because you're pointing to it, but what you need to understand is that Daddy needs to peel the orange before you can devour it. Do you understand?'

'Yeah.'

'Good b—'

'In here, in here, in here, in here, in here, in here, in here, in here, in here, in here. Dadda, Dadda, Dadda, Dadda, Dadda. In here, in here, in here, in here—'

Fuck my fuckin' life.

Antibiotics
Sunday, 11 April 2021

'Can't you do a test to say for certain?' I ask.

'If we swab the back of his throat, it won't be accurate, because there may be other bacteria present that void the test,' says the doctor on the other end of the phone.

'What about a blood test?'

'It takes a while for this type of infection to reflect in the blood work, so again, it won't be accurate.'

'So, you're saying our only option is "not to take any chances" and give him antibiotics based on a high temperature and a phone call to you, yes?'

'That's right. You seem reluctant to give him antibiotics.'

'I am reluctant. I don't believe anyone, especially children, should have antibiotics unless it's absolutely necessary. But it's hard for me to determine if it is necessary because apparently there isn't an accurate way to test him, which puts parents in a challenging position when they're trying to make the best decisions for their children's health.'

'I do understand, but his temperature is thirty-eight point nine degrees, and he's had a cough for over a month.'

'Yes, but the temperature has only spiked in the last eighteen hours.'

'What I think has happened is that Arlo has had a viral infection that he hasn't quite been able to fend off, and now he has a bacterial infection as a result. If you leave him, it's possible his immune system will eventually fight it, but if it doesn't, then it will be difficult to treat him ...'

Arlo, what the fuck, fuck, fuck do I do here? And how have we, as a species that has mastered flight and invented the internet, not found a way to test if an infant has a bacterial infection? I'm chin-to-the-floor surprised that the solution is a spray-and-pray approach using antibiotics. That's like walking into the middle of a burgeoning, lush allotment plot that's teeming with ripe fruits and vegetables and letting loose with a flamethrower, all because there is anecdotal evidence that a rat could be lurking around.

I hate this. I really hate this. But I've got no choice, have I? I either roll the dice and see if you can get through it, knowing I'm putting you at risk of further pain and suffering, or go with the 'don't take any chances' approach and flood your body with merciless warrior-style compounds that go in and do a thorough job of flushing your system out, removing the bacterial infection (if it's there) and hopefully not inflicting any long-term negative alterations on your microbiome.

Parents should not be in this position. No wonder the Western world is rapidly moving up the statistics chart in respect of autoimmune-related diseases. It's in scenarios like this where I'm reminded of the Desmond Tutu quotation: 'There comes a point where we need to stop just pulling people out of the river. We need to go upstream and find out why they're falling in.'[13]

---

13 Look, I'm not a doctor. I'm not offering medical advice. This chapter reflects my opinion based on my research, and it's an opinion I'm ready to revisit any time I learn more. Please don't go making decisions on your children's health – particularly whether to give them antibiotics or not – on the strength of this chapter. Seek advice from a medical professional.

It's 10 p.m. In the last hour, I've driven to four pharmacies. Three of them didn't have the antibiotics in stock, and the fourth wasn't even a pharmacy, which led me to the conclusion that Google is a prick. I guess your antibiotics will have to wait until tomorrow because you sure as hell aren't getting any tonight.

By the way, Arlo, spoiler: today has failed to make it into my all-time top ten favourites.

Antibiotics Acquired
Monday, 12 April 2021

I've finally managed to acquire your antibiotics. Today, your calendar has been wiped clean. All-important meetings and tasks have been rescheduled.

Rest up, buddy.

It's the end of the day and you have begun to perk up. Which is a relief, but I'm still not on board with dishing out antibiotics on a whim.

April Monthly Review
Monday, 19 April 2021

With Mummy returning to work, you starting nursery and the UK slowly beginning to open back up, we've had the

April

busiest month in a long time, and it's demanded a lot of adjustment. But what's great about all this change is that you and I now get more one-on-one time together, either in the morning or the evening. It varies depending on Mummy's shift pattern and whether I have to drop you off at, or collect you from, nursery.

To add to the joy of the increased pace of life, the three of us have spent the majority of the month being ill. As one cold passes, another arrives to tag in. But it's not all snotty tissues and sombre tales, because if I ask you what noise a pterodactyl makes, you yell 'kar-kar!' and if I ask you what Hulk says, you go 'grrrr'.

A few more teeth have cut through, including a couple of molars – *ouch!* Yesterday, you insisted we take a break from cleaning Arlo's teeth so that Arlo could clean Louie's teeth.

Speaking of Louie, he has a lot of company these days as your affinity for soft toys grows. Accompanying you now alongside Louie at bedtime are some of the characters from *In the Night Garden*, usually Makka Pakka and one of the Tombliboos. Bing Bunny is also present.

We've not had as many 5 a.m. wake-up calls, which is a huge improvement on last month, but there's been enough of them to warrant me calling you a little arsehole behind your back a few times.

There have been a few new words that you can say clearly, like 'keys', 'cracker', 'off' and 'Stacey' (from nursery), and once again there's a lot more that you're trying to say, but you haven't cracked the enunciation yet. We've been able to interpret most of them, though. 'Apple' is 'apool' and 'orange' is 'ora'. The biggest leap in your vocabulary was when you strung three words together this month. You said (a few times): 'Sit here, Mamma.'

Staying on the topic of your mother, you've been more receptive to her this month, something that I'm sure her mental health is grateful for, not to mention our stomachs. You were giving her a complex. But all evidence remains in favour of you becoming a daddy's boy. I'm still your number-one preference to read to you before bed. But, if you wake up in the night, it's Mamma that you call for. Good boy. You know how Mummy is; she likes to be wanted. Plus, if it's the middle of the night, then I absolutely support your decision to call for Mamma instead of Dadda.

Your climbing skills have developed. It's got to a point where I've begun encouraging you to take on more challenging routes. I do this because I'm getting sick and tired of telling you not to climb on the table as it's dangerous, only for you to laugh in my face and do it anyway. My new parenting approach is to let you get adept at climbing so you reduce the chances of an injury. Genius, right?

You can open doors, and occasionally you lash out when frustrated, but these occurrences are rare.

You are growing fonder of spending time outside. You like to sweep up and tell Daddy that the nappies he's thrown out the window from the first floor are 'dirty' and that they need to go 'in here', which you say while pointing to the bin. We've had a chap come over and quote us for some work out in the garden. It has become a priority for us to ensure we toddler-proof it and make it a fun environment for you to explore.

Dropping you off at nursery is becoming marginally less of a heartbreak. Reports from staff tell us that you're exploring and playing more. You're also eating lots – *shock* – and napping well.

New reduced lockdown measures mean we can now see other people outside, in groups of six. I've caught up with some of our friends, whom I've not seen in almost a year. Human contact is like air, and it's vital to the survival of our species. Neither Mummy nor I have been called up for our vaccines yet, but I don't believe it will be long.

As always, thanks for another month of dadding.

Get Out Of My Way, Doris
Wednesday, 21 April 2021

It's fallen to me to collect you from nursery. Mummy has the car, so I'm on foot. I commence the operation by launching myself out of the front door and turning 45 degrees to acquire my heading. From there, I set off marching at a pace that would rival a T-1000.

The sun is beating down, but I pay it no notice. My mind is empty of all thoughts, feelings and distractions, save one: to get to my boy as quickly as possible. You see, word has reached my ear by way of a phone call from Mummy that you've had a tough day, one that's been punctuated by long bouts of crying and distress. And your emotional fragility dictates I hurry up.

Hold tight, son, I'm on my way.

Not only have I heeded your distress call, but I bring with me the biggest fucking banana you have ever seen and a *Paw Patrol* sippy cup that's filled with ice-cold filtered water.

Nothing will stop me!

Arlo, something is stopping me or at least slowing me down, which is the same thing in my book. What we've got is a classic Doris-dawdler, drearily dilly-dallying her way forward in the same direction and occupying the same traffic lane as me. It gets worse. Whereas my pace is currently rivalling that of a racehorse, Doris-dawdler's is barely rivalling a past-its-sell-by-date packet of Flumps. I'm like, 'Doris, get the fuck out of my way – my boy needs me!'

I think about whacking Doris across the back with the banana but, after once again checking the size of this thing,

I refrain. It's massive! It's like dragging a bent and out-of-shape lamp post behind me, but one that's more girthy and more yellow. So instead, I sidestep Doris, barely slowing down but doing so enough to throw her a *look*, before taking the next right, crossing the road and entering the hospital grounds. Your nursery is located at the back of the complex.

As I snake my way along the various footpaths and alleys, I attract a few *looks* myself from various individuals. They glance from me to the nine-inch banana and child's sippy cup, wondering why I'm in such a rush. *Let them stare. They don't know what drives me.*

As I approach the nursery, I can see other parents arriving to collect their children. Fleetingly, I wonder if their kids have had a challenging day like you, Arlo, but then I push the thought away because I can't help their children; I can only help my boy.

Despite these other parents arriving before me, they've yet to make it to the entrance, so I speed up, accelerating from racehorse speed to that of a throttle-jammed-down Formula 1 car, swiftly overtaking them and arriving at the back gate. It might strike you as excessive, but we're still observing Covid-19 restrictions, which means we parents have to queue up two metres apart from each other and wait while staff hand over children one by one. I refuse to be stuck in a queue. Goodness knows how your emotional fragility is now – you're probably set to shatter into a billion pieces.

'Hello, who are you here to pick up?' says a staff member.

I puff my chest out, inflating it to the size of an almost-full moon, before responding: 'I'm here to collect Arlo – I'm his dad!'

A couple of minutes later, I see you slowly shuffling towards me with your head and shoulders slumped. But then, you look up. You see me and you smile. And then, you see the—

'NANA!' you scream.
'Would you like this, Arlo?'
'YEAH!'
Come on then, buddy, let's get you home.

Shoplifting
Thursday, 22 April 2021

In Arlo-world, it was fortuitous that the staff at the local Tesco opted to place the oranges on the lower section of the display stand because it was incredibly easy for you to perform your first attempt at shoplifting. And bonus points for determination deserve to be awarded because, even when I returned the first orange that you tried to steal, you went back for a second crack at the heist.

Where To Put The Fruit Bowl
Friday, 23 April 2021

'We need to have a serious conversation about bananas,' Mummy says.
　'I know, he's been a bit relentless of late, hasn't he?'
　'Relentless? All I've heard from him this morning is "Mamma nana, Mamma nana, Mamma nana".'
　'I thought you were going to move the fruit bowl?'
　'That's what I wanted to talk to you about. I don't know where to put it. If I leave it in the utility room, he can reach it. The other day he nearly pulled a bread knife on top of himself because the bowl sits next to the draining board. But if I leave it in the kitchen in its old place near the hob, then he refuses to eat his dinner because he can see the fruit bowl, and he screams at me for a nana.'

'Why not leave it where it is, on the dining-room table? That's where you'd normally find a fruit bowl, right? I mean I'm not an expert, but I definitely have experience in observing fruit bowls on dining-room tables.'

'Shut up, dick! We can't do that, because he can now climb on the chairs, which means he can get on the dining-room table.'

'So?'

'I think the fruit bowl will need to stay in the basement with you.'

'Absolutely not. I have a strict no-fruit-bowl policy that's never been breached. I can't let my standards slip now, not even for you. I'm so sorry, but I can't.'

'Well, what do you suggest?'

'I suggest you stop starving him.'

'That's not helping.'

'NANA!' you scream, having arrived on the scene to contribute to the conversation.

'Arlo, no more bananas till later.'

'Yeah. Nana?'

'No nana.'

Not to be beaten, you immediately begin pulling at the chair next to me so as to climb on it.

'Arlo,' Mummy says, 'what are you doing?'

'Nana.'

'I said no nanas, didn't I?' Mummy continues.

'Pakkerrrrr!'

'You're getting a banana for Makka Pakka?'

'Yeah.'

Say what you will about your obsession with bananas, but I can't fault you for your focus, determination and creative solutions in getting hold of them.

Reusable Nappies, Part 1
Saturday, 24 April 2021

We're failing miserably with reusable nappies. When we encase your midsection in a colourful eco-friendly option that's not destined for landfill, you develop a rash within two hours. And the surface area of said rash is considerable – your bum looks like a pepperoni pizza with extra pepperoni, and you wince as soon as we come anywhere near you with a wipe.

We've tried everything: four different brands of nappies, three types of liners and several different insert options including charcoal, hemp, bamboo and microfibre. We've read blogs, asked other parents for advice and tried several variations of washing, including a strip wash which is a process that removes detergent residue in clothes but also removes any trapped ammonia in nappies. A few eco-specialists we've consulted have suggested that could be the problem.

But nothing has worked. This is incredibly frustrating because we were on a roll last year. Once you were big enough, we were using reusables almost full-time apart from at night.

So why are we facing issues now?

We have a couple of ideas but nothing we can prove. Teething is one theory because it's our go-to diagnosis for anything relating to nappy rash. Teething can increase the acidity levels of waste, meaning we need to change you as soon as we're aromatically alerted to a code brown, because the nappy-rash vengeance is swift and merciless.

The other thing it could be is that you have sensitive skin, and the sensitivity has increased. Like teething, this is something we know for a fact, but we can't say for sure how much it contributes to nappy rash. You're always scratching at your thighs and back, and we have to regularly moisturise you. And when you do yourself a mischief, like walking into something, your skin reacts instantly, forming bruises or bright red welts that serve to evidence how neglectful we are as parents.

So, there you have it: our position is that we're on the losing side of our commitment to go green. But we're not throwing in the towel yet. We're going to have one more roll of the dice. For this test we have strip-washed all the nappies, lined them with a fleece reusable liner and doubled up on the inserts. We've also taken an enthusiastic approach with yellow Metanium cream, the nappy-rash-combatting equivalent of 'the big guns'. It's busted out in emergencies, but we seem to have had a lot of those in our house recently.

Let's see how we get on.

Reusable Nappies, Part 2
Sunday, 25 April 2021

'Mamma.'
   'Arlo, noooo, don't undo the straps—'
   Too late.
   Thud.

Let me pause the scene for a few moments, back up and provide some context. You're standing halfway up the stairs, wearing a reusable nappy and a loose-fitting T-shirt that has – and this is a crucial plot point – no poppers. Why is this a crucial plot point? Because physics dictates that if you un-Velcro a nappy and nothing is there to hold it in place, like a poppered-up vest, then gravity will step in to do its thing. Another key plot point is that you've dropped a code brown. That's why you're on the stairs in the first place. Mummy told you to climb them so she could change you in your nursery. Where am I? I'm in our bedroom getting dressed.

Unpausing the scene and returning to the action, Mummy wasn't quick enough to get a hand to you before the nappy could drop from your midsection and *thud* its way onto the stair you're standing on.

Luckily, it landed preferred side up, and there were no excremental scatterings. Not yet, at least. I say not yet because the nappy is resting precariously on the edge of the stair – its residence there no doubt a temporary one. It's like in a car-chase scene in a movie, where there's a crash and the car has come to a halt resting over a cliff edge or a broken bridge or something else that involves gravity and a long, explosive, steel-wrenching descent.

Mummy is in a similar scene right now. Time has slowed.

Will the nappy stay where it is, or will it fall over the edge? Mummy can do nothing but watch. Remember, Arlo: everything about this scene is taking place in less than a few microseconds.

Will it stay, or will it fall?

Will it stay, or will it—

Fall. It's going to fall. It's already falling. Mummy watches helplessly as the nappy – and its contents – hinges over the lip of the stair and somersaults its way to the ground floor like a Slinky, before creating the second, much louder, *thud* of the morning.

'Daddy!' I hear Mummy shout.

I arrive a second later at the top of the stairs. From my vantage point, not having any idea about what's transpired, I see a smiling toddler on the middle of the stairs wearing nothing but a T-shirt, and a tense and shocked Mummy, who's standing behind you a few steps down. Lying at the bottom of the stairs is an opened reusable nappy that contains what looks like a rained-on mole-mound.

What the fuck?

'Arlo, don't move,' Mummy says, frantically inspecting the surrounding areas for damage.

'I don't believe this,' she continues. 'How did that not go everywhere?'

With you still positioned on the stairs, Mummy quickly recaps the last few seconds, and now I'm clued up as to why she's in a state of shock. Despite a full and open nappy somersaulting its way down half a flight of stairs, there are no visible faecal-particle escapees. Somehow, everything has been contained in the nappy.

Not wanting to risk you pissing on the stairs, I descend to your level, crane you up and away and carry you with two outstretched arms into your bedroom.

After all that excitement, we carry out a nappy-rash inspection to see how we've fared with reusables over the last twenty-four hours.

It's not good news.

Redness has broken out on your bum. It has the circumference of a large mug. Reusable Nappy Experiment 409882 is once again a failure.

I believe this is defeat.

Glasses 2.0

Monday, 26 April 2021

We've come to Specsavers for you to try on some new glasses. You need a new pair because your prescription has changed, for the better.

'I know exactly the ones I want to get him,' Mummy says.

Oh dear. 'You know, I thought we might run into this little wrinkle,' I say.

'What wrinkle?'

'The one where you think you'll be picking his glasses.'

'I most certainly—'

'Can I help?' says a staff member. Her name tag says *Lynn*.

April

Mummy gets in first. 'Hi. Yes, we're here to try on some—'

'Hi, Lynn, I think what my eager and excitable partner meant to ask was if you can direct us to your *Star Wars* selection. Preferably ones that will fit a toddler, but the priority is that they're *Star Wars*. Marvel is also acceptable.'

Lynn laughs, then responds with such a perfect reply that you'd have thought I'd spent fifty quid prearranging the whole thing. 'I'm a big *Star Wars* fan myself.'

'Lynn, you and I are going to get on great.'

'Now hang on, we didn't agree to shitty *Star*—'

'Nana!' On this occasion, 'nana' is toddler-speak for 'banana', and not one of your grandmothers.

'Now, now. Why don't you sort your son out? I believe he requires a banana to pacify him while he tries his new *Star Wars* glasses on.' I strut over to the toddler selection and pick up the first *Star Wars* pair I see. 'Right, job done. We can order these and go home.' I whack the glasses on. You look adorable, cool and badass in equal measure.

'No. Not these ones. They have the nose bits. They'll hurt him.'

Did someone order a plate of gloom?

OK, they do look a tad rigid. Come to think of it, all of them do. I think it's because the older-age-bracket glasses have metal frames, while your baby-blue Eeyore ones are supple, bendable plastic – the frame is virtually indestructible; trust me, you've carried out extensive testing.

The sensible course of action is to try a few more pairs on, except we can't, because you've gone on the run, and now you're over the other side of the shop pulling glasses off the display stand like you're a contestant on *Supermarket Sweep*. By the time I get to you, three pairs are in your hands and three more are on the floor. I chance a quick glance around the shop and can confirm at least four members of staff are staring at us. Is that a win?

What's more, because of Covid-19, any pair of glasses we touch must be deposited in a tray that is then collected so that they can be cleaned before they're arranged back on the shelf. I deposit the six pairs of Arlo-touched glasses in the nearest tray. I then drag you away with the intention of returning to Mummy while also avoiding all the stabbing pairs of eyes.

'Wait ... Arlo. Where have you gone now?'

'He's over here,' Mummy says, laughing.

I arrive on the scene in time to witness you drop to all fours and crawl *under* one of the display stands. And now you're bashing the window that faces out onto the high street.

'Arlo, come here.'

Bash, bash, bash.

You're squealing like you're midway through your favourite roller coaster ride.

'Do you want that banana?'

The change is quicker than instant. The squeals stop. As does the bashing. From behind the display I hear, 'Yeah, nana. Nana. Mamma, nana.'

'Come here then.'

You reappear under the display unit and make a trade, allowing us to strap you into your buggy in exchange for a banana. Now that you're sitting still, you can begin modelling glasses. Once again, Mummy sticks her oar in where it's not wanted.

'What about these—'

'Absolutely not,' I say.

'Why not?'

'Are they *Star Wars*?'

'No, but—'

'Then why are you even speaking to me? Where's Lynn? She seems to know what to do.'

April

'She's gone to look for some baby ones as they're likely to fit better.'

Lynn soon returns with not one, but two *Star Wars* options. Mummy rolls her eyes.

Tragically, neither pair fits well. Despite my early enthusiasm, I'm mature enough to concede there's no point getting you something that's not comfortable, otherwise they'll never stay on your head.

But now Lynn is called away, and her colleague, Chris, tags in. Chris looks like a young wizard disguised as a non-wizard by way of several ill-fitting wardrobe choices. I also suspect he ran out of shampoo a year ago. After a quick chat, we surmise that it's probably best if we get you the same glasses again, but with the amended prescription.

'That's a shame. I liked the *Star Wars* ones,' Mummy says – that's right, *Mummy*, not Daddy!

'I don't know what to say … I never thought you'd come round to *Star Wars*.'

'We could get him one of each?'

One of each? Now that is a smart idea from Mummy. We have two prescriptions so we can get two pairs.

'One can be his Netflix-and-chill, go-outside-and-play glasses, and the other can be for best.'

Chris gives you yet another pair of *Star Wars* glasses and also a very cool pair of *Spider-Man* ones. Both look right on the money, but Chris says that in his professional opinion, the *Spider-Man* ones fit better, and they look more comfortable. I'm not about to argue with a wizard, so *Spider-Man* it is.

Thank you, Chris; thank you, Lynn; and thank you, Mummy, I guess. I know it's not the *Star Wars* option, but *Spider-Man* glasses are still an excellent choice.

Early Morning Stats
Wednesday, 28 April 2021

Arlo, true or false? I love looking at my phone to see that it's 7.30 a.m. and realising I've been up for three hours.

Toddler Inc.:
Half-Year Assessment[14]

'If you want to learn about strategy, then observe toddlers systematically going to town on their parents' mental health – they are true masters.'

Mr Jacobs

The last time Arlo visited the offices of Toddler Inc., he was slow, shaky and unstable on his feet. But no longer. Today, despite being ill, the young tot marched right up to the reception desk to find Mr Jacobs' assistant, Michelle, waiting with his visitor's pass.

'Hello, Arlo. I hope you're feeling better. Mr Jacobs will see you when you're ready,' Michelle said, handing over his pass. Arlo slid through the turnstile and then carried on to the office of Mr Jacobs.

'Arlo, come in. Take a seat. Can I get you any milk?'

'Milk, yeah.'

'How are you taking it these days?'

Arlo uttered a response, but it was a gargled, tangled knot of noise, almost as if he had chosen to reply in cat-speak. You certainly couldn't have accused his words – if he was indeed trying to use words – of being English-language constructs. Whatever he was saying, or trying to say, was incomprehensible to Mr Jacobs.

---

14 This chapter also serves as the May monthly development review.

'Oh, how silly of me,' Mr Jacobs said, and then turned his attention to a large black box on his desk that boasted shiny dials of different sizes and a futuristic-looking display panel. 'I was sent this by my dear friend Elon. It's a translator machine. It scans body language, brain wave activity, vocals – naturally, temperature and pheromone levels and finally the rest of the subconscious that's permanently broadcasting a whole host of confusing bits and bobs. Give me one sec.' Mr Jacobs turned the device on, played with the dials until he was satisfied with the settings and then gave a triumphant nod, the same nod that a man makes when he believes all is right with the world.

'Now then, let's try that again. Arlo, how would you like your milk?'

The machine, boasting the voice of a well-mannered, Oxford-educated Englishman approaching middle age, gave off a thrumming resonance, purring and pulsing, doing its thing before answering on Arlo's behalf: 'Seven ounces, warmed for forty seconds in the microwave, and then add one millilitre of DHA.'

'Excellent. Shaken?' said Mr Jacobs directly to Arlo, and not to the machine.

'Please,' replied the machine.

You see, Arlo didn't need the translator device to understand Mr Jacobs, because he understood him just fine. And Mr Jacobs knew it. It had always surprised Mr Jacobs how baffled parents were when discovering that their children were actually quite smart. It's almost as if they'd totally forgotten their own experiences as children, when they too hustled their way forward in life in search of snack cupboards and delayed bedtimes.

Mr Jacobs relayed Arlo's request to Michelle, and then he grabbed the nearest file from a stack on his desk and opened it up.

'So, you're about to turn eighteen months. Congratulations.'

'Thank you, sir.'

'Let's get right to it. You're here so that we can assess if you're on track to graduate to the terrible twos in November. I want you to start by telling me what tools, tactics and routines you've deployed to create as much misery and mayhem as possible for Mummy and Daddy.'

'I'll start with sleep. I have worked ... tirelessly—'

'Ah. I'm sorry, Arlo, but you're prohibited from performing any unfunny and obvious dad puns until you become a father yourself. It's clearly stated in section 4BBY of the *Guide to Being an Incredibly Unfunny Individual*.'

'Is it really? I didn't know. I'll bear that in mind.'

'Very good.'

'Anyway, I've worked ... hard ... to destabilise any sense of routine they believed they had in place for me. While I still go down at night on time and largely without a fuss, they have no way of anticipating when I'll wake up in the morning. In March, I got up a little after five a.m. almost every day. They hated that – especially my daddy, who remains, when tired, a sad, sorrowful, stale streak of piss. In April, I gave them a reprieve, or at least the impression of a reprieve, by waking after six a.m., only to give it the ol' one-two jab combo every now and then and revert back to five a.m. Again, my daddy found this behaviour particularly crippling.'

'Excellent. Please continue.'

'Staying on mornings, I've adjusted the manner in which I announce my arrival into the day. I used to utter these cute babbling noises and softly call out for Mamma or Dadda. Now I scream in rage until one of them greets me.'

Mr Jacobs chuckled. 'Very good, Arlo, very good.'

'I bash everything I come into contact with, I use my forearms to sweep all inanimate objects from any surface that's low enough for me to access, and I've tripled my climbing efforts to reach surfaces that were previously inaccessible. I leave handprints everywhere.'

'The handprints – this is something that's directed more at your mummy, is that right?'

'Correct, sir. Daddy isn't really bothered about mess, but Mummy hates it. You see, the trick is to learn what their individual nuances are so you know what buttons to press. What works for one parent might not work for the other and vice versa. For instance, my daddy is close to losing his grip on reality when it comes to cleaning my teeth. For my part, I sit there and clamp down on the toothbrush so he can't get a proper scrub. It drives him crazy. Mummy's a lot more patient in that area. But she cannot stand it when I mess up her cushions.'

'You often mess them up?'

'Every chance I get, sir. What's needed is a separate, tailored approach if I'm to succeed in bringing them both down.'

'Outstanding work. Anything else?'

'I spit my drink out and then slap my hands down on the puddle so that it splashes everywhere. I get triple points if there's a folded pile of clean clothes nearby. At other times, I'll insist on something, only to instantly change my mind when they give in to me. For example, I'll state that I want to watch *Bing* so that they put *Bing* on, and then I'll immediately scream for *Hey Duggee*. And when they put *Hey Duggee* on, I'll scream for *Bing*.'

'I see. Simple—'

'But effective.'

'But overall, is your go-to still *Bing*?'

'That's right. That's the show that irritates them the most, so that's the one I request. It's been highly effective, especially over the last few days while I've been ill. I also stick my hands in the toilet regularly, get in the bath fully clothed and turn the taps on, and pull, punch, grab and scratch at my daddy's face. And I will sometimes demand to eat off their plates instead of from my bowl.'

'Yes ... about that. We've received intel. Apparently, that's a ruse on their part.'

'Really?'

'Yes. It worked initially, but they've since caught on to the ploy. What they're now doing is putting more on their plate and setting it aside to make it seem like you're eating their food, but really, you're eating your own.'

'Pity. I was rather fond of that one.'

'I'm sure you'll find a way to respond. Anything else before we wrap up?'

'One more thing, sir. I have found enormous success in turning the washing machine off while it's mid-cycle, the result being that Mummy has to begin the load from scratch.'

'I bet that drives her insane.'

'And then some, sir.'

'I see,' said Mr Jacobs, who was scanning Arlo's file. 'Yes, I've got a record of the email that your daddy has sent to LG on the matter.'

'Fat lot of good that did him.'

'Well, I've heard enough to remove any doubt. It's clear to me that you're on track to graduate your first year as a toddler with distinction, putting you in prime position for a terrible-twos promotion.'

'Thank you, sir.'

'But don't get comfortable. Your parents aren't complete idiots. They adapt well. So you'll have to keep changing it up.'

'I'll be sure to, sir.'

'And, Arlo, try and get that full-blown tantrum out of the way as soon as possible. It's been almost eighteen months.'

'Oh, I forgot to say. It's scheduled for the twentieth of May.'

'Attaboy.'

With the meeting concluded, Mr Jacobs stood and shook hands with Arlo. Arlo then saw himself out of his office and walked back through to reception to drop his visitor's pass off to Michelle.

'Goodbye, Arlo. Take care.'

'Buh-bye.'

May

'Every time I played the guitar or sang, my toddler would whine, "Daddy, that noise make me sad." So I would stop doing the thing I loved doing.'

Dan R, a work colleague

Shopping
Monday, 3 May 2021

Two facts about me and shopping for clothes. Number one: I hate shopping for clothes. Number two: I resent spending money on material things that don't deliver value. Fifty quid on a pair of jeans is hardly a down payment on a Bugatti Chiron, but that fifty quid could be used on books, pay part of a course or even go towards an experience that would create a wonderful long-lasting memory. I can't see me lying on my deathbed experiencing my last ever erection over a pair of jeans I bought in my thirties. Nevertheless, Mummy states that my going over half a decade without buying any new clothes probably needs to come to an end. Annoyingly, she's right.

I end up buying three pairs of jeans and three pairs of trainers. Now we've headed to Primark to buy Mummy something.

'How long will this take?' I ask, already bored.

'As long as it takes,' Mummy says.

'Is that Greenwich Mean Time?'

'It's whatever-I-say time.'

'Er, that's not even a recognised time zone, so you've just advertised yourself to the world as an idiot.'

'No, I did that when I updated my relationship status on Facebook.'

'Er ... well ... why don't—'

'We need to go downstairs. Come on, the lift is this way.'

Damn! Mummy wins this round, Arlo.

As we make our way to the lift, we pass the escalator. Do you remember last year, in *Dear Arlo*, when I mustered the marbles to ascend the escalator going up, but didn't retain my nerve to go back down again? We reach the lift, press the button and wait. *Come on. This is taking forever.* I keep glancing at the escalator. It shouldn't be too difficult to descend it, right? Last time I was a novice, but now I'm ... not exactly a master, but I'm surely beyond a white belt.

'Let's take the escalator,' I blurt out.

'You sure?' Mummy says, with a daring grin that tells me she assumes a) this will terrify me, and b) I'll fuck it up.

'Yes, I'm sure. I wouldn't have said it if I wasn't.'

'OK, go right ahead. Do you want me to help?'

'No, I don't!' I say, regretting that I possess vocal cords.

I am shitting it. My sweat glands have been wrenched open. Backwards down a fucking escalator? What was I thinking! But I can't back out now, otherwise Mummy will win, and she's already posted points on the leader board for that quip about her Facebook status.

I approach the silver-toothed machine, commence a three-point turn and slowly begin reversing on. You're wide awake, looking over the edge. With your eyes you say, 'Come on, Dad, you've got this.'

Mummy stands off to the side watching with a twatty grin spread across her face.

'Are you sure you've got this?' she says.

'I'm so sure.'

'Ohhhh-kayyyyy, baby.'

Christ, I wish she'd shut up. I complete backing on to the escalator, bringing both you and the buggy on as well. We begin moving. I'm startled for a second but, on account of me being a fucking boss, recover instantly. Mummy's standing above, now wearing a look of genuine surprise – *and, fuck, is that respect?* – on her face.

As we near the bottom, my muscles relax and my sweat glands seal themselves shut. The person disembarking the escalator is very different from the one who went on. I've never felt this confident. Once clear, I don't bother to three-point turn the buggy. Instead, I whip it round like a stunt-car racer before catching the eye of an attractive blond who's seen me smash the fuck out of dadding. You can tell she is into me in the biggest way. She's probably thinking up ideas on how to become your stepmum.

'Well done. You did it,' Mummy says.

'Of course I did it – give me something harder next time.'

I'm proud of myself, and I deserve the dadding points. My delightful mood means that Mummy can shop in peace without me repeatedly asking when we're going home. Ten minutes later, she's ready to take the items over to the till, for which the queue extends back a considerable distance. No matter. I've nailed reversing down the escalator, and going back up is child's play.

'Not that I don't think you can do it, but do you want a hand?' Mummy asks.

'No thanks. I've got this. Honestly, it's a lot easier going up than it is going down.'

'You're right. You've got this.'

I race onto the escalator, barely registering my movements because this is all so terribly eas— *Oh shit!*

'BE CAREFUL!'

Turns out that going up isn't as easy as I remembered. We have a three-wheeler buggy, so it can be tricky if you lift the back two wheels up, which is exactly what I did when walking on. I don't know why I did this; I should have rolled it on with all three wheels to the ground, but it seems my prior accomplishment imbued me with a little too much misplaced confidence. Suffice to say that the whole buggy lurched to one side, causing Mummy's heart to slingshot into her mouth and mine to do something similar. Fortunately, I was able to recover in a fashion that meant you didn't die.

After Mummy pays for her items, we return to the lift, where we wait … for ages … and ages … and ages. I don't volunteer the escalator as an option for the way back down, and neither does Mummy.

Damn it, Arlo, this is why I don't do clothes shopping!

Packing, Devon And Mobile Homes
Friday, 7 May 2021

The first thing to understand about packing to go on holiday with a toddler is that it's a terrible idea to have the toddler around, because he's annoying as fuck and gets in the way of a successful packing operation. This little insight has come about from me watching you remove every item that Mummy and I place in our suitcase. That's holiday lesson number one.

Enough is enough. You're going to Nana Feeder's – sorry Nana See-See's – house for an hour to pester her for bananas, except you won't be pestering her at all, because we all know that she'll greet you at the door with a big bright bunch of them, telling you that you can have as many as you like while also suggesting to Mummy that we must be starving you at home.

Last year, we went camping in South Wales, but you were a lot younger. You had just begun crawling. Also, Covid-19 has meant we've not been busy as far as holidays are concerned. All of this equates to me feeling out of practice packing. Still, we eventually succeed, stick everything in the car and hit the road.

Our destination is Devon. The three of us are going, along with Auntie Lisa, Haylee, and Nana and Grandad See-See. We're taking two cars. You, Mummy and I are with Grandad, who will be driving. We've strategically chosen to leave twenty minutes before your first nap and, as predicted (and hoped), you fall asleep soon after we leave, thus ensuring that the first half of our four-hour journey proceeds without event. But then you wake up and announce you want feeding, so we stop at the nearest services.

I often wonder what you feel on entering a new environment. As we walk into the service station, I watch your eyes light up the way mine did the first time I visited Dubai Mall, full of intrigue and wonder. Fascinated, you shuffle forward absorbing the sights of other travellers dashing to use the toilet, grabbing food or having a good old stretch to ease the stiffness and fatigue of a long car journey.

Holiday lesson number two is that it's simply impossible to keep two toddlers corralled in one place without food to distract them. But to get them food, the adults have to queue up and order it – a challenge, because queuing requires patience: the adults want different things, meaning we can't send one to order all the food for our party, and the toddlers want to run into the guide ropes that are in place to govern the queue lines.

'Look at me, Mummy. Am I hilarious?' asks Haylee, whose vocabulary has in the last few months increased by 800 per cent.

'Yes, you are. Now will you come and stand here?' Lisa says.

'Uh-uh, Mummy. I'm standing here.'

'Fine, but don't lean—'

Too late. In putting her full weight on the rope (or queue barrier) she's sunk to the floor, pulling down the two nearest posts on top of her.

I'd love to help, but I have my own problems to deal with because you, sir, have wandered over to a vegan fast-food outlet, and instead of telling the woman at the till what you want, you've decided to cook it yourself. How do I know this? Because you've made a dash through the staff entrance and round the back. I leg it through and find myself strangely privileged to get a glimpse behind the counter of a place where I don't work. The staff find your actions, unlike Haylee's tightrope exploits, to be most amusing.

'Dadda!'

'Yes, I can see you. Now come out from there.'

Instead of listening, you make for the deeper recesses, searching for any delights that a behind-the-counter experience offers. I eventually manage to scoop you up to the sound of you squealing in delight because this is obviously all part of a game, and both of the game's participants are having a jolly good time.

You wave goodbye to the staff, and I relocate us to an empty table, where we sit down to eat.

'Why didn't we grab a high chair?' says Mummy, who's wondering why you're sitting on her lap.

'Because we're hopelessly out of practice. I don't think we've been in an indoor public space together since Arlo became a toddler.'

'Huh. No, I guess we haven't.'

We've bought noodles for lunch, but they're too hot, and you're getting impatient. Mummy cools them down by putting them first in her mouth for a few seconds, before transferring them into yours, like a mummy bird feeding her baby. You don't care. You're like, 'Gimme dem tasty noodles.'

Soon, we're back on the road and you quickly become fidgety. Mummy turns the iPad on, and you guys watch *101 Dalmatians*, which manages to keep you calm, but not Mummy, who's enamoured by your stillness and attention to the narrative.

'Baby, turn around and look at him. He loves this.'

'I realise that because you've asked me to turn around several times already. My spine is not a cloth you rinse out over the sink. We've not even met Cruella yet.'

'OK – face the front then,' she says, sulking.

What the fuck does she think I've been trying to do?

Next, there's an argument over an apple. You want to maintain possession of the apple, but Mummy says you can't if you keep spitting pieces out of your mouth. You lose the argument and gear up for a toddler-rage, but before you can unleash any fury, we arrive at our destination: a mobile-home park.

When we went camping last year, we slept in the same tent as one other toddler and two babies – you being one of the babies. That was an error. This year, we've learnt from our mistakes. Each family has one large, warm, amenity-filled mobile home. I've never stayed in one before, but it takes me all of thirty seconds to appreciate how wonderful they are for families, and they have officially become our new BFF while you remain a toddler.

It's perfect: we have beds, bathrooms and lots of seating that's low enough for you to climb on and fall off without risking brain damage. The space is mostly open, so we can keep a lookout and foil any attempts at badness, like you opening and closing the oven.

Rounding off a successful travel day, we order dinner from the local chippy. It's good to finally get away again. Despite the stress of owning a toddler, I have missed family adventures, and I hope we can make up for lost time.

Roundabouts And The Zoo
Saturday, 8 May 2021

'Arlo, NO! You do not touch the oven. It's very dangerous,' I say, raising my voice to a level that's considered shouting.

'Ha, ha, ha!'

'No, this isn't a game.' Apparently, the whole don't-say-no edict has taken a nosedive.

'Ha, ha, ha!'

I look at Mummy for some suggestions as to what my next move could be, but she just shrugs.

For the record, that's the first time I've shouted at you to tell you off, and it's cut me pretty deep. I hate scolding you at the best of times but shouting brings me zero joy. No matter: it seems I've got myself all upset for no reason because you didn't give a shit. You thought it was a game, which is frustrating for me because I assumed that if I only raised my voice for situations that called for it, then the shock would shake you out of badness and into making better decisions.

Not so.

Eventually, you lose interest in the oven of your own accord and disappear to the bathroom, soon returning with two wet hands.

'Why are your hands wet?' Mummy asks.

In reply, you hold them up to show us that they are in fact wet, along with the cuffs of your pyjama top.

'Did you put your hands in the toilet?'

'Yeah.'

Mummy sighs. 'Let's clean those ... No, Arlo, come here right this instant.'

Lad.

For the record, when you demonstrate that sort of behaviour towards your mother, you're a lad, but when you do it to me, you're an arsehole. I wouldn't want you to be confused, so let this journal entry act as a record, clarifying the matter and avoiding any and all uncertainty.

We eat and get dressed, and then we all drive, in the pouring rain, to a nearby zoo.

'You want to take the second exit to the right,' I say.

'So not the first, but the second,' Mummy says, clarifying my confusing and opaque words.

'That's exactly right, my sweet. If you have two exits on a roundabout, you drive past the first one because that's the first – you can even count it – and then, when—'

'Stop being an arsehole.'

We arrive and park up. It's still raining, but we're equipped with suitable attire to keep warm and dry(ish). The zoo's enclosures are tall and huddled close to each other, reminding me of a town from a fantasy novel, with many-storeyed properties towering above narrow alleyways. We pay for tickets and follow the route that's marked out by arrows on the floor, beginning our adventure.

After spending time in Africa, Mummy and I swore we'd never visit a zoo because ... well, not to come across as a pair of pompous, stuck-up arseholes, but if you've seen the big five up close in their natural environment, then that's not really something you can top, is it?

But as is often the case since I became a parent, my world view has changed; it has moulded and shaped itself into something new. Today, I'm enjoying the zoo because you and

Haylee are enjoying the zoo. Watching you staring at the animals, your eyes tracing their movements and your hands and faces pressed up against the glass-fenced quadrants, is delightful.

The otters are the best. They're sociable and friendly towards each other, and you can't get enough of them. Every time we make to leave, you toddle back to add fresh hand- and nose-prints to the glass, as is the case this very moment. One otter approaches and stands up on its hind legs to get a better look at its spectator. You guys are less than two inches apart, and you're close enough to make out the pigmentation in each other's irises. What are you thinking? What is the otter thinking? I love these moments – tiny little beats in an otherwise frantic and chaotic territory that is parenthood. Eventually, we move on.

'Bir,' you say, pointing.

'That's right, Arlo, birds. How many can you see?'

You point to the nearest while repeating the word 'bir'.

'They're called flam—'

'KAR-KAR!'

OUCH! What-the-fuck-was-that?

My ears flip a coin on whether or not to brick up their canals, permanent deafness being preferable to experiencing that head-splitting cacophony again. It's tails: my ears will remain (barely) operational for the time being while the sonorous ringing dissipates. I look around for the source of the clamour. It wasn't you, Haylee, or any other toddler or any of the animals. It was your mother, who thought she'd try and coax the flamingos into striking up a conversation with her. Except there aren't any flamingos in sight, because Mummy's pitch has caused the pretty pink birds to explode in a loud puff of feathers, and I'm left wondering if Mummy's ancestry is the reason dodos are extinct.

Next up, we observe a couple of pumas. I don't enjoy this encounter, because the fully grown cats are looking at you like you're their lunch, causing a surprising and surreal reaction on my part: I pick you up and don't let you down until we move on. Back the fuck away, pumas – leave my boy alone.

There isn't much to see after that, because most of the animals have sought shelter from the rain, so we get back in the cars and begin the return journey. It doesn't take long for the usual map-reading-demystification conversation to ensue.

'So, you don't want this left, but you want the next one.'

'OK, so drive past this one here and take the next one, yes?'

Kill me now— 'So, you know how you have right and left? And then you have these things called numbers.'

'Seriously, fuck off.'

'I'm willing to, but only if you go first.'

Grandad See-See: The Smartest Person On Earth
Sunday, 9 May 2021

Today, we are off to the beach to build sandcastles in the rain. But before that can happen, we all need to wake up.

'Would you like a normal coffee or a mocha?' Mummy asks.

'Normal, please.'

'We don't have normal.'

'Right …'

Mummy's face is stone. She hasn't done this to be funny, take the piss or for any other reason than to honestly enquire if I would prefer to have *normal* coffee or a (powdered) mocha. And now she's looking at me as if I'm Simon Simpleton who can't seem to find the answers to life's most elementary questions.

'Er, I guess I'll have a mocha. I mean, if that's an option that's available.'

'Right,' she says.

I can tell I've already ruined her day.

'Bol.'

'That's right, it is a ball, but it's not yours, buddy.'

'Bol.'

We're standing outside a shop that sells items to beachgoers: swimming attire, sunglasses, armbands and ... balls.

'Daddy's not really sure how to explain this one, but what you're looking at is a thing called a display stand – a bit like the one you trashed when we went to get your new glasses. Do you remember?' My attempt at parenting has attracted several onlookers who are enjoying the show. 'Anyway, the purpose of a display stand is to advertise products that passers-by might be inclined to pay for.'

'Bol?' you say, reaching for one.

The audience chuckles.

'That's what I'm trying to say. It's not *your* ball, and unless we pay for it, which no one here is about to do—'

'Here you go, Arlo,' says Nana See-See, presenting you with a ball that she's just bought and paid for.

Quick life lesson – if there is anything you want but don't have, ask one of your grandmothers, and I'm confident they'll figure out a way to get it for you.

With the ball episode finished, the crowd disperses, and we walk down a footpath that should, in a few moments, bring us to the beach.

'Whoa, Arlo, look at ... Actually, don't worry,' Mummy says.

'What?' I ask.

'I thought I could see a horse, but it was just a woman in a long coat with a man behind her with a child on his shoulders.'

May

I've said it many times, Arlo: never a dull moment with your mother.

The footpath leads us to Croyde Beach, a small, sandy enclosure looking out towards the Atlantic. Protecting the rear of the beach stands a crowd of tightly packed, short but broad sand dunes capped with patches of well-weathered grass. The only entrance to the beach is via the narrow footpath that we've come from.

You love everything about Croyde Beach. You love the rock pools, you love the sand, you love splashing in the puddles, you love playing with the bucket and spade. It's great to compare your physical development with when we went camping last year in South Wales and visited the beach – you couldn't even walk then.

It's also nice to see how adorable you and your cousin Haylee are together. She mothers you a little too much, and she bosses you around a lot, but it's clear that you guys care for each other a great deal.

'Arlo, you want some of my nummie-nums?'

A 'nummie-nums' is Haylee's term for a dummy; she likes to routinely swaps hers for yours. She pushes you over sometimes when she's bored, and she imitates her mother's vocabulary. 'Oh, for fuck's sake, Mummy,' was a sentence your two-and-a-half-year-old cousin said the other day.

Grandad See-See is also having a wonderful time. On the way back from the beach, he walks ahead of me and Mummy, pushing you in your buggy.

'Do you know, I think that's the first time my dad has ever pushed a buggy,' Mummy says.

'Not even Haylee?'

'He's always been too scared.'

By the time we make it back to the holiday park, I feel drained of all energy. All I want to do is nap, except we need to pack, and I need to look after you while—

'Do you want to go for a pint?' Grandad See-See says to me, and me only.

A pint? Surely that's a joke. In what world does this get sanctioned? But I look at Mummy, who for once is not staring daggers at me. *I think I can ... go ... if I want to.*

Time slows down for me so I can deliberate the question. My first thought is that I probably don't want to go, because I'm feeling ill (your fault), and 'a pint' is code for at least four. If history is anything to go by, those four will be consumed within the hour. I still remember going for *a beer* with your grandad about five years ago on Christmas Day. I had to tip most of my eighth pint of Guinness down the toilet, because I was drinking it less than two hours after I began my first.

But then I consider the alternative: parenting toddlers.

'Yeah, sure, I'll come. I'll definitely come. We should leave immediately.'

Mummy drops us off at the pub and says she'll be back in an hour.

As soon as Mummy pulls up, I know that I made the right decision. 'How have the kids been?' I ask.

'Brutal. Haylee trapped Arlo's fingers in the door, and Arlo won't stop climbing on everything, except for when he's not climbing and he's trying to open the oven door that's hot because Mum is trying to cook. Then I caught them both in the bathroom playing with the taps. How were your beers? You were with my dad, so I assume you had more than one.'

Tumble
Thursday, 13 May 2021

We returned home from Devon last Monday, so this week we've been largely back on our normal schedule. Nana Smurf is at our house today, looking after you. Mummy is also at home, and I'm in the basement working. I'm halfway through typing out an email when I hear what sounds like deep rumbling thunder that ends in an almighty crack.

But I know that sound wasn't anything to do with the weather. Something, or someone, has fallen down the stairs.

I explode out of my seat as I hear wailing.

'*WHHHAAAAAA!*'

I rush upstairs to find Nana Smurf on the sofa looking shaken up. I can still hear you crying, but you're not here.

'He's upstairs. He's OK. He just—'

I sprint in the direction of your voice, finding you on our bed in Mummy's arms. She's desperately trying to calm you.

'It's OK, there, there. Shhh, shh, shh.'

I approach and give you the once-over. I can't see any visible welts, cuts or indications of injury. You're still crying, but you're not screaming, which suggests you're more shaken up than anything. *What happened?*

Turns out there was some miscommunication. Mummy went upstairs to get changed and left the stair gate open. You wanted to follow her, so Nana Smurf shouted to Mummy that you were inbound. But what she didn't do was follow behind.

You didn't reach the top.

Because you fell.

You were extremely lucky: you mostly slid down backwards on your tummy, but at some point, you tried to self-correct, an action that sent you almost cartwheeling down the last few steps and into the stair gate.

How we're not on the way to the hospital, I don't know. But we're not, and we should be thankful that we've had a lucky, knife-edge-narrow escape.

The lesson here is that you can't make any assumptions about what another adult might or might not do in any given situation. Mummy assumed she had made it obvious that she wanted Nana to watch you when she went upstairs, but she didn't give specific instructions. Nana Smurf wasn't 100 per cent on the rules, because Mummy left the stair gate open. So instead, she shouted up to tell Mummy that you were coming. That said, never leave a toddler to climb *our* stairs on their own, because they're too narrow. At some point, I'll have to sit down with Nana and have that conversation. But not today. Today, I'm just relieved to know you're OK.

Apparently, We've Still Not Learnt Our Lesson
Friday, 14 May 2021

Despite yesterday's wake-up call, it seems none of us quite got the safety memo, though thankfully we didn't need you to fall down the stairs again.

This time there was an even simpler cock-up. You and Mummy were at Nana See-See's house. Nana See-See was cooking, and Mummy was pottering. Mummy then went to the toilet and assumed Nana See-See was watching you. But Nana See-See, because she was cooking, assumed Mummy was watching you.

Next thing we knew, you'd vanished, but you responded 'yeah' to shouts of 'ARLO' from both Mummy and Nana. Using your voice as a beacon, Mummy and Nana located you upstairs climbing on the bed.

Enough is enough. Fool me once, shame on you. Fool me twice, shame on me.

New parenting guidelines have been urgently drafted and approved. The policy is this: whenever a parent or guardian leaves the room in which you stand, they must get auditory confirmation that another guardian is on toddler watch. They cannot leave the room until confirmation is acquired. This new policy is effective immediately!

One thing I will say in all the adults' defence: you're a sneaky little bastard and capable of moving at astonishing speeds! I don't want to go back to the newborn stage, but at least then you couldn't go anywhere.

Hopefully, everyone has learnt the lesson.

Fire, Reload, Fire
Tuesday, 18 May 2021

You've been on-and-off ill since you started nursery; in reality, it's been more on than off. You've had colds and conjunctivitis, and now you have a fever that's led to you being the most unwell you've ever been. We've had to test for Covid-19. Don't worry: it's not that.

Seeing you sick is a stark reminder of not only how fragile you are but also how powerless Mummy and I are when trying to keep you from harm. I had similar thoughts when Mummy was pregnant during the first trimester, where there is a high chance of miscarriage. I was outraged by the injustice of our species' ineffectiveness in controlling such eventualities. That's despite the considerable progress and accomplishments we've made in the field of science.

As I've grown older, I've increasingly tried to focus on those things that I can control and submit to a 'what will be will be' mindset for those that I can't. I encourage others to do the same. But when it comes to you, I simply can't do it. The thought of anything horrible happening to you fills every molecule of my anatomy with feelings of nausea and dread.

That said, here's a selfish confession: when you're ill, you need a cuddle, and I like that. It's paradoxical because, of course, I don't want you to suffer. But I never get to have a cuddle with you for more than a handful of seconds, because you're usually so *busy*. I suppose I should submit my dad status to the powers that be so that they can downgrade it from 'needs improvement' to 'utterly selfish', but I know for a fact this is a widespread feeling shared among parents.

The scariest bit about your fever is the temperature. Mummy and I have been battling to keep it below 40 degrees, with a bottle of Calpol being our primary weapon, but it's difficult to predict a winner. The highest it's reached is 40.5 degrees. A high temperature is indicative of your body reacting appropriately to biological enemies, but anything over 40 degrees is a cause for concern as it signals potential high-level threats like meningitis. If I pick you up for a cuddle, I can feel all of your limbs burning against my skin like rods of uranium.

Mummy uses an infrared thermometer gun to take your temperature every few seconds ... literally, every few seconds. She looks like the heroine of a sci-fi action film where the temperature gun is really her laser cannon, which she's using to take down hordes of baddies. Except it's not a horde of baddies, it's the same baddie, and he seems to be impervious to point-blank laser-cannon shots to the head. But what he's not impervious to is getting angry that his view of the television is being impeded by Lieutenant Ellen Ripley.

'I know we need to keep an eye on him, but do you think taking his temperature every few seconds is a bit excessive?'

'But it's going up.'

'I think that's probably the thermometer overheating.'

'Shut up. Go and get him some Calpol.'

'Aye, Lieutenant.'

Your First Official Tantrum
Thursday, 20 May 2021

The fever has broken and you're on the mend, with your temperature finally dropping to a less alarming level. Physically, you're more active, and it seems your appetite has returned as well.

'Cra-ka?'

'You would like a cracker?'

'Yeah.'

Trailed by you, I walk into the kitchen and retrieve the plastic tub that houses our stock of crackers. I then open the lid and select a broken piece approximately half the size of a normal cracker. I do this for several reasons: one, you've never eaten a full one before; two, you always leave a trail of crumbs in your wake; and three, you're in the business of concealing large fragments of cracker in hard-to-see places, like under your play mat.

Are you on board with my logic here? Does my cracker strategy of only giving you half at a time make sense?

'Aughhhh.'

'What's the matter?'

'AUGHHHHH!'

Well, that's a noise I never want to hear again. 'You want a full one?'

'Yeah.'

'If you eat this piece, then Daddy will give you another one. OK?'

'AUGHHHHH!'

Sensing a meltdown, I quickly counter with 'OK, OK', accompanied by some 'you win' type of body language.

I place the fragment back in the box and take out a fully intact cracker. I present it to you, feeling slightly guilty that I've run away from a battle that I should probably have taken on. But sue me.

Slap.

The slap jolts the cracker from my grip, sending it crashing to the floor, where it enjoys the process of shattering.

'Arlo, why did you do that?'

'WHHHAAAAAA!'

Mummy enters the scene, and I quickly recount the last fifteen seconds of my life. *God, has it only been fifteen seconds?*

'He's upset because he wanted to take it out of the box,' she says.

'WHHHAAAAAA!'

'Ah, OK. I can work with that.'

I present the box to you so that you may have the pick of the bunch. You can take a fistful of crackers for all I care.

Your crying simmers down to a whimper as you consider the change in your circumstances. But after a few moments, it seems the thing you wanted is no longer the thing you want. How do I know that? Because—

'WHHHAAAAAA!'

I place the box down to the side, kneel so that I'm on your level and try and comfort you with a cuddle, but you push me away. Still kneeling, I lean back so as to give you some space, but I can't, because you're now holding on to me. It seems you've once again changed your mind, and you *do* want me to pick you up. But of course, when I go to pick you up, you push me away again.

And now real tears are called into action, arriving in numbers, giving themselves over to gravity as they fall from your eyes and join the fragments of the recently deceased cracker on the floor.

You're so upset.

'Here, buddy. Do you want Daddy to pick you up and give you a cuddle?'

'Yeah.'

This time you allow me to pull you into an embrace. I'm still kneeling on the floor. You nestle your face into the crook of my neck, and I begin uttering mandatory soft shushing sounds.

Gradually, you quieten down.

But then ... You start back up again. This time with more ferocity.

This isn't sadness: this is anger, anger towards your father, whose actions have crippled the disposition of one young boy.

And then, as I try and pull you in even closer to me, it happens – the thing I've heard so many parents recount about their toddlers: you go limp.

Like a controlled explosion on a derelict building or a drone that's been blasted by an EMP weapon, you collapse, sliding down my torso and legs before joining what is by now a pretty crowded spot on the floor. You lie face down, arms outstretched, not making any movement. There's now complete silence and stillness on your part.

Mummy is laughing. I am most definitely not laughing. I'm plotting my next move when I suddenly hear the quietest of whimpers rev back up again, continuing on a skyward trajectory until we're back to shouting and screaming.

Oh dear, Arlo. I believe we can record this moment as your first official tantrum.

Can I Please Speak To Chris?
Friday, 21 May 2021

Mummy is in the shower, and she's asked me to get you dressed. I don't get to pick your clothes, obviously; Mummy has left them out on the side for me. But despite her doing this, I'm confused. The items Mummy has selected are as follows: a long-sleeved vest, a short-sleeved shirt and a hoodie. Given my own recent trauma of losing *Who Wants to Be a Good Dad?* I'm confident that this is a fashion disaster waiting to happen. And that might be why I'm wearing a sizable grin on my face.

This is fantastic if she's fucked this up. I visualise the various eye-assaulting discordances that such clothing combinations can evoke. If you're wearing all three layers, then the collar of your shirt will clash with your hoodie, and if you're not wearing the hoodie, then a short-sleeved shirt will clash with a long-sleeved vest, which was apparently the costly mistake I made, losing me the prize, not to mention a night of passion with Jessica Rabbit.

I march into the bathroom to have this out with Mummy. 'Hello, dear. Quick Q and A about fashion. These three items you've left out – were you intending for him to wear them all?'

'Yeah, that's why I left them out.'

'In that case, I would like to say thank you. This is already the best day of my life.'

'How so?'

'Because you've massively fucked up with his outfit.'

'No, I haven't ... how have I?'

'You can't go long-sleeved T-shirt and a short-sleeved shirt.'

'Course you can.'

'Then why did I lose *Who Wants to Be a Good Dad?* you big hypocrite?'

Side note: usually, Mummy doesn't read anything in my journals until they've been collated and transferred into an early draft of what eventually becomes the book, but she's read that particular entry, so she understands the reference.

'That's different from what you did to him.'
'I couldn't agree more. Your choice is much worse.'
'It is not. How—'
'Hang on, let me call Chris and see what he thinks.'

With Mummy still in the shower with the water running, I make an imaginary phone call to Chris Tarrant.

'Chris, how are you? Quick question. Is a short-sleeved shirt over a long-sleeved T-shirt better or worse than a short-sleeved T-shirt over a long-sleeved vest?'

I start nodding, taking it all in.

The best thing about the scene is that Mummy is still watching me, giving me the platform to continue this performance. It hasn't once crossed her mind to duck back under the shower and withhold giving me the satisfaction.

'I see ... Uh-huh. Got it. Cheers, Chris.' I hang the imaginary phone up and deliver the verdict to Mummy.

'Chris said—'

'That you're a cunt?'

'No, but he did say I clearly know more about fashion than you do.' I finish that sentence as I'm dashing out of the bathroom, before Mummy hurls more vulgarities at me.

Friends

Saturday, 22 May 2021

I can't remember the last time we went on a daytime adventure outside of Northampton. Evidently, it's been a while because it's taken us forever to get ready and leave the house. What doesn't help is that you've mounted a tragically successful campaign to delay us. Here's a summary of your achievements:

- Tipping out the contents of Mummy's tampon box on three separate occasions. That's despite me moving the box each time to a seemingly unreachable location.
- Climbing into the bath to play with the bath mat, but then getting bored with the bath mat and choosing instead to play with the taps. Yes, you were fully clothed. No, it's not the first time this has happened.
- Breaking into an impenetrable container of dried pasta: it's clearly not that impenetrable, because there are pieces of pasta spread out over the kitchen floor.

Still, we somehow manage to leave close to the time we intended, 11.35 a.m., which was planned to coincide with your nap. You fall asleep within five minutes of us being on the road. The journey is pleasantly uneventful, and you wake as we're parking up – *perfect*.

Today's adventure takes place at Knebworth Gardens. We've never been before, but if first impressions are anything to go by, it certainly won't be our last visit. Looking out from the car, I'm greeted by a calm sea of green grass. Battalions of trees stand as on-duty lifeguards, supervising the activity of small humans who are screaming with overexcitement and running around in erratic patterns. Near where we're parked is a wooden fort – a huge outdoor play area.

We get out of the car and make ready to find the rest of our group. It doesn't take long, because I'm looking up towards the closest battlement of the fort, and I see a face I recognise staring out above the wooden parapet wall. It's Harry, eldest son of my friend Ian. I've not seen him in almost a year. He's a little taller and leaner in the face, and his voice has changed.

May

'Harry, how do we get in?'

'You go round the side and there's a gate – just walk through it.'

Excellent, don't mind if we do.

I've developed a new world view: there is a 90 per cent chance I won't like any child who's neither my own nor in some way affiliated to me, like my mates' kids. I'll walk you through why I've arrived at such a revelation. You're playing on a wobbly log bridge. You're still too small to be left completely to your own devices, so I loiter nearby, ready to step in if needed. But otherwise, you are the sole occupant of what is a free-standing piece of apparatus. Out of nowhere, a couple of girls (one about six and one about eight) come racing over the obstacle. You are sitting in the middle and they don't even give you a second glance or show the least concern for your safety. It is as if you aren't there.

I am fucking fuming!

When I sent *Dear Dory* out for test reading, one of the comments I received back was regarding the chapter on names.[15] I reflected on how an unfortunate name could land you front and centre of playground bullying taunts. I also originally stated that 'some kids are little cunts'. The comment I received back from a reader was this: 'Can you call kids cunts?' I took the feedback on board as any professional author would, and recast the sentence to say: 'Some of the kids in my class were little cunts.' The specificity of 'kids in my class', as opposed to referring to kids generally, provided

---

15 The chapter I'm referring to in *Dear Dory* is Wednesday, 4 September 2019 'Names, Names And More Names'.

me with a justification for my assertion. Or at least, I assume it did, because I've yet to receive a reader complaint on that chapter. But now I've watched these two girls come tearing past you without slowing down or stopping to wait their turn, I'm ready to admit that I regret changing that sentence in *Dear Dory*. Some kids *are* cunts, Arlo, like these two absent-minded young girls who have put the safety of my precious firstborn son at risk.

Before I can tell them off, they've zoomed over to the net obstacle. But don't worry, those two cunts have been replaced by another two, this time two boys, who are both older than the girls.

'Oi.'

They freeze in their tracks: one has swung his legs up onto the bridge's handhold railing while the other is crouched down next to you. When the first swung his legs up, his feet came dangerously close to your face.

'Wait your turn, please. He's only little.' They remain frozen in place, allowing me time to scoop you up and out of their way.

Bastards.

I honestly don't know how I would react if I saw another child hurt you, particularly an older one who should know better. It's not something I've had to think about before today, but seeing how the last thirty seconds have played out ... I don't believe I'd react appropriately at all. I've never been one for violence, and I certainly don't see me knocking out a seven-year-old for hitting you, but I'm 100 per cent confident that I would wish for the infliction of some sort of pain and misery as vengeance for laying a hand on you.

Once again, I'm reminded that the parenting gig is a peculiar one, but it's never boring or unrevealing.

Soon after the double incident on the log bridge, we congregate with our friends on the grass to have a picnic.

We're using today as an excuse to celebrate the belated second birthday of my godson Eddie, who is Harry's brother.

There's chocolate cake – something you've never had before, and while Mummy and I make a conscious effort to ensure sugar-laden treats are absent from your diet, we both knew there would be occasions where social pressures would trump nutrition. So, when the other parents ask if you can have some, we of course say yes.

Here's a revelation that won't shock you: you love chocolate cake.

Go nuts, son.

Shortly afterwards, the inevitable sugar rush hijacks every child's bloodstream, and you all tear off in multiple directions searching for adventure.

Referring back to *Dear Dory* once more, when we went away to Barcelona, I reflected on the anticipation of seeing you grow big enough to roam around and play with the children of those I hold most dear. Then last year, we went to Eddie's christening. You were still a baby, and so you couldn't join in. Today, while you're still too small to begin cooperative play, seeing you run around with the others is a dream made real for me. It's poignant, it's philosophical, and it is an image that has seared itself upon my spirit. Yes, I know not every social occasion will unfold in such a pleasing fashion, but today's has done. Today there's running, laughing, screaming and shrieking. Today is a good day to be a parent and an even better day to have friends.

Nursery Dilemma
Tuesday, 25 May 2021

When I dropped you off at nursery today, you cried. You also spent the two hours preceding the drop-off in a downcast and pitiful state because, when you woke up, I told you that you would be going to see Stacey. Despite the bond you've formed with her, it's clear you weren't psyched for the day ahead.

While I didn't expect you to be at a stage where you're skipping through the doors singing 'Wind the Bobbin Up', I thought you'd be more settled by now. But you're not. Something nagging at the back of my mind is telling me you're not OK. Call it instinct or schizophrenia. I don't know. But it's something. Mummy feels the same way.

Your room at nursery is a massive area made up of three smaller but still sizable rooms, triangular in layout and connected via always-open doors. It's a wonderful space to explore, with lots of toys. You should be in your element. But rarely do you leave the room that borders Mummy's. Instead, you spend large blocks of time sitting at a nearby table, watching the dividing door that separates your room from hers. Each time the door opens, hope is ignited in your eyes, only for the fire to die out as if doused by a flash flood, because it's not Mummy who appears.

Another component contributing to your unhappiness, we believe, is how busy the nursery is because business is booming. I'm beginning to doubt that the staff, as friendly as they are, have the resources to adequately devote time and attention to the army of small humans that arrives each day to be cared for. Mummy told me that her room can have a maximum occupancy of seventeen babies – *seventeen!*

I get that nurseries are businesses, so of course they want to ensure they're at maximum capacity. But when it's to the detriment of the very people they seek to serve, who, by the way, all happen to be under five years old, then you have to question their ethics and standards and wonder whether management have their priorities in the right order.

Mummy is barely able to pick her feet up high enough to walk over the threshold into our house each day. 'I know I've been away from childcare for a while and I'm getting older, but this place is relentless,' she says. 'You can't get anything done. We spend our days firefighting.'

The situation Mummy is in extends to your room as well. Often – *too often* – she'll call me on her lunch break to say that she's heard you crying for ages without anyone picking you up. And every time I call to check on you, I get the same response: 'He's doing OK, but he still requires a lot of reassurance and cuddles.' *Cuddles that he's not getting!*

So what do we do about all of this? We don't know. I have no idea how your behaviour compares with the other children's and whether it's normal or not. I don't know how psychologically impacted you've been by Covid-19. But I know you attend a nursery that's busier than the London Underground during rush hour. Of course, Covid-19 might have nothing to do with it; you might not be great with large crowds and lots of noise, and maybe this nursery doesn't suit your personality.

You have a parents' evening coming up, so we will voice these concerns then and see what Stacey says. In the meantime, I'd be lying if I said we hadn't thought about going to look around other nurseries.

Annabelle The Apple
Sunday, 30 May 2021

This is the tragedy of Annabelle the Apple, who desired one thing above all else: to be eaten by a toddler. You might think it a strange thing to desire, but some desires are strange, so let's leave it at that.

One day, a fruit-seeking toddler named Arlo climbed up on a chair, and then from the chair he climbed onto the adjacent table and crawled towards the fruit bowl that stood in the centre. In the middle of the fruit bowl lay Annabelle. Annabelle's innards starting tingling, her seeds vibrating with giddy excitement. *Is this the day I'm eaten by a toddler?* she thought.

'Apool,' Arlo said, pointing to Annabelle.

'Would you like an apple?' said Arlo's daddy, a handsome chap with a quite frankly devastating jawline and dashing bright eyes that could penetrate the armour of a tank.

'Yeah.'

'OK. I'll give you an apple, but only if you promise to sit on the floor and eat it, OK?'

'Yeah, apool.'

Annabelle could barely contain her excitement. She practically leapt out of the fruit bowl and into Arlo's hands, whereupon Arlo's daddy relocated Arlo and Annabelle from the table to the mat on the floor.

'Apool,' Arlo said, excited.

'Call me Annie,' said Annabelle – sorry, Annie.

Arlo took a bite. A small bite – tiny, in fact – but a bite, nonetheless. And then he took another bite, one that was even tinier than the first tiny bite, but one that was once again assuredly a bite.

Arlo's incisors sheared Annie's green skin away, exposing what she had underneath: a pale-white interior that shone the way snow shines when it's bathed in sunlight. *So, this is what heaven feels like*, she thought.

Arlo was about to take his third bite ... but then he paused, keeping his small jaws open.

'What's going on?' Annie said. 'Cooee, Arlo. I'm right here, silly. You just need to keep eating me. I'm nice and tasty.'

For some unknown reason, Arlo couldn't hear the apple, and instead of taking a third bite, he put Annie on the floor, stood up and ran away into the kitchen yelling: 'Cra-ka!'

'You now want a cracker?' Arlo's daddy said.

'Yeah, cra-ka.'

Poor Annie. She wept and wept. *Why doesn't that toddler want to eat me? I mean, what's the point of him saying he wants an apple, only to have two tiny bites from me and leave me on the floor? I thought he loved apples. He's always asking for them.*

But all was not lost, because …

'Arlo, you can have a cracker if you sit down and finish your apple first.'

'Yeah, apool. Cra-ka.'

Annie went from dismay to joy in an instant. Arlo came bounding over, dropped to a sitting position, picked her up and began his third bite. But before Annie could think up some positive thoughts about contentment and feeling wonderful, Arlo put her down again. He then got up, ran over to his toy basket and began ejecting his colourful possessions quicker that the laws of science deemed possible. It was like watching a popcorn machine in action.

Annie's once-gleaming pale-white body began to turn an orangey-brown colour. She caught sight of her own reflection from the shiny surface of one of Arlo's toys. *Who's going to eat me now?*

I'm afraid, Annie, the answer is no one.

Soon after, Arlo asked for a cracker again.

'Have you finished with the apple?' Arlo's daddy said.

'Yeah.'

Arlo's daddy conducted a thorough search of the surrounding area (one he completed in under half a second, concluding that the apple was *probably somewhere*), and gave it no more thought as he marched to the kitchen cupboard and fulfilled his son's wishes by giving him a cracker.

And that was the last anyone ever heard from poor Annie …

Or was it?

Three days later, Arlo's daddy was sitting at the table working on his laptop when he looked up from his computer in the direction of the fruit bowl. What he saw made him furrow his brow. It was the brown, hardly eaten remains of Annie the Apple, lying there in a decaying state. Many questions ran through his mind. Is that the apple from the other day? When did Arlo go back and eat more of it? And how did he get it back in the fruit bowl without his highly observant mother or father seeing him?

Sensibly, he ignored all those questions. Instead, he tossed Annie out into the trash, where she found many of her species in a similar half-eaten state, all of them having longed to be eaten by a toddler and each of them convinced that they had been chosen for consumption, only to be abandoned.

The end.

The Return Of Baby Puncher And Baby Puncher's Sister
Monday, 31 May 2021

We're at a friend's BBQ when I get a tap on the shoulder. 'Would you like to buy some raffle tickets?'

I turn around to be greeted by two young ladies whom I don't recognise ... *Hold up, that can't be ... Fuck, it is.* It's Baby Puncher and Baby Puncher's sister, characters whom we last met in *Dear Dory*. I've not seen them since we looked after them that time when Mummy was pregnant with you. Baby Puncher was four, and Baby Puncher's sister was six. You wouldn't remember that enchanting little weekend as you were still cooking in Mummy's tummy, but take it from me, it was a real baptism-by-fire introduction to the world of parenting. That weekend featured the telling and retelling of my own version of *The Boy Who Cried*

Wolf, and me being physically, emotionally, spiritually, and psychologically petrified of the prospect of having to take Baby Puncher to the toilet by myself. Luckily, Mummy swooped in to save the day.

I can't get over how much they've changed, even though it's only been two years. They're taller and Baby Puncher's hair has grown darker. I'm not sure if they remember me, but their expression tells me they don't give a shit either way.

'Would you like to buy some raffle tickets?' repeats Baby Puncher.

'I might,' I say. 'What are the prizes?'

'We've got two great prizes. One's an ice cream and one's an Easter egg, except it's not an Easter egg, it's just a small chocolate egg. Tickets are 20p each, or you can have a strip for 50p.'

I glance at Baby Puncher's sister, who's using a plastic pot to collect the proceeds. There's a fair amount of coins in there. I can see a few notes as well. This ice cream must be the tits.

'What charity are you collecting money for?' I ask.

'Charity? We're not collecting money for charity. This is all for us. We've got stuff we really need to buy. That's why we're selling raffle tickets. Now, do you want one or not?'

Do you know what worries me about their future, Arlo? Absolutely nothing. Those girls are going to be just fine.

In the end, I give them a quid for two strips and don't bother waiting around for the draw. That's if there even is a draw.

June

'It's funny how you go from talking shit with your mates to having kids and talking to them about actual shit.'

Ian M, an old uni mate

How Much Can You Understand?
Tuesday, 1 June 2021

'Mamma?'
   'She's at work, bud.'
   'Whhaaaa.'

The reason you're crying is that if Mummy's at work and Nana isn't here to look after you and it's only me, then that means you're going to nursery.

It doesn't help that we've had an amazing bank holiday weekend, where you've had your immediate family's undivided attention, and you've had a ton of fun. Usually, you only want Louie and your dummy at night, or when you're at nursery. At home during the day, you're not bothered. Until now. Because you know what today is. You've got Louie by the hand, insisting that he accompany you in your high chair while you eat breakfast.

You start crying again as we leave the house and I put you in the car. I do my best to distract you. 'Are you going to school today to play with your friends?'

'Yeah,' you manage to choke out.

'And are you going to play with lots of toys? What toys are you going to play with first? Dinosaurs, cars?'

Nothing.

'Arlo, listen to Daddy.' Your head lifts, and your eyes find mine in the rear-view mirror. 'I know you're upset because you don't want to go to nursery, but you always know that Mummy or Daddy will be there to pick you up again, don't you? You go to nursery for a little while, and then you come home.'

You stop crying.

I've always found speech development fascinating, and I'd love to know how much you understood of what I said. The fact that it's caused an instant change in your behaviour suggests you know more than the majority of parents would expect you to know at that age. Nevertheless, when we arrive you start up again. I'm praying that Stacey is back at work today. She wasn't there last week, and then the week before you were ill. *Come on, Stacey.*

I press the doorbell and we're soon called through the side gate. It's not Stacey waiting to carry you into nursery but another young woman. *Damn.* I can't recall her name, but she takes your temperature and holds out her arms. You refuse to meet them. Instead, you cling to me and quickly work yourself up into a right state. 'Dadda, Dadda, Dadda!' Not since your first week has it been this difficult to hand you over.

As I walk back to the car, I see Mummy, who's popped her head out the door to get a status update. 'Well?'

'Worst drop-off since he started.'

Mummy has rung to tell me that she's had a peek into your room and she could see you crying, holding out your arms to two members of staff who were standing there chatting – completely ignoring you.

Enough is enough. Fuck waiting until parents evening. I've told Mummy to serve notice.

Busy I get, but ignoring a toddler who's crying and lifting his arms up for comfort? No fucking way. I don't know which two members of staff it was, but they want sacking. Management should be ashamed for allowing these conditions to exist. I'm half tempted to list the nursery's name and address as a warning and deterrent to other parents who live close by.[16]

You Are Invited To A Party
Wednesday, 2 June 2021

You've received your first-ever birthday invitation from one of your peers at nursery, a young lady named Lillian. The invitation is red with white stars on it. Seeing it gave me some of the feels. *Your first party invitation.*

So when is this party, what is the dress code, and what are the other key details that we need to know?

It doesn't matter: you're obviously not going.

Listen, buddy, I love you, so, so, so fucking much, but not nearly enough to put myself through attending a toddler's birthday party. Hey, if it were one of our mates' kids, you'd be going. But a toddler party where we don't know anyone? Absolutely not. Here's a small, limited list of things I'd prefer to do with my time:

---

16 The reason I haven't done this is that I thought it was a big step to take, based on my limited exposure to the inner workings of this particular nursery. The truth is that nurseries are tough environments to work in, to manage and, as was the case with Arlo, to attend. That said, I would advise parents reading this always to look at the numbers, paying particular attention to a given room's maximum capacity. In my opinion, the smaller the better.

- Get stuck on hold to my bank for four hours listening to the same crackly song on repeat.
- Kill myself.
- Spend the whole day watching *Bing*.
- Kill myself again, in case I messed it up the first time.

An Old Friend
Thursday, 3 June 2021

My best friend from school, Sean, has got in contact with me to tell me that he found out about *Dear Dory* and ordered a copy. The last time I saw him was almost twenty years ago. He tells me that he has two children, a boy and a girl, and that the elder of the two left school last week. How surreal is that? We're the same age, yet his kids have all but grown up, while my son is still a toddler.

I ask him if he has any advice for me.

'Just enjoy it. For years I've been saying how I can't wait to watch them grow up. But now that they are older and they're out there with their friends all the time, I miss them.'

That's not just good advice for parents, Arlo – it's critical.

Potential Relocation
Friday, 4 June 2021

We've arrived at a potential new nursery for you. Because of the continued relaxation of Covid-19 restrictions, Mummy *and* I can come together. As we pull up, the first thing I notice is how quiet it is compared with your other one. All the children are playing outside but the numbers are low.

The building is a duck-egg blue, and the garden has a bunch of cool things to play with. I can see a mud kitchen, cars, and stuff to climb on and climb through. All fine so far.

We're greeted by Miss Daisy (all the staff are referred to as Miss whatever-their-first-name-is), who takes us through the building and introduces us to our personal tour guide, a small human female with blond hair who's marginally taller than you. She looks familiar, which might have something to do with our tour guide being your cousin Haylee. The nursery we're visiting is the same one that she attends.

Haylee and Miss Daisy take us to the toddler room. It's started to rain, so the children are brought inside. One boy walks up to you, says 'Hi,' and then points at your glasses saying, 'He's got glasses.'

'That's right. They help him see better,' Mummy says.

The other children don't faze you, but that could be because you have your cousin and both parents here. Still, you quickly take yourself over to a chair, sit down and begin demolishing a perfectly arranged wooden-cube toy.

Not one single child is crying.

Haylee takes us to the baby room, where Mummy is devastated to learn that the maximum capacity is five. Remember: hers is seventeen.

I ask about food, and Miss Daisy gives me a menu. I'm not crazy about some of the items, but I'll find out more about the ingredients later. For example, a toddler favourite, jelly, makes an appearance on the menu, and we don't let you have that because we're cruel nasty pieces of excrement. But with jelly and many other desserts there are sugar-free options. Maybe that's what they provide. Regardless, one thing I can guarantee is that I'd rather you have a bit more sugar in your diet and be content in your environment than the other way round.

'Arlo's generally a quiet little boy when he's upset. He doesn't scream or shout. It's more of a silent whimper, and that often goes unnoticed in the nursery he's at now,' Mummy says. *Unnoticed. That's putting it diplomatically.*

'That's one of the good things about having lower numbers. It's easier to pay attention and pick up on things like that,' Miss Daisy says.

Once we're finished with the tour, I'm left feeling convinced that moving you to a smaller nursery is the right thing to do. The word that comes to mind when walking around this nursery is 'community'. Obviously, Miss Daisy and her colleagues want to make a good impression, and they have done so, but seeing simple things like Haylee waltzing in and out of the office room like it's her own home is encouraging.

'We do have a waiting list, but our numbers will reduce mid-July,' Miss Daisy says.

'Perfect – we have to give six weeks' notice anyway,' Mummy says.

We say thanks to both Miss Daisy and our tour guide and leave feeling relieved that we've almost certainly found you a new home for two days a week.

Mummy has served noticed. You have six weeks to go. Although we always try to make the best decisions as your parents, this is one area where I'll hold my hands up and say we got it wrong. I told you when you were in Mummy's tummy that we'd make mistakes along the way, and I don't for one minute envision this one being the last. But, hopefully, today begins to put that one right.

Haircuts And Swimming
Saturday, 5 June 2021

Today we're going swimming, but first, we're taking you to get your hair trimmed. The hairdresser's we're going to is different from the one we've been to before, but having your hair cut has never fazed you in the past, so you should be fine. Mummy drops us off but then leaves to go and pick Haylee up, as she also has an appointment here.

'Mamma?'

'She's gone to get Haylee.'

'YEAH!' It would seem you're deeply excited by this revelation.

We meet a young lady. I forget her name, so we'll make one up – let's call her Amy. Amy will be cutting your hair. She asks, 'Will he need to sit on your lap for this?'

'He should be fine. He's had his hair cut before, and the clippers don't bother him.'

Famous last words.

You begin freaking out as soon as I sit you down. At first, I think you're impatient to see Haylee, but that's not it. You're not one bit on board with getting your hair cut. *Why?* I get that it's a new hairdresser, but you've never reacted this way before. You usually love getting your hair cut.

'Maybe see if he'll sit with you,' Amy suggests.

I gown up and sit you on my lap, where your freak-out level does the opposite of dropping. You start pushing yourself away from me, trying to get down, while also looking over your shoulder for signs of the nasty, evil clippers.

'WHHHAAAAAA!'

'Arlo, calm down, buddy. It's OK. It's just a bit of noise. It won't hurt you.'

Fortunately, Mummy arrives with Haylee. Hopefully, she can succeed in pacifying you.

You're now in a quite uncontrollable state. I switch with Mummy to see if she fares any better with you on her lap. She doesn't. Now it's Haylee's turn. She tries to make you laugh by playing peek-a-boo. But that doesn't work either. Next, she rubs your arm, saying, 'It's OK, Arlo,' which is nothing short of adorable, but once again, success is absent.

Next, we give you a break and tag Haylee in. She sits beautifully, allowing Amy to make quick work of her Rapunzel-rivalling fringe. She's smiling, she's calm, she's relaxed. You can see it all, so hopefully you're amenable to returning to the chair.

Again, negative – you move yourself to DEFCON 1 before we've even placed you in it.

'WHHHAAAAAA! MAMMA, DADDA, MAMMA, DADDA. WHHHAAAAAA!'

Your nose is getting snotty. You want to wipe the snot away, but your arms are trapped under the gown. That doesn't stop you trying anyway, the action ensuring that the already-snipped hair on the gown makes contact with your snot-covered face, sticking to it. So now we have a concoction of hair mixed with snot mixed with real tears, and you're wiping the whole unsavoury lot all over your face and in your eyes.

And I haven't even got to the good part yet.

Your dummy is also in your mouth, but because you're pulling pins from several emotional grenades and tossing them in multiple directions, the dummy is half hanging out, thus allowing for your vocal displeasure to reach the eardrums of everyone nearby. Like your face, it too has collected a thick layer of sticky-snot hair. But don't worry, because Mummy darts in, swipes it out of your mouth, and in a move that constitutes the single greatest act of motherly love since Lily Potter took one in the chest for her son Harry, tosses your dummy into her own mouth, sucks off the sticky-snot hair from it and promptly swallows – *gulp*.

While all this is going on, you've got me and Amy dancing around you, with me trying to wipe your nose with a tissue and Amy trying to work to her job description. She eventually gets about two thirds of the way through, but it's been an uphill battle all the way. Mummy loads up *Bing* on her phone for you to watch. Your agitation marginally reduces, but soon ramps up again.

Luckily, I've had another idea. 'Arlo.'

You turn to face me.

'Do you know what we need to do? We need to sweep up all the hair. Would you like to watch Daddy do it?' Your eyes display the faintest glimmer of interest, which is more than enough for me to cling on to. I ask Amy for a brush, and I begin sweeping up the place. It doesn't quite match Mummy's sacrifice, but picture the scene for a moment: your dad on his hands and knees sweeping up hair with a dustpan and brush, because he knows how much joy you will derive from this activity. The rest of the staff are looking at me like I need to be sectioned, but I don't care as long as it works.

And it is working—

'WHHHAAAAAA!'

And now it's not.

And now I've run out of ideas. So has everybody else.

Mummy has no choice but to hold you in place while you display the most displeasure I've seen since your first day of nursery. Mummy's about to cry; I'm standing there like a fucking moron with a dustpan and brush in my hands; Haylee is standing there looking like less of a moron but as clueless as I am about what to do.

At long last, Amy finishes.

The moment you're out of the chair, all evidence of a 'scene' vanishes, and you're back to your happy, chirpy self.

That is as frontline-in-the-trenches a toddler-parenting experience as you can get. At least we've got swimming to look forward to.

The BBQ
Sunday, 13 June 2021

The sun is beating down upon us, bathing the scene in 24-degree rays. Clouds are absent from the sky. We've been invited to a BBQ by our friends Matty and Jasmine. They have a daughter, Harper (five months old), and a son, Oakley (not long turned two).

Their garden is arranged in such a manner that it has lots of toys for toddlers strategically strewn about, almost as if the space were an outdoor nursery. Sure, there are red flags and things to watch out for, but the adult-to-non-adult ratio favours the adult population – four in total – so we're in a position to relax, enjoy the weather and the company, and watch you and Oakley spend time together. Perfect.

A couple of hours into our afternoon, Mummy and Jasmine, along with Harper, head indoors to do ... something. I forget what, but whatever it is, they're no longer with us. From the adult population, only Matty and I are left outside.

You're playing in a shallow paddling pool, and Oakley is playing on your bike, which we brought along with us.

'Can you watch the kids? I need to go and grab the meat,' Matty says.

'Sure,' I say, like the complete idiot that I am.

At that point, a few things happen inside the region of my brain that houses the prefrontal cortex. The first thing it does is send me a message telling me that I'm a twat for agreeing to Matty's impossible and absurd demand that I care for two toddlers. Next, it relays an order to another area of my brain, with instructions for my adrenal glands to release all available stores of cortisol. Finally, it deploys a follow-up message reminding me that in case it wasn't clear the first time, I'm still a twat.

I should also add that when I described *what* you and Oakley were doing – you in the paddling pool, and Oakley on your bike – I didn't bother to say *where* in the garden you both were. It didn't seem important then. It does now. You're at the top of the garden, close to where I'm standing, and Oakley is shuffling his way towards the bottom of the garden, still on your bike. Oh, and it's a big garden!

Despite my less-than-calm demeanour, I mentally get to work, plotting a course of action that results in you and Oakley not dying, or at least surviving long enough for backup to arrive.

OK, so I've got Arlo in the paddling pool. It's shallow, and he's no longer a baby, so he's probably fine, but I'm sure I read somewhere that you need to keep an eye on infants at all times when there's water concerned and that even a depth of an inch can sometimes have fatal consequences. Then there's Oakley, who's sitting on Arlo's bike, shuffling his way towards the bottom of the garden, where there's a series of three stone-paved steps for him to fall down. He's almost certain to do himself a mischief if he doesn't get off the bike, pick it up and walk down. So who do I care about more? Well, obviously, I care more about Arlo, but it's not like I don't care about Oakley – the thought of any toddler in pain from an accident pulls at my heartstrings. In fact— Stop! You're getting sidetracked. Make a decision. What are you going to do?

I decide on my plan and spring into action. First, I bound over to the paddling pool, scoop you up and place you near a plastic mud kitchen that has bowls of water on it – something that should capture your attention. Next, I tell Oakley to get off the bike and walk down the stairs. He doesn't listen, so I make to run after him. But then he stops, gets off the bike, performs a 180-degree turn and begins playing with a nearby water sprinkler. *Fine.*

I turn my attention back to you only to discover that you've lost interest in the mud kitchen, and you've now tottered over to the dinner table and picked up the nearest bone-china dinner plate. *Not fine.*

I swiftly relieve you of the plate and shoo you off with hand gestures back towards the mud kitchen. But because you're such a magpie, something else has distracted you, and now you're sitting under an umbrella playing with purple kinetic sand. *Back to fine.*

And now Oakley has mounted your bike again and is once again progressing towards those damn steps. *Back to not fine.*

And now you're eating the purple kinetic sand. *Also not fine, but less not fine than what Oakley is doing.*

And now I'm running towards Oakley.

And now I'm not, because a quick look back reveals you're now headed towards the BBQ – the three-foot-high naked flames serving to attract your attention.

'Arlo! Hot. That's very hot. You can't go near it.'

You stop in your tracks, lean forward and begin blowing at the flames to cool them down, like we do when Daddy leaves your dinner in the microwave for too long.

'ARRGH!' shouts Oakley.

Now what?

Oakley has begun his descent down the steps on your bike while simultaneously arriving at the conclusion that this was all a terrible idea – something I can very much relate to.

There's no way I'm leaving you standing on your own to blow out the BBQ flames, so once again, I scoop you up and march quickly to Oakley, but not too quickly. After all, I don't want to look like I'm panicking, in case Mummy and Jasmine are looking out of the window at me. Thankfully, before I can get to Oakley, he negotiates the final two steps without falling over.

Matty arrives with a plate of meat and two beers. He can't have been gone for more than forty seconds. *Bloody toddlers!* I put you down and snatch both beers from Matty.

Seems Fair To Me
Tuesday, 15 June 2021

'So, nursery have said that he needs to stay off for at least twenty-four hours from the last occurrence,' Mummy says.

The word 'occurrence' in this case means diarrhoea. You seem fine in yourself, but take it from my nose, you're not a well little boy.

'It's OK. I've told them I'm not coming into work today,' Mummy continues.

'But that means you won't get paid, right?'

'Right.'

'But do we still have to pay for Arlo?'

'We do.'

'Even though they're the ones who have told us not to bring him in?'

'That's correct.'

'In what world does that make sense?'

'In the world where the nursery doesn't lose any money.'

'Oh, that world. I see.'

The good news is that if you're not at nursery, then that only leaves us with four more weeks before the big relocation. Actually, three weeks. I've taken the last week off so you and I can log some serious lad time and get up to mischief—

Frrrttt ... braaaaapppp ... braaappp ... pat, pat, pat.

Come on, son. Let's go and change your nappy.

Mop Buckets And Zooming
Wednesday, 16 June 2021

I've had two uneventful and, to be quite honest, pretty average days. But they weren't totally uneventful. And 'pretty average' is as per what it says on the tin: 'pretty average'. Not 'below average', and not 'worst-day-ever average'. No. Thanks to you, there were a couple of high points.

Yesterday's high point was you inviting me to come and stand with you in the almost-full mop bucket to partake in a spot of splashing.

Today, we developed a new game while out for a much-needed walk to the park. The game was that I would tilt your buggy back so that you were facing the sky and simultaneously sprint over the road holding on to the buggy with only one hand, and with the other I'd reach in to tickle you. You loved it, and I can assure you that the whole thing was 100 per cent responsible parenting on my part because we got to the park alive.

It does make you stop and think, though. Yesterday's mop-bucket game barely lasted a minute, and today's tilt-the-pram-and-run-across-the-road game wasn't much longer, yet those are the two occurrences that will stay with me. There are several lessons here. One: you can always turn things around in your favour. Two: you will find joy in the unexpected as long as you're open to receiving it when it presents itself. And three: truly wonderful and poignant experiences can come and go in no time at all.

My final point is that I would almost certainly have forgotten these moments over the course of my life. But now I won't, because I took the time to write to you today, and that is as powerful a memory-retrieval tool as I've ever come across.

Mummy's New Job
Thursday, 17 June 2021

Aside from Haylee's nursery (soon to be yours too), Mummy went to look at another. I couldn't go, because they only allowed one person in owing to the usual Covid-19 restrictions.

We chose Haylee's nursery for you because it makes sense practically. Nana See-See will be collecting you each day, and it's closer to her, so she can get you and Haylee at the same time.

But Mummy said the other nursery was also brilliant. She said they represent everything about early development that she loves and that she would much prefer to work for that nursery than the one she's currently at. Mummy rang them up on Monday on the off-chance that they were looking to hire and asked if she could interview.

Fast-forward to today, and she's been offered a job. She interviewed this morning and apparently did phenomenally well. Go Mummy!

'Does this mean we're getting a takeaway to celebrate?' she says.

'Yes, it does.'

Surprise!
Friday, 18 June 2021

'Right. Say goodbye to Daddy, Arlo,' Mummy says.

'He's not coming?'

'Nope.'

'Oh, buddy, come and give me a big cuddle.' I scoop you up and give you lots of kisses, which you find irritating, and then I put you down and say goodbye. I honestly don't know when I'll next see you.

I leave you in the capable hands of Nana Smurf, who I presume is babysitting you, and then Mummy and I get in the car to go to ... I have no idea where. Mummy has planned a little Father's Day surprise for me. She told me to be ready to leave bang on 5 p.m. and said that I had to pack my cycling gear. As it's a Father's Day surprise, I assumed you'd be coming with us, but evidently that's not the case. I found it difficult saying goodbye to you. I'm once again reminded of the conflicting emotions that parents feel when leaving their children. I still believe it's vital to take time off from mumming and dadding, but it's easier said than done.

But you'll be pleased to know I quickly forgot about you as I focused instead on trying to guess what I'm doing for the weekend.

Let's start with what I do know: I'm going cycling. I'm also – and Mummy doesn't know that I know this – going with my mate Ian. I know this because Ian saw a message from Mummy to his wife, Cara, saying something about 'their Father's Day surprise'. While exchanging messages guessing what we're doing, we agreed that it's critical we play dumb and act surprised if we see each other. Our partners won't find out the truth until this book comes out.

Mummy also gave me a clue that referenced having 'eight sore cheeks'. Which means we *might* be going cycling as a four with Ian and Cara because four people each have two bum cheeks, and if you add them up, you get eight! How I don't own a detective agency, I don't know.

But the thing that's confusing me is that Mummy asked me to pack my cycling gear, which means it must be more than a jolly jaunt by the canal followed by a picnic, right? It's possible that this is a dads-only surprise, in which case, I get to hang out with two more of my mates and presumably without kids. This weekend is shaping up very well.

June

'Stop looking at the satnav!'
'I'm not.'

I am. I can't see where we're going, but I can see it's going to take us an hour and forty minutes to get there. I carry out more fine detective work and calculate that unless there is traffic, which I don't believe there is, because I can't see any red or orange lines that indicate traffic on the map (the one I'm supposedly not looking at), then it's about thirty minutes longer than the usual time it takes to drive to Ian's.

Are we not going to Ian's? Are we going to someone else's house? Are we going to a hotel or a lodge, or are we camping? Isn't this exciting, Arlo?

Turns out the whole journey time was a ruse, because Mummy purposely took the scenic route to Ian's so I wouldn't know where we were going. It worked: for a minute, she threw me off the scent.

'Right, bye then.' Mummy says to me.
'What, you're not staying either?'
'Nope.'
'But the clue said eight sore cheeks, so if you're not coming, that means there's no way Cara is coming. No offence Cara ...'
'None taken.'
'So does that mean we get to hang out with two more of our mates?'
'Jackpot,' Ian says.

Mummy leaves and Cara orders pizza.

Eddie, my godson, wanders over with a book about dinosaurs, and implies with some fancy arm-waving that he would like me to read it to him. Eddie has not long turned two.

I recently learnt that humanity's dinosaur knowledge is more concentrated in children and in parents who take an active interest in their children's interests. That's amazing. The depth of an adult's dinosaur-related education relates directly to whether or not they have children. Before today, I would have struggled to name more than ten species of dinosaur. But that's no longer the case. Here are some new ones that have been introduced to me: *Troodon, Corythosaurus, Quetzalcoatlus, Torosaurus, Albertosaurus, Kronosaurus, Dimorphodon, Elasmosaurus, Iguanodon* and *Baharriasaurus*[17].

I spend my evening playing with the kids, eating pizza, drinking beer and watching football.

Arlo, I bloody love Father's Day surprise weekends!

Sightseeing
Saturday, 19 June 2021

Ian and I are certain we'll be sharing our Father's Day surprise with James and Martin. We believe that James is coming because he has a spare bike (I don't have one), and Martin is coming because he's the closest other mate who happens to be a dad. Oh, and I may or may not have seen a message flag up on Mummy's phone from Martin's wife, Jess. Again I ask: why don't I own a detective agency?

We're right. Martin and James soon arrive and they're exuding as much joyous astonishment that they've got the day off from dadding as Ian and I are. Next, we're all invited by the mummies to a Father's Day WhatsApp group, where we quickly receive another clue.

We deduce from the clue that we're supposed to take a train somewhere. We're not sure where or at what time,

---

[17] It's times like this when I'm thankful I don't have to narrate the audio versions of my books. Over to you, Andy.

until Cara suggests that maybe one of us has a recently downloaded app on our phone.

'It's me. I've got the tickets,' says Martin. 'We're going to Cambridge.'

We cycle to the station and make the train on time. When we arrive, we go and find a pub to have breakfast and wait for our next clue.

It doesn't take long to arrive:

> *Now Cambridge is lovely, there's much to explore,*
> *And to boss you all day would be quite a bore.*
> *So pick out a landmark or maybe choose two,*
> *Then send us a photo to get your next clue.*
> *There's a church in a circle, a big old bronze horse,*
> *A load of old bricks and the uni, of course.*
> *So run wild and free, but please keep in mind,*
> *That come 4 o'clock there's a new place to find.*
> *The last stretch on your bikes will be roughly an hour,*
> *So try to reserve just a little more power!*

'They want us to go sightseeing,' says a confused Martin, who immediately rereads the clue to see if we've missed something.

A waitress brings over four beers.

'Is it illegal to cycle when you're drunk?' Ian asks.

'Nope,' says James.

'Well, we're not going sightseeing, that's for sure,' Ian declares.

'Hang on. I've got this,' I say. I google some of the sights that the mummies suggest we visit, and send stock photos to the Father's Day WhatsApp group. I ignore the fact that we've supposedly covered all the sights on their list of suggestions in a handful of seconds and that all the images I sent have Shutterstock watermarks on them.

We search for 'extreme things to do in Cambridge', but punting down a cold river ranks top of the list. So instead, we find another pub, this one with a shuffleboard, and we settle in for the day.

'Hang on. If we don't get our next clue until around 4 p.m., then we're definitely checking in somewhere,' Ian says.

'What, so we have a lie-in tomorrow, without the kids?' I say.

'I think we should get very, very drunk ... Excuse me,' says Martin to a passing barmaid, 'can I get four steins?'

In the few years that I've been writing these books to you, Arlo, I've covered a lot of ground, including some essential life lessons. Here's another one. Regardless of your achievements and how you usually conduct yourself at home or in public, never underestimate how rapidly your maturity level can plummet when you're in the company of your drunken best friends. I've spent the last thirty seconds riding naked and high-fiving Ian and Martin while James fixes a tyre puncture. This behaviour, while highly amusing to us, is also illegal. Thankfully, our antics are taking place away from the city centre in the countryside, where there is not a single person in sight – and I can see pretty far ... despite blurrier-than-normal vision.

With our clothes back on and the puncture fixed, we reach our final destination, a houseboat situated on the River Cam. Sainsbury's have also swung by to deliver alcohol and snacks, and breakfast for the morning. Arlo, if you've ever heard me slag Mummy off behind her back, know that my words were only in jest and that I think she's the most perfect woman and I'm the luckiest man on the planet. But now you'll have to excuse me as I'm about to throw up!

Father's Day
Sunday, 20 June 2021

It's late afternoon by the time I arrive back from Cambridge. As soon as I walk through the door, you manage a perfunctory half smirk before taking your *Hey Duggee* chair to the back door, asking for the keys.

For Father's Day, you've painted me a card and bought me some lovely bath stuff. Yes, that's right. I'm now sober and away from my friends, so I'm back to my respectable deep-thinking self who loves to ruminate on life in the bath while in the company of classical music, candles and a few drops of lavender oil.

Mummy tops off a stellar weekend by cooking a roast dinner. You are one hungry, grumpy toddler, but you cheer up after you devour what's on your plate, and the two of us log some solid playtime with me chasing you around the house with the 'ooofer.'

We put you to bed, and then Mummy says, 'Would you like me to run you a bath with your stuff in it?'

Talk about icing a cake.

June Monthly Review
Monday, 21 June 2021

This is a couple of days late, I know, but you'll have to forgive me as I was busy being an absent father and getting drunk with my mates. Anyhow, let's see how you're getting on this month.

We're still under Covid-19 restrictions, but they've softened enough to allow us to return to some family-fun adventures. Swimming and soft-play parks have reopened. It took you a little while to build up your confidence again in both the pool and in soft-play, but not all that long. Soft-play in particular is fun to revisit because of how stable and confident you are on your feet now. I love watching you totter off flapping your arms like someone's glued springs to them, with your excitement levels off the scale. It's great.

You spend the majority of your time on this planet asking for food. You have a list that you verbally cycle through: 'Cra-ka, apool, oran, nana, bottle, cra-ka, apool, oran, nana, bottle.' Sometimes, if you're told 'later' in response to a request for food, you'll walk away for half a second before returning, assuming that 'later' has arrived and that you can begin cycling through your list of food preferences. It's cute and comical but a little annoying at the same time.

You've not really added many new words to your vocabulary this month, but you have upped the two-word phrases, and even some of three-word ones. Mummy assures me this is a massive development in your language. You say: 'I see you', 'I did it', 'one more' and 'sit here'.

Colours confuse you. You can say 'purple' and 'blue', and you correctly say 'purple' when we point to a purple object, but you also say 'purple' to any object we point to that's not purple. Still, I think colours are about to become a big part of your life. I'm sure Mummy will come up with a clever way to teach them to you.

The other day, you were playing at your tool station, and I asked you to go and build me a chair. You grabbed your hammer, walked into your nursery and started bashing on a box that you periodically exclaimed was a chair. I was beside-myself impressed with you.

You know not to walk on your own in the road. And you know to sit down as soon as you enter the house so that we can take your shoes off.

Your awareness of television has reached the point where you request certain episodes of your favourite TV show, *Bing*.

There's one about a Hoover that's naturally your favourite, but there's also one about a slide and another about a fire engine. We watch those same episodes every single night before bed.

Bedtime has been a bit rough on us all this month. There's a lot of protesting on your part. This might have something to do with us swapping your sleeping bag for a duvet so that you have more room to move. Or it could be a phase. If it is, can we get past it quickly, please? Because it also includes you waking up at 5 a.m. – *again*! – and yelling, 'Mamma. Dadda. In there!' In other words: 'Take me into your bedroom, and turn the TV on.'

Something you're loving at the minute is seeing a lot of Nana Smurf. She's moved back in with us for a few months while we renovate her house. You might recall that last year we managed to pick up the keys a week or so before the first mandatory lockdown. Her house needed work, and now we're finally getting round to doing it. A loan from Auntie Lisa is funding the project.

I've had my first Covid-19 vaccination, and Mummy's booked in to receive hers next week. The UK was supposed to exit lockdown at the end of the month, but the date has been pushed back until July, because of a new strain (the Delta variant) that's causing trouble. Don't worry, though. Disney are still releasing *Black Widow* next month.

As always, thanks for another month of dadding.

He's So Far Up The Other End
Tuesday, 22 June 2021

I've taken Nana Smurf with me to collect you from nursery. On our way back, we're at the traffic lights. You're sitting in your buggy. I lean over and stroke your head. The action attracts the attention of another boy who's standing with his mother nearby. He's about four. After a few seconds, he walks right up to you and strokes you on your head in the same way that I did.

The action catches me off guard and I'm unsure how to respond. At first, I stiffen up, wondering if he was about to hurt you, but his mother quickly intervenes and apologises. He doesn't hurt you, so I tell her there was no apology necessary, but I'm still a little bit stunned as to what's just happened.

Nana Smurf leans in and whispers, 'He's so far up the other end.'

'The end of what?' I whisper back.

The lights go red, the cars stop and the little man goes green, telling us pedestrians that we can cross the road. The boy who's apparently 'so far up the other end' and his mother cross the road, quickly – very quickly.

'I'll eat my hat if he isn't,' continues Nana.

'Isn't what? Mum, what are you on about?'

'That young boy. He's massively on the spectrum, you mark my words. I'd even bet my house on it.'

Huh!

I instantly felt for that mother, and not because she has a son who may or may not be on the spectrum. But because, if that is indeed the case, I wonder how many apologies she dishes out to others on a daily basis. How often does she have to react instantly and tell strangers that her son has a condition, and that it's not his fault? I cannot comprehend the ongoing emotional exhaustion, Arlo. She must have to do that every day. I bet her worry levels are even worse when he's not with her. Can you imagine what sort of wreck she must be when she sends him off to school? I hope his needs are catered for.

Also, I probably need to sit Nana down for a chat because I'm not sure that 'he's so far up the other end' is recognised by the *New Oxford Style Manual* as the correct way to describe someone on the spectrum.

July

'When my son was a toddler, he spent the first night in his newly decorated Thomas the Tank Engine *bedroom. Come morning, he'd torn off a third of the wallpaper.'*

Sarah K, the author's mother

Gunfight At The O.K. Corral
Saturday, 3 July 2021

A red sun smothers the town in suffocating heat. Beads of sweat fall from those who have the misfortune to be out in its company. Outside a local drugstore, two gunslingers stand facing one another. They ignore the heat and everything else. Nothing distracts them.

In a few moments – each slinger will intuitively know when – the time will come for them to draw their weapons.

Any moment now.

DRAW.

'I'm pushing the buggy!' yell both gunslingers at once.

But it's the daddy who beats the mummy to the draw. Which means that when the family enters the drugstore in a few moments, it's the mummy who will be responsible for somehow containing the mischievous little errant of a toddler who'll no doubt be intent on pulling things off the shelves and throwing them on the floor, things that they've yet to purchase or have no intention of purchasing, while the daddy gets to sit back and observe the affair with a great deal of amusement.

As they enter the drugstore, the mummy begins to protest, looking for a way to somehow alter the outcome that has left her in the horrendously unenviable position that she now finds herself in. 'But you pushed it last time,' she pleads.

'Sorry, but I called it first. I know it's frustrating when the cards don't fall your way. Now, watch Arlo. He's already dashed off and wrapped his hands around something he shouldn't.'

'Arlo! Wait there! PUT THAT DOWN!'

How About You OPEN THE FUCKING DOOR AND LET HIM IN!
Sunday, 4 July 2021

We're at a birthday party for the four-year-old child of one of my friends.

It started out great because as soon as we walked into the noisy and populated back garden, you took yourself straight off to go exploring. As parents who worry that your confidence has been hampered by Covid-19, we find this behaviour deeply reassuring. Another thing that I like is that you still get a lot of attention from other parents because of you being an undoubtedly handsome young man in glasses.

But twenty minutes in, my cheery mood threatens to dissipate entirely and be replaced by rage. Why? Because you're trying to open the door of a playhouse at the bottom of the garden, and there's another boy who is at least five years old preventing you from doing so. He's holding the door shut from the other side, looking at you dead in the eye through the Perspex door panel and shaking his head and saying 'no.'

Only Mummy and I can see what's happening. Everyone else is deep in conversation, and there are a lot of kids here, so any audible evidence of kids not playing nicely is tuned out.

In hushed tones, Mummy and I have an adult discussion about what's happening.

'Why won't he let him in the fucking house?'

'I think it's because Arlo's too little.'

'Well, he's big enough to walk over there and open the door, so just let him the fuck in.'

'Calm down.'

'I will not. What a little prick!'

'It's OK. Arlo's not bothered any more.'

She's right, you've abandoned your campaign. Instead, you've tottered over to the sandpit to begin digging for dinosaur fossils.

Minutes later, that *kid*, which I'm putting in italics because I want the reader to really know I mean 'little cunt who I don't like', walks by. He doesn't look at me, but I burn lasers into the back of his odd-shaped head.[18]

This is now the second time in the last few months where I've displayed an emotional response to other children older than you who were either being unkind or who, through their own absent-mindedness, almost hurt you.

It's bonkers when you think about it – an adult male in his mid-thirties getting worked up over something like this. Am I overreacting, or is there something more to it? Since becoming a parent, I've found that some of my responses to certain things are wildly at odds with my personality, and I've questioned whether it's some primal reaction; an outdated piece of biological code that's still live, residing in my DNA.

---

18 Truthfully, there was nothing odd about the shape of his head, but by that time, I'd gone into full Sith mode on him and had let my emotions take over. Sorry, Master Yoda.

I'd speak to another parent but I doubt it's socially acceptable to ask, 'Do you ever glare at a five-year-old at a kids' party like you want to hammer-throw him into a tree because he's not letting your little boy into a playhouse?'

Obviously, I'm exaggerating, and I wouldn't want any actual harm to come to this kid ... probably. But inside I'm fuming, and I don't like him. If he came up to me and asked me to help him with something, I'd either do it but be cold and frosty towards him to make a statement, or lie and tell him I didn't know how. That'd learn the prick.

Carer Day
Tuesday, 6 July 2021

Historically, my carer days have sucked. But not today. Why? Well, for starters, you're not ill. OK, technically you are because you've got the runs, and the latest episode occurred well within the last twenty-four hours, meaning you aren't allowed to go to nursery, although we still have to pay. But regardless of all that, you're in a relatively buoyant and chirpy mood, so I believe we can get away with doing something cool today rather than watching *Bing*.

The reason it's me on carer duty is that neither of your nanas are about – don't worry, I've told them they obviously don't care about you – and Mummy took the last shift. We take it in turns to make it fair to our employers because an unplanned day off work has a wider impact on the people we work with.

But enough preamble. We enter the trampoline park.

We're ten minutes into a parent-and-toddler session, and I'm being told off for doing something that I'm apparently 'not supposed to be doing' by a young lady whose name, according to her badge, is MFD. It should be clear to even a single-cell organism that MFD is an abbreviation of Massive Fucking Dickhead.

And I disagree with her statement. Because I *am* supposed to be doing the thing I'm doing (which I'll get to soon), and I have a long list of qualifications to prove that fact. Let me first tell you about that long list, Arlo, and then I'll tell you what it is that I'm doing, and you can see if you agree with me, which of course you will because I'm right.

First, I'm in the correct attire. I've got loose-fitting clothing on, as have you. And we've both got the correctly branded socks to go with our outfits. I questioned why we had to have *their* socks, which cost £2.50 a pair – yes, even the toddler-sized ones – but I was told that it's a 'safety procedure'. I said, 'No. Wearing surgical gloves while performing surgery is a safety procedure. This isn't that.' But I was ignored.

Next, I completed the health and safety documents and ticked all seven – that's right, seven – disclaimers waiving my rights to ... I assume both our lives, but we all know I didn't read shit, because no one ever does. I'd also like to highlight that the parent-and-toddler session lasts an hour, and if I had carefully read all of the documentation instead of scrolling through it as quickly as possible, then not only would we not yet have performed a single bounce, but we'd probably also have had to pay for a couple of extra sessions. Anyway, I ticked all the boxes, so any personal injuries sustained are on me. Fine. Can we go and jump up and down now?

We can't. Because next we have to watch a safety-briefing video. MFD is blocking the entrance to the park, ensuring all participating parents and toddlers are watching the said video. But this is a problematic endeavour because the toddlers are looking at the bright, alluring colours of the trampoline park, and one toddler in particular, you, has decided that safety-briefing videos are boring, and so you've set off up the short flight of steps and into the park. The management have not thought this through!

And now MFD is telling you off, saving me the job so I can instead focus on absorbing the important points of the safety video.

Breathe. In through the nose and out through the mouth.

Look, MFD, you obviously don't have kids, or you'd understand that you can't expect a toddler to stand still and look at a destination that they have the desire and capability to get to. There's one insight for you. Also, how about I be the one to run point on telling my son what to do?

On a closer inspection of MFD's name badge I realise I've got it slightly wrong. It's actually SMFD. The S stands for 'Super'.

Finally, the safety video ends, and we can get set to leave these last few excruciating minutes behind us and log a bit of jumping!

But wait ...

We can't!

Because now, another video has started. This one's a warm-up routine. Surely not? SFMD, how about you get out of the way and let us into the park, and I'll do a lot more than warm up. I'll burn up, on account of my badass jumping-agility skillz.

But alas, Arlo, it seems we can't possibly skip this vital health and safety step, a step that you and every other toddler didn't get a memo about because you're all standing there looking at your respective parents like they're idiots. Eventually, the warm-up ends, and we're finally granted entry. Now, we can start having some fun.

And it's fun we have. Just a boy and his dad testing their physical and psychological limits, with smiles on their faces and beads of sweat dripping from their heads. I'm about to surmise that I'm unlikely ever to have another carer day as good as this one when—

'Oi! You can't do that in here.'

Even though I arrived in the correct attire and purchased the correctly branded socks, even though I ticked seven separate disclaimer boxes waiving my rights, even though I kinda watched the safety briefing and kinda performed the warm-up, I apparently can't do the thing I came here to do, and that's bounce.

That's seriously all I'm doing. I'm standing in the exact centre of the trampoline, bouncing up and down. I'm not doing any reckless moves like somersaults. I'm not bouncing from one trampoline to another. There aren't even any other parents or toddlers around for me to accidentally bash into.

And where are you while all of this is taking place? You're right by my side, of course ... hanging upside down ... Don't worry. Daddy is holding on to your ankles real tight.

Chair!
Friday, 9 July 2021

We've gone for one of our obligatory walks to the shop to buy some fruit. Once inside, you spot one of those circular two-step stools that shelf-stackers use to access the upper reaches when they're replenishing the stock.

'Chair!' you say, and you begin tottering off after it.

'It's not a chair,' says a male staff member who's walking past.

Your mother is horrified. She whips a glare around and hurls it into the back of his head, firing off daggers, lasers, supernatural spells and any other analogy I can think of to describe someone directing silent wrath at another person.

'Look, Arlo, you're right. IT IS A CHAIR. Because if you say it's A CHAIR, then it's A CHAIR. And Mummy wants to come with you and also sit on THE CHAIR.'

Though I didn't have the same reaction that Mummy did, I'm well and truly on her side. You're under two, so what gives? Why didn't he shut up and let you pretend it's a chair?

By the way, Mummy never sat on THE CHAIR. She intended to, but after she got close enough, she surmised that its hygiene level wasn't quite up to her standards, so her rebellious intention performed a 180-degree about-turn and quietly went home.

What Do You Expect Me To Do About It?
Saturday, 10 July 2021

I shit you not; you've had a tantrum because we were looking at an aeroplane in the sky, and then it went behind a cloud and we couldn't see it, and you naturally thought these were all variables that I was controlling.

Lads' Day
Wednesday, 14 July 2021

I've got the day off, and it's just you and me, buddy. We're kicking off today's adventures with a parent-and-toddler swimming session.

I divide the forty-five-minute session between standing back and letting you walk around the ultra-shallow section where the water barely comes up to your knees, and taking you into a deeper region of the pool, pulling you through the water or holding you by your waist and encouraging you to kick your legs.

Once we're finished, I reflect on the experience and consider the lessons I've learnt:

- It pays to exit the pool quickly when the session ends so you can bag a family changing room.

- Stripping you of your swimming costume *before* wrapping you in a towel is a smart thing to do.
- And finally, 100 per cent of my attention should be on you when you're in the water and not drawn to attractive members of the opposite sex. Good job Mummy wasn't with us to catch me out. Luckily, she'll never know about my betrayal of the eyes.

After swimming, we go to a soft-play adventure park. Soft-play parks are, at your age, a little overwhelming. So, we take it slow and I do my best to judge when to push you, like dragging you down the big slide, and when to stand back and let you explore for yourself. Because you're more aware of your surroundings, you're less confident than when we were here eight months ago in between lockdowns. I remember you had no problem throwing yourself down the big slide without encouragement then.

Once our day is over and I get you settled for bed that night, I all but collapse on the sofa next to Mummy, who, it has to be said, is wearing one of her annoying, wanky facial expressions that means: 'It's hard looking after toddlers, isn't it?'

The truth is, she's wrong on this occasion. You're at a stage where you're reasonably easy to manage, but I'll freely admit that neither of us have to look after you full-time any more – we have help. Still, you enjoy activities, you're stable on your feet, you listen (most of the time), and you behave beautifully. Also, your speech continues to develop, meaning that you can communicate what you want and don't want, even if it is only through body language and grunting. As things stand, parenting you is easier and a lot more fun than it was earlier in the year because you're less of a threat to yourself.

By the way, there were fewer attractive members of the opposite sex in the soft-play park, so I was altogether a much better and more present parent in the afternoon.

Nursery: Round Two
Thursday, 15 July 2021

Next week you start your new nursery. But before you do, and as with your previous establishment, you have a couple of settling-in sessions to get used to your new environment while Mummy and I are close by. We're both anxious. We're all too aware of your last nursery experience, and we hold ourselves accountable.

We've been preparing you for weeks. Every time we drive past the building, you shout 'there', because you know it's where your cousin Haylee goes to nursery, and when you do that, we always ask if you would like to go there and play, to which you scream: 'Yeah.' Teachers have been preparing Haylee as well because she's been coming home and explaining that 'sometimes, Arlo will play with his friends while Haylee plays with hers'. This preparation serves as a way to lessen her compulsion to mother you, something you don't always welcome.

The plan is for Mummy to head to the office and complete paperwork while I sit with you and help you integrate.

We arrive and we're welcomed by Miss Daisy. Miss Daisy invites us in and quickly throws a curveball: 'Why don't you both come with me, and we'll leave Arlo alone to play outside.' Mummy and I share a nervous glance, but then we shrug. You only have two of these sessions, so we might as well get an idea of what we're in for. We take you outside, and then another staff member leads you to a space where several red and yellow Little Tikes cars are ready and waiting for test-driving.

With you distracted, we disappear inside to fill out paperwork and spy on you from a window. You get teary as soon as you notice we're gone, but Haylee and a staff member are able to quickly distract you by leading you over to the mud kitchen.

You're loving life. You are surrounded by other children, but you don't mind occupying a populated space. The collective attendance in this nursery produces a volume of significantly fewer decibels than that of the children in the last one. It's something that I noticed during our first visit and something that I'm pleased to see has remained noticeable this time round.

At 3 p.m., Auntie Lisa arrives to collect Haylee, leaving you to complete the rest of the session without her. This brings on more tears and shouts of 'Dadda, Dadda, Dadda.' It's hard for both me and Mummy not to run out and reveal our presence, but we don't, because we won't be there next week, so we give it a few moments to allow the staff to do their thing, which they do – effectively. It doesn't take long for the tears to stop and for you to find your way inside a wooden hut. Next, you point at a red ladybird bike. Then you return to the mud kitchen.

Tears do not make a reappearance.

If reassurance was a scale, then Mummy and I would be right at the top end, jumping for joy.

At the end of the period, we venture outside and ask you if you've had fun. You respond, 'YEAH!' We ask if you would like to come back tomorrow, and you give the same answer. We thank Miss Daisy and the other staff, and we wave goodbye to your small human colleagues. We leave beyond content that the decision to move you to a smaller nursery was the right one. *Thank Christ!*

Second Settling-In Session
Friday, 16 July 2021

'He cried when I dropped him off, but he quickly settled when Miss Daisy took him out to play in the garden. But then he got really upset when she changed his nappy, which happened to be just as I went to pick him up, so I could hear him crying from outside.'

Ouch. 'OK. Do we think he was all right for the rest of it?'

'He was fine.'

'How do you know?'

'Because Haylee has given me a full report. She said, "Arlo cried a little bit, so I rubbed his back, but he didn't want me to do that, so I did this," and she showed me the dance she did, and then she said, "And that made him OK, and he didn't cry any more."'

Good girl, Haylee. Look after your cousin.

It was always going to be a tough handoff because we were leaving you at the door and saying goodbye. But I'm encouraged by the fact that you settled quickly and had fun playing outside. You do bloody love the outdoors. Fortunately, we have some warm weather coming up, so as long as you're slathered in sun cream you should be fine, though Tuesday might be rough, as Haylee won't be there. To be continued.

July Monthly Review
Monday, 19 July 2021

You've started to speak in complete sentences. The results are adorable because 99 per cent of the words are gibberish. In the computer game *Super Mario*, Mario has a green lizard pal called Yoshi. When Yoshi eats something, he makes this cute, funny *gulp* sound. The majority of your sentences are filled with Yoshi-*gulp*-type words before ending in a word that we can make out. For example, 'yum ya gulp ah gulp park' is Arlo-speak for 'I want to go to the park'. What's fascinating is that these aren't random sounds, because if I ask you to say the sentence again, you repeat it in exactly the same way, with the same pronunciation and enunciation. I've said before that I was most interested to observe up close how an infant learns language, and I am continually amazed and impressed by these speech developments.

You've added new words to your lexicon. You can now say 'lolly', 'park' (as in parking the car – you point to a space and say 'park'), 'stars', 'stick', 'stairs' and 'knee'.

Colours are another area where you've made significant progress. You know purple, blue, green and grey. You also know yellow, black, orange, red, brown and white but you can't say them clearly. Red is 'rrr'; orange is 'orra'. You're almost there with pink, though you often confuse it for purple. The rest are mainly grunts, but if we listen carefully, the grunts you utter are nuanced in such a way that we can tell you are trying to say the words. If we ask you to point to an object of a particular colour, you do so correctly each time.

Your hearing is impressive. You can hear sirens (you call them 'nee-nees') and aeroplanes before anyone else. We'll be in the garden; you'll look up and say 'errr' (which means 'aeroplane') and I'll hear nothing, but then a few seconds later I'll catch the faint but unmistakable sound of an aeroplane, and we'll begin scanning the sky to locate its position.

You know what each key on my set of keys unlocks: this includes both the front and back doors, even though the keys are identical, save for a small purple nail-varnish marker on the back door key. You point to our garden chairs saying either 'Dadda', 'Mamma' or 'Lisa'. You do this because we had lunch out here over a month ago, and you can remember where each of us sat. If we go a different way to the park, you're quick to twist round in your buggy and clarify whether we're definitely going to the park.

Nana Smurf is still living with us, which you love. Her house is almost ready, but I think she'll be here for another few weeks. Every Thursday, she takes you to play with the balls at the trampoline park – your favourite thing to do.

She's even met SMFD a few times, and we are in iron-clad agreement that I translated her initials correctly. Nana tried to take you last week but arrived only to learn that the toddler session was cancelled. She almost cried. Luckily, she spoke to a nice man at the train station who let you guys through so you could sit on the platform and watch the trains come and go. You loved it.

Sometimes, you randomly grab your arm or leg and indicate that it hurts. Mummy tells me there is such a thing as growing pains. I'm not surprised: as of today, you are 92 cm tall. The last time we measured you was in February, when you were 87 cm. That's 5 cm growth in five months!

Another thing we've noticed this month is that you've become funnier. And you know you're funny and act up to make us laugh. This is something you've always showed signs of doing but, thanks to your recent physical and mental developments, you're able to amp it up. A fun game is watching you disappear, then hearing you rummaging around somewhere and finally seeing what you reappear with. For instance, we were out in the garden yesterday and you kept nipping indoors to retrieve stuff. First, you reappeared with a bag of ice cubes, then it was my Bluetooth speaker, then it was one of Mummy's make-up brushes and then it was a tube of aftersun cream. Each time, you marched towards us wearing a huge mischievous grin on your face, which you directed at us until we broke out into smiles.

Something that's the opposite of funny is you using a blue-ink biro to vandalise the coffee table.

Aside from you turning twenty months, today marks another occasion: Freedom Day, a day that represents the removal of the majority of the UK's Covid-19 restrictions. Nightclubs are open, and there are no attendee limits at big affairs like weddings and sporting events. Face masks are no longer mandatory, though the government is encouraging the public to be sensible, and many businesses are still insisting that people wear them. We've each had our first jab and are due to have our second in the coming weeks. We're still a while away from being rid of Covid-19, though there are many who are saying we'll never be rid of it (a bit like the flu), but hopefully it will be downgraded from being a global pandemic. A quick search online tells me that across the planet over 4.1 million people have lost their lives to the virus.

Tomorrow, you begin your new nursery. I'm not expecting it to be easy, but hopefully you'll adjust and settle in well at this one. I have complete confidence in you.

Thank you for all the smiles you've created this month, and best of luck on your big day tomorrow.

Déjà Vu
Tuesday, 20 July 2021

Despite an assiduous campaign to drum up as much excitement as possible, dropping you off at your new nursery was the most excruciating thing to happen to me in my dadding adventure this year. It was even worse than the drop-offs at your previous establishment. I know that you'll be well looked after and comforted, and that going to nursery will ultimately – *hopefully* – be the best thing for you, and that this setting is better for you than the last one. However, you don't know that yet. You believe I'm abandoning you, and the look you gave me while simultaneously crying and waving goodbye was, as I said, excruciating.

I half expected things to play out this way, and I half expect them to be like this for the next few weeks while you go through your *second* period of nursery integration in five months. But that doesn't make it any less painful for any of us. I feel we let you down by having to do this again because we fucked it up the first time.

The woman who greeted us at the door isn't someone we've met before. Also, Haylee isn't here to comfort you. Both of those variables do not contribute to making the start to your day any easier. I manage to garble that Louie and a dummy are in your bag if needed, like right now, then I turn and walk away as quickly as possible, hearing you cry out 'DADDA! DADDA! DADDA!'

As I walk out to the car, I can see Mummy peering round behind a bush. We agreed it made no sense for both parents to walk to the door. But it matters not because … 'I can hear him crying from here. He never cries that loud. He's calling for you,' she says.

'Let's just get away from here as quickly as possible. There's nothing we can do.'

9.41 a.m. 'I've called, and he's fine. He's playing outside in the garden.' Mummy says.

12 p.m. Another report from Mummy. 'Just got off the phone to them again. Apparently, he's sitting at the table eating his lunch beautifully.'

2.30 p.m. Mummy and I arrive to collect you. We can overhear another staff member talking to you while she changes your nappy. She asks if you've had a good first day, and if you're looking forward to seeing your mummy and daddy. You reply enthusiastically: 'Yeah!' Once you've been changed and you've put your shoes on (it's great that you're not made to wear shoes inside in this heat), you're brought to the door.

Every time you were picked up from your last nursery, you would burst into tears without fail as soon as you saw us. Today, not a peep. You waltz out and over to a nearby table and start rifling through a lost-property box that's left out for parents. I share a quick 'he's absolutely fine' glance with Mummy before Miss Lorelle introduces herself and says that she'll be your key worker. She then gives us your daily stats: you ate all of your lunch (a beef chilli burrito), you had a few wobbles, but you have mostly enjoyed yourself. Finally, she says you slept for forty minutes. Normally, that would be a concern because you usually sleep for two hours, but this is your first full day, and also – wait for it – you went down for your nap *without* Louie and without a dummy.

This is massive, Arlo! You don't usually budge an inch without both of those vital comfort aids attached to you, especially in your last setting. While I'll never get over seeing you upset when dropping you off, I'm now stacked with confidence that we have finally made the right decision for you concerning your preschool education.

This will be your nursery until you go to school. May it be a place for you to learn and develop, explore and discover, flourish and bloom; a place for you to grow and build upon what you already are; a pillar of possibility, purpose and potential. Your life is an unmarked map with no borders or boundaries. You can chart whatever course your heart desires – you have only to walk it. And you can do so knowing you have the belief and backing of your parents.

Day Two Of Déjà Vu
Wednesday, 21 July 2021

'He didn't cry as we were walking to the door, but then his bottom lip went as I said goodbye. But it was a million times better than yesterday.'

'That's good news.'

'Yep. I've also just rung them to see how he's getting on and they said he's already playing, but he often seeks a cuddle and a bit of reassurance from someone.'

'But it took almost a month for him to get to that stage in the last place, right?'

'Exactly. He's doing really well. I told them to let him have Louie and his dummy for nap time, and I'll call them again later.'

It's afternoon and you've returned from nursery with a bag. In it is a laminated sheet of photos of your first week. You never once arrived home with anything from your old one, aside from a bag of dirty clothes and another child's dummy.

We are top-of-the-chart proud of you. Well done, buddy.

I Will Not Give In, Goddamn It
Friday, 23 July 2021

I'm standing in the utility room with the laundry basket on my head, and I've been in this position for over a minute. I'll tell you why. We're supposed to be playing hide-and-seek, but you're being selfish and unfair. It's been your turn to hide for the last ten rounds, and now I want a turn at hiding. I even said to you, 'Can it be Daddy's turn now?' and you said, 'Yeah,' so I went and hid. But you haven't come to find me, because you've gone off to hide yourself – if I had to guess where, I'd say on the rug outside the back door, because that's been your go-to spot since we began playing!

'Daaaadddaaa.'

I'm not responding to your demands. You need to learn to take turns.

'Daaaadddaaaa.'

'No, Arlo. You have to come and find Daddy.'

This stand-off lasts for a few minutes, which, when you're on your own with a laundry basket on your head, feels a lot longer than that. I should also add that I've been pretty consistent at working out this week and the inside of the basket smells worse than an all-night orgy in a South American prison cell.

Eventually, and I do mean eventually, you totter into the utility room and slap me in the nuts to indicate that you've found me.

What Did She Expect?
Saturday, 24 July 2021

'How's this happened?'

'Well, for starters, you went out of the house and left me and Arlo to our own devices, so I don't know what you expected to walk back into.'

'I was only gone an hour.'

'And if we're being honest, you've had a lucky break because we can usually accomplish a lot more in that time.'

'It's everywhere!'

'Don't be dramatic. It's not everywhere, it's just on his clothes … and a little bit on the kitchen worktop. But I took his clothes off and put him in the shower because I always practise responsible dadding.'

'Hmmm. So that's why his clothes are still on the worktop covered in shaving foam.'

'Exactly right, my sweet. I thought to myself, *The best thing I can do right now is get Arlo showered*, so that's what I did. Like I said – responsible dadding.'

'Hang on a minute, the shaving foam was on the top shelf. How on earth did he get it?'

'I would have thought that one was obvious. I gave it to him.'

The First Throw
Sunday, 25 July 2021

It's dinner time, and it should be noted that in the last five minutes you have attempted to retrieve and eat a purple lolly from the freezer on no fewer than eight occasions. Each time, your efforts have been thwarted by either me or your mother shutting the freezer door and saying, 'You can have one after dinner.'

After dinner, you're finally rewarded with a lolly, which you promptly go to town on.

And now having finished it, you've asked for another. This is a first. You've never requested another lolly before.

'No, Arlo, that's enough now. Dinner is finished,' Mummy says.

Since you became a toddler, you've been trained to accept that when dinner is finished, it's finished, and your next action is usually to hold up your hands, signalling that you're ready to have them cleaned so you can get down from the table and find something to trash.

But not this time.

No, sir!

Instead, you glare at your mother and then you lift your sippy cup and throw it across the table, logging the second first of the evening.

While you've steadily increased the rate of toddler-tantrums, this is the first time you've sought assistance from a third-party inanimate object to help you express displeasure.

At first, we're shocked. But then it becomes one of those times when it's difficult not to break out into a smile. Of course, we don't, because that would send a critically wrong message to you.

'He's never done anything like that before, has he?' I say, knowing the answer.

'No, he has not, but this is just the beginning.'

'The beginning?'

As if to confirm Mummy's words, you shift your glare from her over to me, and I swear you perform a blink-and-you-miss-it nod.

I personally think you're bang out of order. It's still a little under four months until you reach the terrible twos, so could you maybe lay off throwing sippy cups across the dining-room table?

The Rain
Tuesday, 27 July 2021

It's morning, we're in our bedroom, and it's raining the hardest I've seen it rain all year. The view is so spectacular that I would never forgive myself if I didn't share it with you. I lift you up so that you can look out of the window for a few moments. Once I think you've had enough, I put you down again. You quickly leave the room, no doubt heading off to make good on your commitment to magic up hourly mischief and mayhem.

After a few minutes of silence, Mummy deploys herself on a field mission to secure your location and to report back anything of interest, along with an itemised list of things that have been damaged, hidden or drawn on.

'Quick, come here,' she hisses to me from ... somewhere.

I follow the sound of her whispers to your bedroom, where you are. You've dragged your bookcase over to the window and climbed on it so that you can continue watching the rain.

I'm now standing in the doorway with Mummy watching you watch the rain and trying to imagine what could possibly be running through your mind in this moment. I can see from the reflection in the window that you're not even blinking. You're lost in thought – wholeheartedly absorbed in the moment. I'd love to know how you interpret the image you perceive before you.

What is it that you see? Falling rain? Or something else?

Would you like to know what I see when I watch rain fall from the sky?

I see the power to fuel all of life; a substance that can battle flames and quench thirst; a force with the might and will to erode earth, sand and rock. I see an unlimited multi-lane motorway, a hub for travel and a way to carry large masses across the planet and to ferry creatures through lakes, rivers and oceans. I see a tool to rid us of dirt, and to aid us in cooking. I see a child's ally in the sun; the main ingredient for a myriad of fun, shriek-inducing activities; ammunition for super-soakers and water bombs. I see, hear and smell the essence of our existence. It's so profoundly comforting that I could stay in this moment and observe the rain falling for eternity.

Another thing I see is that we need the builder to come over and fix our gutter!

July

It's later on in the day. Nana See-See collected you from nursery, but she's dropped you off to me. Mummy and Nana Smurf are working, so you and I have some lad time to kill before I think about getting you ready for bed.

I'm about to suggest getting your dinosaurs out when the rain returns with a force similar to that of the morning's downpour. You immediately totter off to the back door, place both hands on the glass and stare. Then you look at me and say, 'Out there!' while pointing outside. You're wearing socks, joggers and a long-sleeved T-shirt.

I look from you to the rain.

'Dadda. Out there?'

Hmmm. I mean, his mother would kill us both, but she's not here ... and I was planning to bath him before bed anyway ... Fuck it.

'Arlo, do you want to play outside in the rain with Daddy?'

'YYYYEEAAAHHHH!'

I open the door and you hurry outside. You quickly find a place to stand. You hold your arms out, palms facing the sky, face looking upwards. An ear-to-ear grin is spread across your face; water fills all the small creases that a less-than-two-year-old face can produce. The sound of the rain falling all around us is bordering on monstrous, but the temperature is mild and almost pleasant, so we're all set to enjoy the next few precious minutes together.

Within seconds, we're both completely soaked through. We play chase, then we jump in the puddles, then we kick water at each other. Next, I pick you up and, holding on to you securely, run laps with you around the garden, crashing through curtains of lashing rain and dodging obstacles. You release a medley of long, drawn-out, delightfully cute squeals.

'More, more, more.'

'More? Daddy is getting tired now.'

'More, more, more.'

On it goes. We run round the table and up and down the decking, sliding past see-saws, bikes, garden chairs and flowerpots.

My lungs beg me to stop, so I slow down the pace, bringing an end to our frantic fun. I take you back into the house.

'More.'

'We can't, mate. Dadda really is about to collapse.'

'One more?'

The choice is a pair of collapsed lungs and a heart attack, or living with the image of disappointment in a toddler's eyes. *Which is it?*

'You want one more?'

'Yeah.'

'OK, buddy. Back out in the rain we go.'

'YEAAAHHHH!'

August

'The name Persephone was on our "maybe" list of names. In hindsight, naming my daughter after the Greek queen of the underworld would have been quite apt in view of her exploits as a toddler.'

Tom M, an old uni mate

The First Of Many, I Suspect
Tuesday, 3 August 2021

I went to collect you from nursery and I was rewarded with a bit of paper. This is what it said:

> **Accident and Incident Form**
> Accident or Incident? *Accident*
> Name of child: *Arlo Kreffer*
> Date: *3/8/21*
> Time: *12.15 p.m.*
>
> **What Happened:**
> Arlo was swinging on his chair and not sitting correctly. He fell off the chair.
>
> **Injury:**
> Slight bruise on forehead.

Action Taken:
N/A - didn't notice mark until later on.

I suspect we'll be getting many more of these.

Buh-Bye
Friday, 6 August 2021

For her birthday, I'm taking Mummy away to the Peak District for the weekend. You're not coming. This will be yet another first because we've not left you to go away before, and this will be for two nights. Mummy is excited but apprehensive. She worries that you'll get upset when we say goodbye. She's also upset because she'll miss you.

But her concern for your emotional state is unwarranted, as you happily stand by the front window with Nana Smurf and wave us off. We haven't even left your field of vision before you scramble down from the window, having concluded that we've finished saying our goodbyes and that it's time everyone got on with their lives.

'He's not even bothered,' Mummy says, while a small crack appears in her heart.

'Hang on. You were worried he'd start crying. It's good that he's OK.'

'It damn well isn't. I'd rather him cry – little bastard!'

Glorious Morning And Another Buh-Bye
Saturday, 7 August 2021

I'm flying. Bodysurfing on soft, wispy clouds that fold over themselves like waves in the sea, but calmer in how they move. And now I'm descending to an aesthetically pleasing metropolitan area, gliding past a handsome knot of trees in a park. The trees themselves whisper to me, telling me how wonderful this morning is. Their voices carry through the air on a relaxed, passive breeze. I can feel rays of sunlight bathing my face. I land delicately, weightlessly, on the ground. Passers-by wave at me, though I'm not entirely sure why. The sun's rays warm up my face even more as the world around me begins to ripple, distort, and slowly vanish.

A dream.

I open my eyes to be greeted by those rays of sunshine, lancing through the window of the bedroom of the 300-year-old stone-built cottage we're staying in.

I spin round to find Mummy already awake.

'It's OK,' she says, 'I've already checked the monitor. Arlo is fine.'

Of course she's checked the monitor. I bet she was checking it through the night as well.

'What's the time?'

'Gone seven.'

'Seven? I'd forgotten that was even a number you could wake up to.' *No wonder I was dreaming.*

The thing with parenting, or at least our parenting gig, is that our day kicks off with a starting gun: a big, loud *bang*. We can't slowly ease our way into it. We usually wake to your urgent demands for liberation from your cot. Mummy then has the delicate task of affixing your eyepatch while I go downstairs and make us all a drink. We then enjoy a few peaceful moments while you down your bottle, but we're talking minutes at most. Next, you divide your attention between watching snippets of television, kicking me in the nuts and trashing our bedroom. Then I go downstairs to write, Mummy feeds you breakfast and gets you dressed, and you deliberate on how much of the day you want to spend opposing our instructions. When 9 a.m. finally arrives, we feel like we've each done a day's work – and that's not far from the truth.

But not today. Today, we can get up when we want.

Let me be clear: that's not resentment you can detect from me. It's really not. You know how much I bloody love my dadding gig, but it's nice to have a change of pace. I feel the same kind of gratitude when I get time away to hang out with my mates.

And I do miss you. So does Mummy. She's clawing away at her skin like a drug addict trying to kick the habit by going cold turkey.

'Do you want to video-call Arlo?'

'Yes, let's do it right now.'

Ring ring.

Nana Smurf answers the phone. You guys are sitting at the breakfast table in the kitchen. Your face lights up when you see us.

'Mamma! Dadda!'

'Hey, baby boy, did you have a good sleep?' Mummy says.

'Yeah.'

You're busy emptying the contents of your cup on the worktop, something that you know you're not supposed to do, because Mummy always tells you off for that. But she's not there. Nana is, and Nana lets you do whatever the fuck you want ... which I now know to be a common characteristic of grandmothers.

'He's just finished breakfast. He didn't wake once in the night, and he woke at six thirty.'

Six thirty! *You bastard, Arlo, you absolute little bastard.* I know I've had a lie-in today, but a 6.30 a.m. wake-up time for you is pretty much the equivalent of a three-day spa retreat for me. Why don't you normally do that?

'Buh-bye,' you say, clearly done with the conversation.

'Oh, OK,' Mummy says. That small crack in her heart that appeared yesterday gets noticeably bigger.

Before you know it, you've hung up on us.

'He doesn't want to even talk to us.'

'He's fickle – he's a toddler. Come on, let's go and have breakfast.'

Mummy's Birthday
Sunday, 8 August 2021

It's Mummy's birthday today, and I kick things off by telling her that we're a couple: one who's in his mid-thirties and another who, as of today, is in her late thirties.

It's pouring with rain in the Peak District, so we've decided to head home early. However, our weekend of not parenting isn't over yet. I've worked out that the time we will get home will be about the same time as when you go down for your nap, and that's a piece of information I made sure to include a dozen or so times when I presented my argument to Mummy, explaining why we should be driving straight to the cinema. I tried to say I was doing this for her birthday, but she gave the *mum look*, so I went back to repeating your nap times.

No traffic on the roads means we're back in Northampton in good time. We go to the cinema and watch *The Suicide Squad* (which is bloody terrific), and then we head to Nana See-See's house. Nana See-See collected you yesterday from Nana Smurf. The plan is for us to spend the afternoon there and have a Chinese takeaway for dinner. Your Auntie Lisa and Haylee will be joining us.

We time our arrival perfectly because as we walk through the door, we can hear Nana See-See talking to you, asking if you slept well and if you're ready to come downstairs.

When she appears with you, you launch yourself out of her arms and into Mummy's. It's a lovely moment. I get some affection as well. A few minutes later, Nana See-See gets her shoes on ready to take Grandad See-See to the pub, which means we get a bit of time to catch up, just the three of us.

'Car?' you say, while walking away from your parents.

'You want to come with Nana and Grandad in the car?' Nana says.

'Yeah.'

Thirty seconds later and Mummy and I are standing in the doorway, watching you wander off, saying 'buh-bye' while waving, but without looking in our direction. And now Mummy is crying. I'm not crying, but I am absolutely gutted. For Mummy's birthday you've got her a Santa-isn't-real moment, and they were obviously on a buy-one-get-one-free offer as you've given me one as well.

Happy birthday, Mummy.

Let Me Refer This
Tuesday, 10 August 2021

'Arlo, I'm just going outside to hang the washing out,' Mummy says, at a volume that's thirty decibels higher than it needs to be, especially when you consider you're standing right in front of her. I'm in the other room, yet I still hear her declaration clearly.

Hmmm.

Fortunately, I'm a writer, and I have a list of contacts I can refer to who specialise in language. First, I send Mummy's statement to a friend of mine who's a retired linguistics professor, who in turn reaches out to ten of his younger colleagues who are not only active in their field but also leading authorities, having dozens of published papers between them.

It gets better.

HAL from *2001: A Space Odyssey* has got wind of all of this, and he's stepped by to lend us his views, along with Alan Turing, Noam Chomsky and the local librarian. I've also somehow managed to acquire three quantum computers to assist us.

To say I've got all bases covered is an understatement.

From there, we're able to arrange a quick video call with everyone to share our findings as to the meaning of Mummy's words.

Everyone unanimously concurs with one another.

Here's the original phrase again: 'Arlo, I'm just going outside to hang the washing out.'

Now, here's what it actually means:

'Daddy! I'm leaving our only child in your sole charge, therefore if he dies, it's on you. So how about you come and sit with him, and try not to fuck anything up before I get back? Understood?'

Thank God I was able to rustle up so much support; I would never in a billion years have figured that one out!

LG, Part 2

Wednesday, 11 August 2021

Hi LG,

Me again.

I'll start by begging your forgiveness for the putrid, pungent pong that emanates from where I stand; it's such an acrid, humming stench. It's infiltrated the digital atmosphere, invaded every cyber-molecule of this email and no doubt commenced a savage assault on your nostrils.

Once again, I have no clean clothes.

I'm sure you can guess why.

That's right. My darling little toddler is at it again, turning off our washing machine mid-cycle with ruthless efficiency and regularity. I am a man in despair. My partner is even more distraught.

I fall before your feet, hands pressed together in prayer and at your mercy, desperate for my plight to chance upon a sympathetic ear. I need – *need* – your engineers to reconsider their stance on the specifications of the child-lock safety feature.

Allow me to once again present my arguments.

You claim that allowing the power button to remain functionally active when the child lock is on is for safety reasons, because it allows for the machine to be turned off quickly in the event of an emergency. Can I first ask you what LG defines as an emergency? And then can I ask if your definition includes a mother decapitating her son with a throat punch? Because if it doesn't, it needs to be considered.

Back to your claim – I'm pained to admit that I need to go right ahead and call bullshit.

First, if there were such an emergency, pulling the plug from the wall would be just as quick as pressing the power button, and even if it were marginally slower, we're talking hundredths of a second at most.

'Perhaps the plug isn't easily in reach,' I hear you say. Well, why don't we revisit the idea I pitched in my last email and code the machine to kill the power when selecting two buttons simultaneously? I mean, it really is that simple.

'But what if the operator gets flustered and panics?' you ask. Easy. Just add a couple of arrows to the buttons in question. You can even add a shiny label that says something like: *Press these two buttons simultaneously to turn the machine off when child-lock is engaged.*

Mankind has cracked landing on the moon, breathing underwater and bendable straws. I'm sure we're capable of figuring this one out, right?

If you're still resistant to the multitude of simple solutions that I've graciously provided to you free of charge, then I have one more roll of the dice; one final swing of the bat; one last-ditch attempt at swaying you towards seeing some semblance of sense.

I propose that you keep your damn power button! That's right, keep it.

All I ask is that you place it somewhere else on the machine and not on the main control panel. Because when that panel is turned on, it presents a vibrant light show that could rival a Disneyland end-of-the-day firework display, and for a toddler's inquisitive fingers the allure is too powerful to resist – like how a moth is drawn to a flame.

I'll end this email by showing you an image that was taken from the kitchen CCTV camera in my house. As you can see, the small human is in mortal danger. Would you look at this:

I hope to hear from you soon with an acceptable outcome.

Warmest regards,

An end-of-his-tether dad

Games

Thursday, 12 August 2021

'DADDA!'

'Yes, Arlo?' I shout from down in the basement.

Bang bang bang.

I respond to the summons by heading upstairs, and when I open the door, I find you waiting on the other side. You don't say anything; instead, you take me by the hand and walk over to the other staircase, the one that has a stair gate in front of it. It's open, and there are cushions and a mummy dotted about on the floor.

I give Mummy a curious 'what's this all about?' glance.

'Daddy, Arlo is inviting you over to his house for tea.'

'Is that right, Arlo?'

'Yeah, Dadda. Sit here,' you say, pointing to a spot on the floor. It's a little cramped, but being uncomfortable is the last thing I'm concerned about right now. You shut the stair gate, turn around smiling, delighted to be hosting guests.

'Are you going to make Daddy a cup of tea?'

'Yeah.' You hold out your hand with the imaginary cup, while I wonder if parenting ever gets better than this moment. What's unfolding before my eyes is 100 per cent perfection – a beautiful moment. I take the imaginary cup from you, and you watch me take a sip. I can tell that you're anxious for my validation and approval of your tea-making abilities.

'Do you know something, Arlo?'

'Yeah?'

'I think that's the best cup of tea I've ever had. Thank you very much.'

It's not only the introduction of tea parties. There are other games that we've recently started playing. Like when you pick up a 'phone' (literally anything you can lift to your ear) and begin a telephone conversation. It plays out the same way every time. I ask you where you are, you tell me you're in the car, I ask you if you're going to the shops, and you say yeah, and then you tell me what you're going to buy. It's always apples and oranges, and sometimes 'nanas'.

Then there's hide-and-seek. You now ask for my help to lift you into our pan drawer which is large enough to fit you in it, and then you ask me to shut it. I then commence a thorough search of the surrounding area, all because I couldn't possibly have the faintest idea of where you could be hiding.

I love it. Games with a toddler are the best, if a little repetitive at times.

Hotels
Friday, 13 August 2021

We're going away again for the weekend, but this time you're coming with us. We've booked a hotel in Bury St Edmunds. The plan was to try and leave Northampton at 4 p.m., but the afternoon got away from us, and it was closer to 5 p.m. by the time we hit the road.

The later-than-expected departure means we need to rethink our plans. The trip takes about an hour and forty-five minutes, so there is no way you're not falling asleep. Usually, this isn't an issue, because you're pretty good at allowing us to transfer you from your car seat to your cot, and you either stay asleep or go straight back to sleep. But I can't see that working today, as we need to check in and get the room set up. Also, we haven't eaten yet. I guess we can order room service, but I don't know what we can and can't get away with as we'll all be in the same room together.

We don't have a lot of experience in dealing with scenarios that impact on your routine, like late nights in places that aren't home. And as is so often the case with parenting, any previous experience we did have is null and void, because you've once again grown into a different person than you were even a month ago, so I guess you'll be dictating how things play out this evening.

It's 6.45 p.m., and you woke up about two minutes ago, having enjoyed a one-hour danger nap. We park up and get out of the car. Your eyes are full of wonder.

'Blue, purple, grey,' you say.

'Are you looking at the different-coloured cars, Arlo?' I ask.

August

'Yeah.'

We check into the hotel and inspect our room. It's family-sized so we have plenty of space, and they've erected a travel cot. All fine.

Your danger nap has fully restored your energy reserves. If anything, they've been over-replenished. *I suspect dinner time is going to be interesting.*

The hotel restaurant is modest(ish) but it has several different areas, and even though it's early, it's busy, which brings us to our first parental test of the weekend. Since you started walking, we've always tried to take a step back and allow you explore as you see fit. We do this even if there is a small chance you might have a tumble or do yourself any sort of mischief. It can be hard, but it's one parental area where Mummy and I are fully aligned.

Trouble is, we're still getting used to being around people. Outside of soft-play adventure parks that are specifically built and designed to foster the curious wonderings of children, we've not been in any contained, populated spaces where we can let you roam around.

Before we can decide what sort of boundaries we're going to set, you've zoomed over to a fire exit on the other side of the restaurant that happens to be open. And now you're outside climbing down some *big steps* leading to a lawn so you can enjoy the last remnants of evening sunshine.

After I retrieve you for the third time, your brain registers that this is a game. For now, the remainder of the restaurant's diners are enjoying this display, but I'm sure their patience and goodwill has an expiry limit.

After the fifth time, Mummy steps in to distract you with a toy, and we're able to order food and drinks. I'm thinking of—

You're gone again. Along with your toy.

This time you've taken yourself off to go and sit on a step – the same step that grants the *only* entry point to this particular section of the restaurant, apart, of course, from the open fire escape that you've already become well acquainted with.

Waiters are trying to serve people their meals, but first they're having to circumnavigate a toddler who's naturally chosen to sit in the middle of the step. Parental etiquette probably dictates that I go and get you. However, I'm not always uncomfortable with you inserting yourself into an environment in a way that might be a hassle or inconvenience for others. In fact, I often find it amusing.

Fortunately, Mummy has made sure you're wearing your glasses, which means we're able to rely and capitalise on the effect you have on onlookers. Even the staff manage a few smiles in your direction. I'm about—

'DADDA! CHAIR!'

Everyone in the room breaks off from whatever they're doing and allows the sound of your voice to hijack their attention.

Christ, you've definitely inherited your mother's vocal strength.

'How long until food, do you reckon?' I say to Mummy.

'There's no way he'll agree to going in his high chair until he can see food,' she says, picking up on where I was going with the question.

Fast-forward a few seconds, and now both of us are sitting on the step playing with one of your toys. I've tried to coerce you into sitting on the far side, but you refuse; you want to sit in the middle, and you want me to sit next to you.

'I'm so sorry,' I say a million times to staff.

Arlo, you might be a cute glasses-wearing under-two-year-old, but I am not. I'm an adult in his mid-thirties, and I'm not as easy on the eye. I doubt I warrant the same level of patience and leeway from strangers as you do.

Fortunately, you tire of sitting on the step and instead wander to a nearby table that happens to be the only one in the restaurant that isn't occupied.

'DADDA! HERE!' you shout, pointing under the table.

'You want Daddy to go under there?'

'Yeah. Here!' you say, stabbing a finger at the exact spot where you want me to sit. I look at Mummy, and she shrugs. *I guess I'm going under.*

I mean, when you think about it, it's the easy choice. If we try and make you sit in your chair and wait patiently, you'll kick off, and the only reason we'd be doing that in the first place is because we're worried what other people think, and we feel that we *should* be setting an example of how to behave in public. But I can't bring myself to do it. You're not yet two, and I'm sure we've got time to finesse our hotel etiquette.

Moreover, and I tell myself this all the time, how long are you honestly going to want me hanging out with you under a table? We're talking a few short years, maybe less. So, right or wrong, regardless of anyone's opinions and the impression we're making on those around us ... son, if you want me with you under a table in a busy restaurant, I'm there! Just you try and stop me.

After a few minutes, I take myself out of the game we're playing and chance a quick glance around to see how many judgemental looks we're receiving.

Can you guess how many?

Zero. Absolutely zero.

It's the opposite.

I see warm, loving smiles from people I've never met before. There's a young woman nearby: she's done up to the nines, with eyelashes that look like they were freshly plucked from an in-season male peacock. She's clutching her boyfriend's hand, smiling at our behaviour and whispering in his ear.

I can't hear what she's saying but I've a fair idea. There are others. Mainly older people. They've stopped eating, put their cutlery down and are watching us play.

When you were first born, I reflected on the experience one has when holding a newborn baby, and what people see when they stare into a new baby's eyes. I'm having a similar moment now as I watch other people from my uncomfortable, cramped, all-fours position under the table. What do they see, Arlo? Do they see flashes of their children at your age in similar settings, maybe? Or do they see regret? Maybe they were those parents that told their children to sit quietly at the table and wait for their food. Perhaps society and social norms meant they had no other choice. Maybe they're reminded of their grandchildren, and the time they've lost because of Covid-19. When you observe a situation unfolding before your eyes, you bring all your life experience with you, and all those past interactions mould and direct how you make sense of what you're seeing. I've always found other people's stories fascinating: the paths they've trodden and the roads they've travelled, having no doubt journeyed in many unexpected directions.

As I exit my moment of reflection, I travel back to the present, where you're holding out a cupped hand to me with an expectant look on your face.

'Is that a cup of tea for Daddy?'

'Yeah. Tea.'

'Thank you very much.' I take a sip. 'Aah. That's a lovely cup of tea.'

Mummy summons us: 'Arlo, Daddy – dinner!'

I guess the show's over for the moment, folks, but no doubt we'll be back soon for an encore. *And, hopefully, a million more.*

That's A Niche Company, Isn't It?
Sunday, 15 August 2021

We're driving back from Bury St Edmunds when something wonderful happens, something that probably ranks as one of the greatest experiences of my life. Are you ready for this, Arlo? Make sure you're paying attention because this is brilliant.

'That's a bit bloody niche, isn't it?' Mummy says, nodding her head at the van in front, which has the words *Gecko Decorating* painted on the back.

'What's that?'

'A decorating company that specialises in painting geckos.'

What? Surely ... she can't think ... 'What is it that you think they do exactly?'

'Go around finding geckos and painting them, I guess. I can't imagine they get much business, but I suppose they must do, as their van is a twenty-one plate.'

Arlo, there are some moments in life that are beyond perfect, where every single star in the universe aligns just for you. This is one of those moments.

'Oh dear,' says Mummy, who's apparently had an 'aha' moment about exactly what services Gecko Decorating offers. 'They don't paint geckos, do they? They're just a normal decorating company ... Wait, why are you laughing at me?'

My chest is on fire. Red-hot molten embers the size of gobstoppers are *pinging* around my lungs like balls from a pinball machine.

'Stop laughing!'

'I'm ... tryi—'

'It was an easy mistake to make. The branding threw me off the scent!'

'Please stop ... I can't take much more.'

'Why have you got your phone out? Heeeyyy, come on now, you can't put that in one of your books. It's got fuck all to do with parenting. You're only supposed to write it down if it's to do with parenting!'

'I'm sorry, baby, I really am, but I do the world a disservice if I don't allow it to share in the magic. But don't mind me. Keep your eyes on the road – you never know, you might spot a gecko who's in need of a new paint job!'

Maybe You Are Picasso After All
Monday, 16 August 2021

I'm having a horrendous day at the office, and I'm a nanosecond away from smashing up my laptop.

'Daaddaaa!' I hear from upstairs.

'Is that Mr Arlo shouting me?'

'Yeah!'

Welcoming any excuse to leave my desk, I take a break from contemplating laptop destruction, and instead heed my summoning call. I enter the dining room to find you at the table with Nana Smurf, wearing an enormous grin. You're drawing on an empty A4-sized envelope. As soon as you see me, you drop your pen, pick up the envelope and hand it to me.

'Dadda.'

'He's been very insistent that he's drawn this for you,' Nana Smurf says.

Really? Wow, that's a new one. 'Have you made that for me, Arlo?'

'Yeah,' you say, while continuing to proffer a hand holding what I'm sure is an exquisite piece of modern art.

I happily accept the gift and review it. I'm looking at a collection of blue biro-drawn swirls and jagged shapes. According to the artist, one swirl in particular represents your interpretation of me. My heart swells, not because I like to keep all of your drawings, but because this is the first time you've actively drawn something with the specific intention of giving it to me.

'Thanks, buddy. That's just what I needed today.'

I abscond with my present – one that has turned my shitty day around. I then write the date on it along with these words: *Another Arlo Kreffer masterpiece – given to his daddy as a gift.*

Honestly, mate, these creations you've made at the start of your life really are the most invaluable inanimate possessions I own.

Choice Versus Control
Tuesday, 17 August 2021

When Nana Smurf was pregnant, there were several suggestions made by those closest to her that she should get an abortion. She didn't. When I was eleven, my auntie and uncle helped my mum and me escape from an abusive relationship. We relocated to another town, and I had to move schools. On my first day at my new school, chance sat me next to a boy called Sean. He became my best friend. When we finished school, I decided to enrol on a college course in public services, because that was the course he had chosen. There was no other reason. During college, I met a lecturer who said I should aim to go to university, but I didn't have the grades – until that person worked extra hours tutoring me, helping me get the results I needed in one particular subject, ensuring I had enough marks to go. They had no reason to do this, and to this day, I don't know why they did. When I applied for universities, I had two criteria: my university had to be in the Midlands because I believed that the cost of living would be cheaper, and it had to have a higher female-to-male student ratio. That was it. Northampton was the first university to offer me a place that fulfilled my criteria, and I accepted. I didn't bother going to view the campus beforehand. I wasn't even too sure what to study, but I fancied joining the police so someone suggested I study sociology. I can't remember who that was, but I listened to them and enrolled in the course anyway. I hated it. I skipped most of the lectures to watch films. Then our university had an outbreak of mumps, and I missed almost an entire term's worth of lectures. I was about to fail the year when Nana Smurf helped me reframe my predicament – proposing that this was not about failure, but about opportunity. I repeated my first year, but I chose a different course. I chose film. When I graduated, I had a mate who said he could get me a job in a bank working in fraud. I shrugged and accepted. Years later, while still working for the same company, I met a woman called Taci (pronounced 'tah-see'). She invited me to her wedding, where I met an obnoxious, loud young woman whom I didn't think much of. Taci invested a considerable amount of time telling me that I had misjudged the woman. Eventually, and I have no idea why, I relented and took her out on a date. We fell in love. We wanted to start a family, but doctors told us it wasn't possible. And then she fell pregnant. Once again, for reasons completely unknown to me, I jotted a few lines down in my journal about discovering I was about to be a daddy. And look what that has led to.

So much of my life has been down to chance, or the result of making big decisions without even realising they *were* big decisions, using little or no brainpower in making them.

My life is a long list of turning points and crossroads, of junctures and pathways, of highways and thoroughfares. Try as we might, Arlo, we cannot control our external circumstances or always make sense of everything around us. Such aspirations are destined to result in, at best, failure, and at worst, misery. But I ask you, where's the fun in being in control all the time? Sometimes, being in control can be like living in a cage with no space to move, your view to the outside world compromised by a set of thick iron bars. By all means create plans, develop a solid strategy for executing them, and iterate them along the way. But never ever fool yourself into thinking you're in control. And then relish that fact.

A New Piece Of Legislation
Wednesday, 18 August 2021

I do hate to be the one to enforce an absolute blanket rule, but sometimes situations call for regulatory assistance, and it's a parent's job to ensure such rules are respected and obeyed, otherwise they're seen as optional, which destabilises the very definition of the word 'rule'.

The following new piece of legislation is effective immediately. Non-compliance will ensure swift action is taken. The rule is:

> Under no circumstances is Arlo to hit his grandmother with his hammer.
> Or anything else, for that matter.

August Monthly Review
Thursday, 19 August 2021

When we settle you down in bed, we now say 'get comfy' as part of the routine. You respond by following the instruction to the letter, and then you say 'buh-bye' as we leave the room. Usually, we don't hear from you until the morning, but *when* in the morning is still a lottery. This month, 6.20 a.m. has been about average. Some days we get lucky. Other days ... not so much.

Speech development has slowed this month. You seem almost embarrassed to give new words a go. It's the same when we play music and encourage you to dance. You become shy. Yet you remain an excellent communicator, making do with the words you can say and choose to say, and with pointing and grunting. It's rare that we're not able to understand you and vice versa. Mummy says she's not worried about language, and that she's not comparing you to other children that she sees at nursery. I nod in agreement, but I'm pretty sure she's lying, whereas I'm honestly not bothered. You might struggle to say certain sounds, but that's all. And unlike me, who suffered from terrible hearing problems as a child, problems that still impact on both my spoken and written communication today, your hearing is brilliant.

You have learnt a few new words, though, and my favourite is what Mummy has decreed we call the female reproductive organ. She calls it a 'foo-foo' (which she's always done since I met her), and you can say it as well. You can also say 'BOOM', which is always accompanied by slapping your hand down on a nearby surface and a big grin.

You're more curious and inquisitive when one of us is on the toilet. 'Poo poo, there,' you say, while either pointing to your bottom or trying to point to one of ours while it's in use, which, as I'm sure you can imagine, is fantastic fun for me and Mummy. I guess these are initial signs that we perhaps need to think about potty-training, but we have vowed to ensure that's one activity that will not be taking place in 2021.

One final point on reproductive organs: you do like to give yours a bloody good yank – to the point where it makes me wince. But then Mummy tells me all the boys your age are like that at nursery, and that makes me smile and think, *lads being lads.*

You're quick to get agitated, and you use physicality to express yourself when you're pissed off. Things get thrown, pushed and mishandled in a way that tells us that you're not a happy bunny. But you're also quick and easy to distract if we're on our game, which we usually are. We can extinguish a lit fuse by asking if you would like to read a book or go for a walk, but Daddy is not on his game before 6 a.m., and he usually defaults to: 'Arlo, stop that horrible noise.'

Stuff goes missing: keys, remote controls and mug coasters. But when asked, you're usually able to show us where you've hidden them. The other day, Mummy had completed one of her weekly rearrange-everything-in-the-house chores, which meant Nana Smurf was unable to locate your high chair. You were able to show her exactly where its temporary new home was.

You're doing amazingly well at your new nursery. You still get a bit teary during drop-off, but by the time you've hung your coat and bag up, you've stopped crying. When we arrive to collect you, you waltz out with a wide grin, happy to see us, and you're not frantically dragging us towards the car like you would before. Naturally, I'm relieved by this as I still can't help but relive some of your past nursery experiences – an exercise that brings me no joy.

A trip to the park has once again become an all-round favourite thing for us to do. You're physically confident and you love exploring. One of our new favourite games is when we climb the stairs leading up to the bandstand and *fly* around it like aeroplanes. Then I pick you up, and I fly you around until I get so dizzy that I think I'm going to drop you and throw up.

Your imaginative play continues to develop. It's one of the best things about you at the moment. I love it when you make me a drink or bring me a lolly or invite me into your house. It's wonderful.

I was about to end your monthly review when Mummy called me upstairs to show me a small boy who wasn't wearing a nappy, but was instead wearing a pair of red and blue pants. The heartbreaking thing about this image is that they really suited you, and even though it's August, it won't be long until November rolls around, and we'll be celebrating your second birthday. *Ah, man!*

Is This An Uncommon Strain Of Parent Guilt?
Friday, 20 August 2021

Here's a strange example of parent guilt – or maybe it's not strange, I don't know. If we're playing a game and you're pretending to do something like, say, sweeping the floor, then I'm all too happy to humour you and pretend you're doing a great job sweeping, even though you're obviously doing a terrible job because you're under two. I'm fine with that, and I love that you love being praised. But say I need to do a chore like the hoovering, and you want to help. I feel guilty when I manipulate you into going and getting your Hoover and then asking you to vacuum a spot that I've already done. Is that not bonkers?

I believe my guilt comes from the notion that when you've got my full attention and I'm playing with you, it doesn't matter what I say and do because I'm fully immersed in the narrative of what we're doing, but when I'm using your imagination as a tool to manipulate you, for instance to bugger off to the other side of the room so that I can finish the hoovering without you trying to assist me, I feel terrible for taking advantage.

Like I said, I've no idea if that's a widespread feeling, or if it's unique to me. But it's something I feel I need to get off my chest, and I have.

LG? El-Geeeee, Are You There?
Sunday, 22 August 2021

Hi LG,

Just checking in to see if you received my last email.

Warmest, kindest regards.

A Minute In The Life Of Arlo
Monday, 23 August 2021

I don't understand why my daddy is in such an arsehole mood. All I want is a lolly.

'No, Arlo. You've already had one.'

Well, I damn well want another one. Now get out of my way, you great big oaf, I'm trying to open the freezer.

'Arlo, I've said no. Go and play. You're not having another lolly.'

'ERRRAHHH.' Take your hand away, you big mean prick.

'Arlo, I'm not—'

'AHHHH.'

'Stop it. Look, why don't we go and play with your toys?'

FINE! But not before I throw that fridge magnet on the floor in protest ... wait, what are you doing? Daddy, I did not permit you to lift me up and carry me into the living room. PUT ME DOWN.

'There you go, now ...'

Stomp, stomp, stomp.

'You're going back to throw the fridge magnet on the floor, aren't you?'

You better believe it, sonny. It's the white octagonal one I want, and it's the white octagonal I'll get, you mark my words.

'Arlo, why don't—'

THUD.

There, that's much better. Wait ... why does my daddy appear in such a dejected state? It was only a fridge magnet, Dad, which, by the way, wouldn't have got thrown if you had given me a lolly. So don't be standing there in such a sorry state, you silly sack of sagging substance. You get me?

Not One Single Drop …
Wednesday, 25 August 2021

I've just dropped you off at nursery and you didn't cry. There wasn't A SINGLE FUCKING TEAR! Not one! There weren't even signs of your eyes glistening over with that shiny sheen – a precursor to teardrops falling to the floor. Your bottom lip remained firm and unquivering, and when Miss Lorelle asked you if you would like to go and play, you confidently responded with a 'yeah'.

You go and have yourself a good day, son; play with dinosaurs and cars; play in the sand; maybe do some drawing and painting; just have fun. Daddy will see you later.

I'm literally skipping back to the car while sending a message to Mummy that says: *NO TEARS!*

I'm bloody proud of you, my boy.

Foreshadowing
Thursday, 26 August 2021

'I feel horrendous. My chest feels really heavy,' Mummy says.

Truth is, she's felt rundown since Monday, but this is the first time where she's complained of a heavy chest, which is a Covid-19 red flag. 'Let's go and take a test,' I suggest.

The Wrong Kind Of Positive Test
Friday, 27 August 2021

'Fuck, I'm positive. I've got Covid.'

'Shit, no wonder you've been feeling off.'

Beep, beep. That's my phone. It's the NHS with my results.

'Well, do you have it or not?'

'I don't. It's negative.'

'That's not fair! Eighteen months of this bullshit, and now I get it.'

She has every right to be pissed off, but it's not that surprising. Apparently, even if you have had both vaccinations (Mummy has only had one), there's still a 20 per cent chance of catching the latest Delta variant. Given Mummy's age and health, symptoms were never expected to be severe, but that doesn't guarantee her an easy time of it ahead. I said she's been feeling rundown but that hasn't done it justice. She has no energy, she wants to lie down a lot, and she's still reporting pain in her chest.

It is for these reasons that Mummy has been banished to the bedroom. It's just you, me and Nana. But Nana feels a little under the weather as well, so now she's taken a test; the results should arrive today.

I find it odd that I'm negative, but then I have had both vaccinations, and I don't work in a nursery. To be on the safe side, you and I are to begin taking tests twice a day.

I take you to the park. We find some ducks to feed, and you attempt to jump in the lake for a swim. We return home and I'm about to enlist your help in cleaning the house when Nana makes an announcement. 'Guess what?' she says.

'Covid?' I ask. She nods. We're dropping like flies, Arlo.

'I feel fine. Maybe slightly rundown, but otherwise OK.'

I head upstairs to the infirmary and relay the news to Mummy. I also announce that while there's not an awful lot I can do for you and me, I am going to wash all the towels on a 60-degree cycle.

'You mean two cycles?'

'No, I mean one.'

'You can't do that – there are grey and white towels, so you'll need to separate them.'

'Is that your main concern? Not that your chest feels like it's bench-pressing a tank or that the two most important men in your life remain healthy?'

'Well, obviously I care about Arlo.'

And Daddy ...?

'And you, of course.'

'Of course.'

You and I soldier on for the afternoon, killing time in the garden and trashing the house. Well, you do the trashing, I do the thing where I politely ask you not to trash, and then you ignore me and double down on trashing, leaving me to wonder if I make things worse by opening my mouth and asking you not to trash in the first place. *I'm sure there is a parenting-philosophy lesson in that.*

We make it to bedtime when two things happen that set off a few more alarm bells to accompany the already massed cacophony of jingles and jangles that the other Covid patients in our household have set off. First, you start coughing. Second, I start feeling rough!

Interesting ...

You and I each take a test, and then I put you to bed. Then I return back downstairs to review our results. Still negative.

It's 7 p.m., and sick-note Mummy has come downstairs to fill up her water bottle. She should probably message me to do it, but honestly, even if we can't see it, you and I are bathing in Covid-19. Turns out that needn't concern us anyway, because ...

'You've got Covid!' Mummy says.

'What? The test was negative!'

'Well, now it's positive.'

She's not wrong. There are two clear, distinct lines. We do a quick review of your test, and although the second line is fainter than mine, it's there. Looks like a full house of Covid-19 victims.

Rough Seas Ahead
Saturday, 28 August 2021

'I'm feeling better today so I might get up and do a little bit of cleaning,' announces Mummy. Arlo, her 'little bit of cleaning' involves pasteurising the house and our lungs with a Dettol aerosol spray and then using another Dettol product, this one a surface cleaner, to further fumigate the rest of the house even more.

You and I both still feel awful, and I'm all but certain we have the virus. Still, I take us to a drive-in clinic for another test – this one is called a PCR test and it's more accurate than the home kits we've been using thus far. The results come back eight hours later. As suspected, we're both positive.

We had next weekend booked in for us to go away, child-free. We were once again going to offload you onto your grandmothers, something we're become quite proficient in lately. But now we can't, because we need to isolate for ten days from when we first had symptoms. That means next weekend is cancelled. I don't believe I'll be going back to work for a few days either.

Ah, fuck a duck! I've just realised this also means I won't be able to go to the cinema and watch the new Marvel film, *Shang-Chi*, on opening day. Seriously, Covid, FUCK OFF!

Symptoms
Sunday, 29 August 2021

I usually wake up with a horrible taste in my mouth. But not today. Today, I can't taste much of anything. And my chest feels heavy. It's not painful or unpleasant, but it's surreal and disconcerting given that I know why it feels the way it does. It's like someone's placed a small folded-up pile of clothes on my chest, though the feeling vanishes as soon as I get up and walk to the bathroom.

The lack of smell and taste is a strange experience. They haven't completely gone, but they're flickering like the flame of a candle, coming and going rapidly. If I breathe in a single inhalation through my nose, my sense of smell comes and goes several times throughout that one intake of air. It's the same with food. I'll have a bite of something, and it's like a toddler is at the helm of my taste-bud controls, annoyingly turning them on and off like they do with every light switch they can reach.

I also feel rough as fuck, but then so does everybody in the house. We're just going to have to muddle through together as best we can. It will be kind of fun ... right?

A Tough Day
Monday, 30 August 2021

What's that, Arlo? You want to watch Disney Pixar films all day, have snacks whenever you ask for them and generally be allowed to do whatever the fuck you want so long as none of the adults have to exert themselves too much? You got it, buddy.

Once again, no one is loving life today. We're going to take it one minute at a time and hope that you nap for a minimum of twenty-two – sorry, two – hours.

Ring ring.

It's a female operator from the NHS Test and Trace team. She wants to ask me some questions about where we've been and where we might have picked the virus up from. During the conversation, I admit that I took you to a soft-play adventure park earlier in the week before Mummy was diagnosed.

'Do you think it's possible that you caught the virus at the soft-play park?' she asks.

Is she really asking me that? 'I'm sorry, you want to know if one of five hundred high-on-sugar, screaming, snotty-nosed kids tearing around the place *might* have given us Covid-19?'

'Yes.' Not registering, or perhaps ignoring, my sarcasm.

'Well, we probably can't afford to rule it out, now, can we?' I say.

'Did you get close to anyone then?'

Jesus fucking Christ. 'I would say so, yes.'

'Government guidelines advise you should be aiming to stay at least two metres away from people who aren't in your household.'

'And does the government have any practical advice for parents on how to get toddlers and infants to follow those rules in a soft-play-park environment?'

'I guess that might be a bit tricky.'

And I guess you don't have children.

'Is there anything you want to ask me?' she continues.

'Yes. Am I allowed to break my isolation period to go to the cinema to watch *Shang-Chi*? It's just I never miss a Marvel movie on release day, and my isolation period is what you call a real fly in the ointment. What does Boris say? Surely this qualifies as a special circumstance.'

'Erm ... Well, no, it doesn't,' she says.

Today is the fucking worst!

By the way, I know that was a daft request and, truthfully, I have no intention of going to the cinema and infecting other people, but I assumed we were playing that game where we each take turns to ask silly questions.

We've somehow traversed the day, but Mummy and I are worried about you. Your temperature has spiked at 38.6 degrees. You've lay cuddling your mother for the last two hours. Even when you've been ill before, you've never sat idle for this long. We've given you Calpol to help control your temperature, but it's barely done anything to help your situation.

'I think I want him in with us tonight,' Mummy says.

'Forty-one point seven degrees!' Mummy exclaims.

'He can't be that hot, surely,' I say.

'Look!'

We're all in our bed, and it's gone midnight. Mummy takes your temperature again and shows me the reading. *Fuck, fuck and FUCK!* 41.7 degrees. Anything over 40 degrees is when you need to be seriously concerned. If memory serves, the highest it's ever been is about 40.6, and that was almost a hospital job.

I call the NHS 111 number and have a chat with a woman named Julie.

'Are you sure it's that high?' Julie asks. 'Can you test the thermometer on yourselves so we can rule out it being faulty?'

'Sure.' Mummy takes readings on me and on herself. Completely normal.

'Ours are fine,' I say.

'God, that's high for the poor little man.'

Next, Julie guides me through a series of tests to rule out meningitis and a host of other life-threatening conditions.

'Is he responding to you?' she asks.

'I think so ... Hang on ... Arlo, Arlo?'

'Dadda, hdsahasfh haslfhlahf balls?'

Of course that's what you want to do. 'He's asking me if I can take him to the trampoline park.'

'OK, and what's he like when you shine a light on him?'

'Well, he's been in a dark room since six thirty p.m. I don't think he's going to love it.'

'I'm not sure how to respond to that,' Julie says.

'Well, no one likes having a light shone in their face at night, do they, Julie?'

'Dadda, hdsahasfh haslfhlahf balls?'

'Arlo, Daddy will take you to the balls another day. OK?'

'I just need to know if he's really sensitive to the light,' continues Julie.

'Park?'

'I'll take you to the park another day as well,' I say to you, before mumbling to your mother to turn the torch on her phone on and then shine it in your eyes.

'Pool—'

You recoil from Mummy's phone, which has this second become brighter. I'm still sticking with my ingenious theory that it's night, and your eyes aren't calibrated to accommodate an LED-generated beam from a flashlight.

'Well, is he sensitive?'

Christ, this is getting exhausting. 'It's like I said before, Julie. It's dark, therefore he's reacting the same way anyone would when having a flashlight shone in their eyes. However, I don't think he's any more sensitive than usual.'

Julie continues asking me a mix of sensible and stupid questions while you interject with delirious requests for me to take you to the trampoline park, the normal outdoor park and the swimming pool.

Fortunately, during our conversation, your temperature reduces ever so slightly, leading Julie to conclude that it's *only* a severe fever that's probably caused by the virus.

'I am still concerned about his temperature as it really is very high. But if you can get it below thirty-nine degrees, then I don't think he needs to go to hospital. What you can do is use a wet flannel to help.'

'OK, thank you, Julie.'

I end the call. Two things, Arlo. Thing one: fuck going to the hospital. Can you imagine how unpleasant the experience would be for all of us? We all feel shit, but at least we feel shit in our own bed in the quiet and in the dark. If your temperature rises that high again or you develop other symptoms, then we'll have no other choice, but until one of those criteria is met, we're staying put. Thing two: I'm not on board with the wet-flannel idea. I suspect that's now defunct advice. We were always told *not* to do that when tackling temperatures. But advice changes all the time, so I'm unsure.

Mummy takes your temperature again and it's fluctuating between 39.7 and 40.4 degrees. However, it's been almost four hours since your last dose of Calpol so hopefully your next lot will work to bring your temperature down to less terrifying levels.

It works.

Just.

We get it to the low 39s, and you cease uttering delirious requests for me to take you out of the house and do stuff. Eventually, you drift off to sleep.

Since this virus business began, I've always mentally prepared myself for the probability that we'd all catch it at some point, while knowing that the statistics are on our side and that we should, and would, be able to ride it out.

But I'll hold my hands up and say that when I saw that thermometer reading, I wondered if Mummy and I had made a terrible mistake and grown complacent and careless, and if, as a result, you'd paid what could have been a terrible price. Believe me when I say I never want to see you register a temperature that high again.

Another Tough Day
Tuesday, 31 August 2021

I'm tired.
You're tired.
Mummy's tired, and so is Nana Smurf.
We're all tired.
But we have cause for celebration because you successfully traversed the night, your temperature eventually falling to a non-volcanic level.

We spend our time tag-teaming our way through the day, looking after one another. You invite us to tea parties, demand things on TV and *help* with the cooking. Mummy is feeling much better now. Her chest pain is gone. But she's quick to tire, so she needs to take it easy.

If I had to use one word to sum up the day, it would be 'purple'. You drew a picture of your purple mud kitchen on a purple piece of paper using a purple pen. You selected a purple chalk when continuing your arts-and-crafts activity outside on the paving slabs; you requested many other purple items such as your purple bottle, your purple dinosaur and your purple blocks; and you generally spent a large portion of your day pointing to things that are purple.

I'm sure some other stuff happened, but I've not been paying much attention today. Sorry. Call it shit dadding on my part.

September

'Having seen a lifelong friend look up at Paw Patrol *on the television and declare the episode to be "one of the good ones", I have committed to never having children.'*

Jamie A, a childless man

How Much Longer?
Thursday, 2 September 2021

Isolation is beginning to take a toll on us all. It started when you asked for a cracker, but there was only a single half left in the box. I made the mistake of telling you that you had to eat that half first before I would open a new pack. By the time I realised what a stupid battle that was to pick, it was too late. Then you started bashing the dinner table because your food wasn't ready in time – food you later refused to touch unless you were allowed to sit on the floor and eat it. We ended up granting the request but you still didn't eat anything. What you did do, though, was slap your mother because she wouldn't give you yet another cracker. And then, obviously concerned that you hadn't quite got the message across, you ran after her into the kitchen and gave her another slap for good measure.

Then there was the incident where you started screaming 'MAMMA' even though MAMMA was right in front of you trying to discover what you wanted. Turns out you wanted your toy duck, which we call 'The Mamma Duck'. We won't be making that naming-convention mistake again. Then there was the response to me asking you to put your grey pen away – a response that saw you hurl the pen across the living room. Finally, you really lost it when I told you to stop playing around with the buttons on my height-adjustable desk.

It's fair to say that we've all had enough of this isolation period now.

Ahh, Man
Friday, 3 September 2021

Good news: my sense of taste has partially returned.

Bad news: *Shang-Chi* comes out today, and I can't go and watch it (insert sad face).

More bad news: my sense of smell has now completely gone, as has Mummy's and also Nana's, which is worse news for you because we can't tell when we've got a code brown on our hands unless you volunteer the information or we remember to check.

Even more bad news: you continue to be a stressed-out, violent, bored little bastard.

Freedom Day For Mummy
Saturday, 4 September 2021

'Right, see you later,' says Mummy, who is wearing a face full of relief because she can finally leave the house.

'Have the best time,' I say, with a look that's a mixture of passive-aggressive jealousy and undiluted resentment.

She's literally skipping out the door, pausing briefly to do the Carlton dance. Fuck her, Arlo. We don't need Mummy anyway; let her abandon us to go and see her friends. Mummy is such a stupid-head. We'll have tons more fun without her.

And it's fun we have …

OK, that's a lie. We have no funs at all.

Not even a single fun.

For anyone who's counting, that's zero funs.

If I surveyed 10,000 people and asked them how many funs I had being stuck at home with you, they would all say: 'No funs.'

'All together now! Three, two, one … how many funs?'

'NO FUNS!' roars the crowd.

Freedom Day For Nana Smurf And Arlo
Sunday, 5 September 2021

Confusion.
Images.
Sounds.

Fragments of my life flash before my eyes. The clippings pass too quickly for me to make them out. And I hear sounds. Fluttering, distorted audio extracts from a scene that I can't place as past, present or future. It's mostly static. Like a broken radio recovered from the war-torn streets of a once-beautiful European village during the First World War.

Is there anyone out there?

Slowly, order begins to emerge and the flashes become clearer, like a thousand-piece jigsaw puzzle that's correctly arranging itself before my eyes. What was once an awful acoustic assault gradually eases off until it's all but gone. In its stead arrives a sound of such beauty that my senses explode with joy and life.

'Say that again,' I tell Mummy.

'I said, Arlo's period of isolation ends today so I was thinking of leaving him in his pyjamas and taking him straight up to my mum's. I'll only come back when it's time to put him down for his nap. Is that OK?'

'Let me go and get his shoes for you right now.'

'Well, can I finish my—'

'I've got them! Arlo!' I shout from the hallway. 'Come here, son, you're getting in the car to go and see Nana See-See.'

Look. I love you more than you can imagine. It's a love that you won't possibly understand until you have children yourself. But … I'm ready for each of us to have our own space for a few hours.

'Buh-bye.'

Don't rush home!

Freedom Day For Dadda
Monday, 6 September 2021

FREEEEEDOM!

'Years from now, we'll look back at this time and remember it fondly and recall how we all experienced this piece of history together,' says Nana Smurf, who I presume is suffering from brain damage.

Arlo, listen to me. If, when you grow up, you hear Nana reflecting about how wonderful this time was, tell her from me that she's a fucking liar and that there was next to no enjoyment about having Covid-19 and being forced to isolate together, especially with you being the angry, demanding, cracker-grabbing little bogan that you are.

Lego
Sunday, 12 September 2021

'Arlo can build a tower out of Lego all by himself. Isn't that amazing?' says your mother, who genuinely looks like the proudest woman on the planet. That's a shame because I'm about to make her pride disappear quicker than a rock vanishes when it's dropped in quicksand.

'That is amazing. Or at least it would be if it were true.'

'What are you on about?'

'Well, first, it's not Lego he's using. Second – and please feel free to challenge me here – I'm ninety per cent sure that your definition of a tower is him clicking two pieces together.'

'Hang on, you weren't even there. How the fuck do you know?'

'OK, you tell me. How many pieces—'

'No, the other bit. How was it not Lego?'

'Because Lego and Duplo are two very different products, and I'm willing to bet half the contents of my penny jar that it was Duplo he was playing with.'

'Well, you're wrong, and I'm going to prove it right now.'

Mummy gets out her phone to research the various plastic-brick products on the market while I wait for the uncomfortable silence that's sure to follow.

A few seconds pass.

Mummy's expression turns from a frown to disbelief and then to annoyance. She's swiping away at her smartphone a bit like you would when trying to swat a fly that's chanced an emergency landing on the tip of your nose.

A few more seconds pass, and annoyance turns to dejection.

'How you are getting on?' I ask.

'Well, you were right, but you didn't need to be such a dick—'

'I'll stop you right there. Lego is one of the most important subjects on the childhood curriculum, even more important than *Star Wars* and Marvel movies. You cannot – *cannot* – wantonly bandy about false claims like that and get me all excited. You know I can't wait to build cool shit with Lego. So no, I won't apologise for being the smartest person in the room when it comes to Lego knowledge, and you'll do well to remember that. Also, please answer me.'

'You haven't asked me a question.'

'How many bricks did he stick together to construct this mighty tower of his?'

'How about a million, you prick!'

'So it was two. I thought as much.'

September Monthly Review
Sunday, 19 September 2021

Your nursery confidence continues to grow. You rarely cry when we drop you off, and if you do, your sadness is quickly remedied by the promise of food. For those moments during the day when you are upset, staff take you off to the reading corner to have stories and cuddles until such time as you're ready to go it alone again.

If I had to suggest a theme for this month's development, it would be tantrums. Oh boy, have they amped up. There's a lot to sift through here. First, tantrums occur almost exclusively when you're trying to do something but can't. If you're in a good mood, you'll persevere with an activity for a while before asking for help. Asking for help is something we've been drilling into you for months. But often, there are times when you're not in such high spirits, and you either forget to ask for help or choose not to. That's when fists are balled, shouting erupts and, often, things are thrown.

In one sense this is amusing to observe. In another, it's not, because you're a toddler, and you don't have enough understanding of the world to process and control your emotions. And by the way, that is something you will need to practise for the rest of your life because adults struggle with this too. Including me.

I've noticed you testing and pushing boundaries more often. Let me give you an example. You'll be lying down when I'm changing your nappy, and you'll start stroking my arm. Then you'll start lightly tapping it. This is followed by me giving you a warning look, one that says, 'Arlo, I'm watching you. Remember we use kind hands.' You'll go back to rubbing my arm before slapping it as hard as you possibly can, often while smiling. As you can see, there's a clear difference between you losing control and you being in control.

That's not to say you haven't lashed out aggressively. You have been known to chase after your mother so that you can deliver a wallop, your action serving to clearly communicate that you're angry with her. I've also been fortunate enough to receive my first anger-driven slap to the face from you, though I forget the reason why you hit me.

Nana Smurf has moved back into her house. You've adapted quickly to her not being here, though you missed her the first few nights, and you often ask where she is. However, we're not entirely sure if it's her company you miss or the fact that she would let you go into her room and watch cartoons during the day, something we don't allow you to do. On the other hand, it's been tough on poor Nana. We calculated that she has spent more of your life living with you than she has without.

Still slow progress on the language-development front. Recently, Mummy rang the community healthcare worker for a chat (told you she was worried). It was a short chat. After Mummy explained her concerns, the woman asked, 'Can he understand what you're saying?'

'He understands evvvvverything.'

'Then I'm not concerned.'

So for now, that's the end of that.

Next up is swimming. You love it. And now that we've recovered from Covid-19, we've committed to you having regular pool time. It's amazing to see your progress in only a couple of sessions. You can get in and almost get out by yourself. You can hold on to the side of the pool for a handful of seconds, and you're getting good at kicking your legs.

I'm going to end the monthly recap on a high note. And that's to tell you that you've become *even more* affectionate of late, regularly opting in for cuddles, which is a nice counterpoint to the increased periods of anger and rage. I love Arlo cuddles. They're the best.

Asking For Help
Monday, 20 September 2021

In yesterday's review, I said that we encourage you to seek help when you're frustrated by not being able to do certain things. I believe that's worth digging into a bit more.

Wanting you to ask for help doesn't mean we don't want you to solve your problems independently, because we do – it's an important life skill. But at your age, you've just embarked on your introduction to the world of emotions, and they're complex little buggers. So, our parenting approach is to reduce the chances of you blowing a lid. And having assistance can often achieve that.

That said, another important life skill is being comfortable with asking for help. People often believe that's the same as admitting you've failed at something. But please don't subscribe to this philosophy, because it's not. Asking for help is anything but failing. The real failure comes from letting your pride get in the way of you seeking assistance when you want and need it. I can tell you now that I have achieved nothing of worth all by myself. I've had a lot of help along the way. And I'll continue to rely on help for the rest of my life. You would do well to adopt my approach.

I Must ... Comply ...
Tuesday, 21 September 2021

'Dadda!'
'Don't you dare call Daddy. He will say the same thing.'
'Daddaaaa!'
I answer the summons, and find you outside, standing in the mop bucket which happens to be situated directly underneath the outside taps. Your desire is clear: you want me to fill the bucket up while you stand in it. It's a request I hear often, and I rarely refuse. But Mummy has spoken, and I *need* to back her up.

I'm finding that tough.

Biological protocols are emailing my brain with clear instructions ordering me to turn the taps on; I'm fully on board with your view that this all seems like jolly good fun.

But before I can take another step towards you, laser beams begin searing through the back of my eye sockets, beams that Mummy is projecting in my direction, willing me to think carefully about whom I side with. Accompanying the lasers is 'the glare' – *the dreaded Mummy glare* – and a frown. Imagine a B-2 stealth bomber in a nosedive position, and you will have some idea of what one of Mummy's frowns looks like.

'Daddaaaa – here!'
'Daddy, don't you dare!'

My face is like that of an android who's activated two conflicting protocols that cause him to convulse until his circuitry overheats and he explodes.

'Daddaaaa.'

'Now, son, what did Mummy say?' I ask, with a complete lack of authority or conviction – a proper drip of a man.

Ignoring the question, you look at me with a frown of your own, but this one sits atop a face of confusion. You don't understand why I'm not dancing my way forwards so I can hop, skip and jump in with you.

'Dadda?' you say, with a *what-the-fuck?* shrug of the shoulders.

'Arlo ... It is with great sorrow ... and regret' – *must ... support ... the Matriarch* – 'that I must decline-your-request-for-me-to-turn-the taps-on!' Before you can mount what is likely to be a successful campaign to flatten my resolve, I retreat inside the house, run upstairs and lock myself in the bathroom to begin hyperventilating. I'm sorry, son, but Mummy has spoken, and we are an unbreakable, unified team that's built out of carbon-infused dragon scales.

Your Son's Being A Prick
Wednesday, 22 September 2021

Ring ring.

'Hello—'

'It's taken me five minutes to convince your arsehole of a son to get in his car seat. He's bit me, he's screamed at me, he's punched me in the tits—'

At least he's getting near 'em.

'—and in the end, I had to bribe him with Louie.'

'What did you do that for? We have a strict policy of not negotiating with terrorists.'

'Well, I was trying to corral a toddler, and they're worse to deal with than terrorists, so I had to negotiate with him.'

'What are you trying to say?'

'I've already told you. Your son's being a prick.'

'Oh, I see.'

Another First
Thursday, 23 September 2021

Mummy has rung to bring me up to speed with another milestone that you've apparently reached.

'So, Arlo purposely stood on the nappy cream when I was changing him, and, just like any good parent would, I called him a "little fucker".'

'Naturally.'

'But Haylee was in earshot, and she said, "Arlo, you little fucker." And then Arlo said "fuck".'

'That's the—'

'Yep, that's his first "fuck".'

'I'm just glad this was your fault.'

'Piss off. You swear all the time.'

Road Trip
Saturday, 25 September 2021

We're going away for the weekend, and we have a three-hour car ride ahead of us. Twenty minutes into the journey I can report the following: you insisted we play your playlist on repeat, one that consists of two songs: 'Wind the Bobbin Up' and 'We Are The Dinosaurs'; you got your thumb stuck in your Etch A Sketch toy; you demanded orange segments quicker than my speed and agility would allow for; and finally, you rubbed your citrus-juice-covered fingers in your eyes, causing a stinging sensation that you responded to by screaming in my ears.

And now you've got your thumb stuck again in your Etch A Sketch toy.

What a wonderful time we're all having. Arlo, can you believe it's only two hours and forty minutes until this journey comes to an end?

Welcome To Parenthood
Wednesday, 29 September 2021

'MAMMA! DADDA!'

Like a pair of stage performers moving in sync, but without a trace of enthusiasm, Mummy and I turn onto our sides, look at our phones and then let out a groan. It's just gone 6 a.m. At least you've allowed us to have what I'm devastated to report is something we consider a lie-in. Mummy drags herself out of bed, shuffles down to your bedroom and retrieves one unhappy toddler and one unhappy toddler's chimpanzee. Then, she places you in my arms and heads downstairs to make drinks.

'Whhaaaa!'

'What's the matter, Arlo?'

You shake your head while continuing to cry. 'Calm down. Breathe. Now, try and use your words. What's the matter?'

'*Bing.*'

'Would you like Daddy to put *Bing* on for you?'

'Yeah.'

'Then I will. You don't need to get so upset. Just say to me, "Dadda, *Bing* please."'

I've always hated *Bing*, but I've recently come to see him as an ally. I don't know how I'd traverse the first hour of the day without him. Before I can ask you what episode you would like, you erupt again, throwing poor Louie away and hitting me in the arm.

'Arlo, I know you're upset, but please don't hit Daddy as it hurts. Can you say sorry and use kind hands?'

At first you say no. But then, slowly, without making eye contact, you slide your hand up my arm and give it a fleeting rub – a toddler's way of saying sorry.

I press play on *Bing*, and we have a few moments of peace. Soon, Mummy returns with your bottle. Despite her practically sprinting over to you to get it in your hands, you erupt yet again, screaming and crying.

This behaviour has become something of a common occurrence. I'll level with you: I'm finding it tough. I recall confessing that I wasn't Superman when I lost patience with you after having a less-than-stellar day earlier in the year. When I told you that, I was reflecting on what was then a one-off(ish) incident. That's no longer the case, and I find myself unable to maintain patience with you at times.

While Mummy too is struggling, she understands how emotionally difficult it is for a child of your age. Her words and actions help me to acquire the empathy and understanding that are critical to parenting. Arlo, understand that, trying as this stage is, I am in no way resentful towards you. I get that this is an age thing and not a personality thing. But that doesn't mean I'm having an easy time of it right now.

After *Bing*, I ask you what you would like for breakfast. You select two different types of cereal. I don't bother asking you to pick one. Instead, I let you have some of each. The next job is for me to add the milk. I'm careful to involve you in the entire process, lest I risk another tantrum. I ask you what type of milk I need to get out of the fridge.

'Blue,' you say.

'Blue milk it is. And where should Daddy pour it?'

'In there,' you reply, pointing to your bowl. I begin pouring the milk—

'WHHHAAAAAA!'

'Now what?'

You continue screaming while at the same time shaking your head and trying to tip your bowl over. I have no idea what I did wrong then, but I clearly did something. Sometimes it's easy to guess the problem and rectify it. But not this morning.

I'm already exhausted. I've made one decision and one realisation. The decision: I'm dropping you off at nursery as soon as their doors are open. Realisation: I love my day job more than anything, and eight hours of being stuck in a basement with next to no natural light is the equivalent of heaven.

I've been a member of Dadding Inc. since you were born, but looking back, my time on the job thus far has been my probation period, and I'm about to discover what parenthood is really like.

The worst part about this morning when I drop you off at nursery, bang on 8 a.m., is the look of sadness that you give me when I hand you over. You don't cry or scream, but you drop that famous bottom lip of yours and wave to me ever so slowly while looking at the ground. You cannot imagine how heart-crushing that is, especially since I've spent the morning wanting to get rid of you. I walk back to the car, missing you already, feeling bad for dropping you off early but in no way promising it won't happen again.

Welcome to parenthood, where toddlers have access to an inbuilt biological keyboard that's wirelessly connected to your emotions and where every keystroke initiates a metamorphosis of your current mood, testing your patience and resolve every waking moment.

October

'Toddlers are like hurricanes: they're noisy and destructive, they cannot be reasoned with, and they will cause complete devastation of your home. But then they say something like "I lub you" and they become a lot less terrifying, if only for an instant.'

Dom A, an old uni mate

Time Away
Friday, 1 October 2021

You and Mummy are going to Ireland for the week to meet some of your extended family members for the first time. You don't fly until tomorrow, but I'm leaving you today to go to Liverpool for a friend's birthday. This means we're all set to be parted for a new personal best of eight days. The previous record holder was a five-day skiing trip, before Covid-19 really started to kick off.

I'll miss you, but I'm looking forward to the first few days, at least. Don't take it personally, but if someone gave you a choice between waking up naturally and being woken up earlier than your body clock would prefer by a screaming toddler shouting for Mummy and Daddy, what would you choose?

Something I am gutted about, though, is that I'm missing out on your first time on a plane. I can see exactly how you will take to the scenes: going through security scanners, wending your way through the airport and then boarding the aeroplane. You will be totally fascinated, and it would be wonderful to watch. Still, in your almost two years of life, I believe this and your first ever nursery settling-in session are the only things I've missed out on, and that's a statistic I'll forever take comfort in.

Safe flight, buddy; have fun!

The Drinking Stamina Of A Parent
Saturday, 2 October 2021

Last night, I went out in Liverpool to celebrate the birthday of a friend, as I mentioned yesterday. He's a comedian. Our group comprised two parties: old uni mates who are now all fathers and other comedians who have no children. Of the two groups, one collectively left early and was home in bed before 1 a.m., while the other strolled in at 4.30 a.m. How many doctorates do you need to figure out which group came home first?

The Best Hangover In Years
Sunday, 3 October 2021

I'm enjoying the best hangover I've ever had. The reason is fourfold. First, my drinking stamina once again rivalled that of a dead pig, and I found myself in bed at a reasonable time, meaning I wasn't dead the next morning. Second – and again, I'll remind you not to take this personally – I arrived home with zero parenting or partner commitments. Third, I spent the afternoon watching Bond films. Finally, because I was hung-over, I had a takeaway while feeling not an ounce of nutritional guilt – you don't when you're hung-over. All in all, a bloody great day!

Oh, and as suspected, you *loved* being on an aeroplane. Mummy captured some beautiful photos of you looking out of the window. I'd tell you more about it, but I've still got a couple of Bond films to rewatch so I'll probably leave things there.

FaceTime
Monday, 4 October 2021

Despite enjoying being on my own, I have begun to miss you already. But thanks to smartphone technology, we can still connect by way of video calling.
Ring ring.
As soon as I see your face, I'm hit with the realisation that, as terrible as Covid-19 was and is for anyone experiencing loneliness, I'm thankful that the technology landscape is where it is right now, because while this form of digital human contact and connection cannot entirely remove and abate loneliness, it can reduce the symptoms. I never thought about that deeply until now, because we at least had each other for company when we were in lockdown.

Now I'm alone, I'm grateful that I can see your face while chatting to you, even if you're quick to tire of talking and you bugger off out of the frame on some important business, whatever that important business is.

With you otherwise engaged, Mummy gives me a general summary of your trip thus far. While she's talking, I observe something wonderful. It's you. You've reappeared in the frame, in the top-left corner. You're creeping towards your mother with a mischievous grin. I'm not sure what you're up to, but I'm not about to ruin the moment by alerting Mummy to your presence.

You continue sneaking; the grin spread across your face is getting deeper and broader, full of malevolence.

'… so, then we thought we'd go and see Granny …' Mummy says.

Suddenly, you strike, like a bird-eating spider. You wrap both arms around your mother, and you sink your shiny-white ivories into her shoulder.

'OUCH! Arlo, we do *not* bite, do we?'

You immediately lower your head and slowly shake it with the demeanour of a little boy who regrets his actions. But you're still smiling, so no one buys it. I have to turn the phone away so you can't see me laughing, though Mummy can tell what's happening.

'Oi! It's not funny!'

Except is it.

Step Aside, Dad
Tuesday, 5 October 2021

Ring ring.

Yes, Arlo! I eagerly accept the call and see your bright, adorable face on my screen. 'Hey, buddy, how did you sleep?'

'Ooofer?'

'The Hoover? Do you not want to talk to Daddy?'

'OOOFER!'

You little prick! 'Fine, I'll go and get the Hoover.'

Once Again, Dad, Step Aside
Wednesday, 6 October 2021

Ring ring.

'Good morning, Mr Arlo. How are—'

'Ooofer?'

For fuck— 'I'll go and get it.'

You're Really Taking The Piss Now
Thursday, 7 October 2021

Ring ring.
'Good morning, Mr Arlo. You OK?'
'Yeah. Balls?'
'What do you m— You want to watch a video of you at the trampoline park?'
'Yeah!'
'Buddy, I can't, because I'm using my phone to talk to you.'
'ARRGGGHHH.'

Home
Saturday, 9 October 2021

You come home today. I've cleaned the house, and I've been to the shop to ensure we've got whole milk for you and semi-skimmed milk for Mummy's tea addiction. I've tried to use my final day without distractions to be productive, but honestly, it's not going well. I'm excited to see you and that's all I can think about. Hopefully, we'll have a good old catch-up.

I say 'hopefully' because past experiences have taught me to temper my excitement. Those experiences include you consistently behaving like a bellend towards me all week on video calls. I've prepared myself not to burst into tears if you're not in the least bit excited to see me.

'Hello, Arlo.'

'DADDA!'

Yes. Yes, yes, yes, yes. You are pleased to see me!

I should have known that you would always do the opposite of what I expected you to do. I mean, you *are* a toddler. It's in your DNA. But in this instance, you doing the opposite of what I expected has wonderful consequences. We have cuddles, look at pictures from your holiday and play with Duplo. I make a dinosaur which isn't totally unrecognisable as a dinosaur. Considering it was made by my famously unartistic hands, I'm quite proud of it. I even take a picture to document the accomplishment.

It's great to have you home, buddy.

My Birthday
Monday, 11 October 2021

It's my birthday, and I'm trying to figure out who was in charge of selecting my cake. It's a Bing Bunny one. Any idea?

Tantrums 2.0
Wednesday, 13 October 2021

I recall documenting what I proclaimed to be your first *official* tantrum. Do you remember? The one where you let your body go limp and collapsed on the floor over half a cracker. To me, that felt like a proper 'event' moment, one that was important for me to record in your journey from conception through childhood.

These days, 'event' moments happen more often than the minute hand completes a full rotation on a clock. If the slightest thing in life upsets you, you lash out in a loud and violent manner, aiming to lay waste to your surrounding area. I've previously reported that this has been quite the adjustment for me as a parent. But luckily, I'm adapting quickly.

Let me give you the Arlo-tantrum highlights from today.

You shouted at me because I gave you half an ice lolly instead of a full one. I did this because yesterday you erupted (I forget why) and threw your complete ice lolly on the floor. The action split it in two, resulting in one half going in the bin and the other going back in the freezer.

You screamed at me when I selected the wrong angle to push you on the swing at the park. You exploded with rage when I suggested you put your shoes on first before going outside to play with your umbrella. And then you went suicidal because you knocked on the door and I opened it. That's right, you read correctly. Apparently, you wanted to be the one to open the door. That's despite you hurling mixed messages my way by knocking on the door in the first place.

A regular farce of a performance is walking you over to the Hoover and asking you to apologise for 'hurting' it. It wouldn't move in the way you wanted it to move, a way that naturally ran in contravention of the laws of physics, and so you attacked it.

I've confessed previously how difficult it is to maintain a straight face during some of your tantrums. The momentum and determination you muster to attack a specific object are at times, I'm sorry to say, comical. Often, you'll chase after an item that you've flung away in protest so you can throw it again. It's all but impossible not to laugh at some of these demonstrations.

But the hardest thing – the thing that beats me every time – is when either Mummy or I have to drop down to your level and have a talk with you after you've performed an act of misbehaviour. We'll say something like: 'We mustn't do that, must we, Arlo?' and you'll vigorously shake your head from side to side, but all the while smiling, sometimes laughing, as if it's all part of a comedy-sketch routine that we've done many times. Often, I'll need Mummy to take over admonishment duties while I go to another room to release a laugh that I've been confining to my lungs, and vice versa. At least we can laugh about it because otherwise we'd be doing the thing you do when presented with half an ice lolly.

Mr Moo Cow
Monday, 18 October 2021

Haylee has returned home from holiday with a present for you. It's a soft-toy cow, one she made herself at one of those build-a-bear type places. She has decided to christen the cow 'Mr Moo Cow', which in itself is already awesome, but it wasn't until later that we realised that Mr Moo Cow comes with his own maker's name tag. Before I tell you what it is, let me remind you that Haylee isn't three yet and definitely can't read. Anyhow, the real name on Mr Moo Cow's birth certificate is Mr Moo Chow Cow! Isn't that brilliant?

October Monthly Review
Tuesday, 19 October 2021

Let's start with swimming. You still love it and it's currently your favourite activity, having overtaken the park and the 'balls' (remember: that's toddler-speak for trampoline parks). You climb in and out of the water unaided, and your kicking has grown in strength and stamina. When we pull you through the water, you aim your torso, pointing it in the direction of where you want to get to, while Mummy or I use our hands to ensure you don't slip beneath the surface.

You've started gymnastics. It's another activity that meets your approval. I guess it's like the trampoline park, but it features more toys and less intimidating apparatus. It's great. Mummy sends me videos of you running, jumping and climbing, and generally having the best time.

This month, your interest in music has grown. You request songs, and your playlist boasts more than two entries. You rarely listen to a track for longer than ten seconds before requesting another, which quickly becomes painful, especially in the car, but it's great to see your enthusiasm.

Once again, there's been little progress with your speech.

I spoke about tantrums last week so I only have one other point to add. It's all too common for me to hear you upstairs throwing toys while I'm trying to work, and then hear the mandatory dialogue between you and Mummy in which she explains that you must look after your toys, and you say yes. But then you throw them again two seconds later.

But toddler-tantrums are overshadowed by an increase in love and affection on your part, which has once again continued to ramp up since last month. You're heaps cuddlier now. You put both hands on our faces to give us a kiss, but you still find my chin stubble irritating, so you'll lower your head instead, permitting me to kiss your forehead.

I guess that concludes my final monthly review of Year Two.

The Tip
Sunday, 24 October 2021

We're at the tip, and there is a sign that says: *No Children.*

But you know what else there is? A massive JCB digger that's being manned and operated as we speak. There is no way on earth you're missing out on this opportunity, so I ignore the sign, walk up the ramp and stand with you in my arms a safe distance away from the digger, allowing you to absorb the sight, which you do with a big grin and some enthusiastic pointing.

As if parents should be expected to withhold that experience from their children! Why do they bother with the sign anyway? OK, probably for some health and safety reasons, but safety, schnafety – my boy needs to see a digger diggering!

Hot Or Cold?
Monday, 25 October 2021

With word development still not ramping up, though it's by no means stalled, you're still reliant on body language to communicate a number of wants and needs. This is not without a generous dose of charm, though, to the point where I'm now certain I'll miss this stage when looking back on your life.

My new favourite display of body language arrives whenever we ask you if you want hot or cold Weetabix. If you want it warming up, you point to the microwave. But if you want it cold, you wrap both arms around your torso and pretend to shiver, saying 'brrrr'. Is that not just the sweetest thing of beauty?

Dino Kingdom
Saturday, 30 October 2021

Today, we're driving to Nottingham with Auntie Lisa and Haylee to visit an attraction called Dino Kingdom. It's situated in a place called Thoresby Park, a huge expanse of ground that's more than equipped to welcome a large collection of animatronic, life-sized dinosaurs.

We've been showing you pictures all week to engineer as much interest and enthusiasm as possible. Whenever we ask you where it is we're going, you respond with a roar. Everyone's excited, and we're all set to have a roarsome time.

But what's not too roarsome is the long walk from the car park to the entrance, a walk that you personally insist on performing instead of allowing us to throw you in your buggy and shred our strutting time from 'this is taking forever' to 'yay, look, dinosaurs'.

Another noticeably unroarsome variable is the weather. It's started raining. You and Haylee are wrapped up in enough layers, but Mummy and Auntie Lisa are not attired for anything other than a spot of light drizzle, which is what was falling, but not any more. Now, sheets of rain are lashing down like a never-ending battalion of watery lemmings marching off a cloud and splattering themselves on dinosaur-park explorers of all ages. Also, despite bringing an appropriate number of waterproof garments to protect you, your parents have committed a double-major fuck-up. The first fuck-up is that your nice warm hat is made of wool. The second fuck-up is that we haven't brought any gloves for you. I did try and blame this all on Mummy, but she was having none of it. *She's so unreasonable at times.*

You're still refusing to accept buggy support despite the brutality of the elements, which now include wind that is ... well, brutal. You want to walk – slowly. *Come on, buddy, let's pick up the pace.* It's as if we're being made to wade through a river of setting amber sap, each footstep requiring more effort than the last.

Your hands are now noticeably swollen, but I'm not about to ask to borrow an EpiPen, because I believe I'm good to go with the assumption that it's the cold causing it. I try to hinge the hood of your puddle suit over your head, but it's too small to cover both your head and your large woolly hat, which is now wet and heavy.

My rain jacket is about as efficient as you could wish for, and it's withstanding everything the gods hurl at me. If only I could say the same for my bottom half, which boasts zero water-repellent fabrics. I'm wearing a pair of black jeans, and I now look like a gender-reassigned version of Catwoman wearing a decent raincoat.

Eventually, we make it to the entrance in time for the rain's efforts to be accompanied by hailstones, the small orbs of ice assaulting us from several directions thanks to the ever-increasing ferociousness of the wind.

We meet a few dinosaurs, but it's hardly the encounter we've been fantasising about all week. Haylee remembers she's scared of dinosaurs and doesn't want to go anywhere near them. You aren't at all scared of the dinosaurs, but you don't like them as much as the fairground rides you've spotted and towards which you are valiantly marching.

No one is having fun.

Everyone is wet.

I'm pretty sure I've got eight strains of trench foot.

Even if the skies were to clear making way for the sun, our party is too waterlogged to mount a rescue attempt on the day. I look around, and I can see families abandoning the park. With great reluctance and disappointment, we consign ourselves to joining the fleeing masses.

But you don't want to leave. You begin crying. Not tantrum-crying; it's the crying where mine and Mummy's organs turn to mulch because of your inconsolable disappointment. It's our fault for drumming up so much excitement in you. We now know never to do that again, especially for an activity that's weather-dependent. There is a tiny part of me that's reconsidering leaving, but a quick touch of your hands returns a temperature reading of ice-cold. We need to warm up in the car. *I'm sorry, buddy. We've had rotten luck with the weather.*

Getting three adults and two toddlers out of wet clothes is a mission. And my and Mummy's organs show no signs of becoming un-mulched when we realise that your puddle suit has done a poor job of keeping you dry. Every single layer of clothing that you're wearing is soaked through.

To cap this disaster off, we make it five minutes into our return trip home when the rain stops and the clouds do one, allowing the sun to beat down on us. Had we arrived even forty-five minutes later than we did, I'd be recounting a very different set of events from today!

At least we've got ninety minutes of you and Haylee arguing over the Spotify playlist to look forward to.

Roar!

Trick Or Treat?
Sunday, 31 October 2021

Last Halloween we dressed you up as an Ewok. The outfit elicited a great deal of fanfare from friends and family, so we've garbed you in the same threads again this year. Don't worry; it still fits comfortably. With regard to footwear, you're in *Star Wars* wellies, so you're officially a welly-wearing Ewok.

We've headed to a quiet little neighbourhood that, according to Mummy, is 'the place to be' if you're gunning for a half-decent trick-or-treat experience, which is of course exactly what we're here for.

I'm not sure when you last went out on an on-foot adventure after dark, but the absence of light certainly isn't fazing you right now, because you're one excitable young man. I recall that, as a child, being outside at night was a big deal.

Mummy has already explained the rules of trick or treat but she goes over them one last time. 'Arlo, what do you have to do?'

You respond by holding up your arm and knocking on an imaginary door.

'That's right, and then what do you say when someone answers?'

'BOO!'

'Good boy.'

You grab my hand and usher me forward, declaring 'more', which is toddler-speak for 'Mum, Dad – less faffing and more knocking'.

We approach the first house. The owners have set-dressed their garden as a graveyard. Skeletons are arranged so that they appear to be clawing their way out of the earth. Bats hang menacingly from the front porch, spiders lurk in the centre of their webs and pumpkins radiate warm, mood-setting orange hues from within, casting frightening shadows on the wall. It's impressive stuff.

Since becoming a parent, I've become appreciative of the efforts people make decorating their houses for child-friendly occasions such as this one. At the same time, I think, *That must have taken them bloody ages to set up*. And I'm in no rush to begin competing.

Instead of stopping to appreciate the decorations, you march up to the front door and give it a knock while Mummy and I hang back, allowing you to take the stage all by yourself.

Such confidence.

The door is answered by a nice woman in a pair of devil horns. She smiles and marvels at your appearance. 'Aww, look at you!' she says, holding out a plastic-pumpkin bowl that's filled to the top with sweets. You take a look at the bowl, and then glance towards me and Mummy, at a loss for what to do next. I approach and explain to you that you can take a sweet and deposit it in your bag. You do as instructed, though it's clear you remain ignorant as to what sweets are. I was certain Nana See-See would have shoehorned them into your life by now. *Looks like I underestimated her.*

Our trick-or-treat adventure welcomes two new participants, Haylee and Auntie Lisa. Together, we stroll around the neighbourhood having the best time. This is a ton more fun for me than I was expecting. I believe it's because you're so confident. There's a momentary dip when someone first opens the door: your 'BOOS' are more like 'boos', but other than that, you're loving life.

Mummy is shepherding you through this new experience as a teacher and as your guide. 'No, Arlo, pick *that* bag of sweets. Mummy prefers those ones. No, not those ... yeah, those ones. Get Mummy a bag of those.'

'More?'

'Erm ... go on then, why not.'

She comes skipping down the garden path, exclaiming, 'I love Halloween! Arlo has stocked up my sweet cupboard a right good 'un.'

The next participants to join our party are Taci and her family. You may recall from *Dear Dory* that Taci is responsible for getting me and Mummy together, and she can arguably take some of the credit for your existence.

'Arlo, what are you supposed to be?' she asks, with a look that combines confusion and disgust.

Jumping to your defence, I say, 'He's a terrifying and ferocious welly-wearing Ewok.'

'But that's got nothing to do with Halloween.'

Unlike your opinion, apparently.

Usually, I'd march straight onto the battlefield with a prepared salvo of powerful, witty verbal missiles ready to hurl at my opponent. But I don't, because I'm a little preoccupied with something else. I'm embarrassed to admit it, but one of my basic needs must be met quickly. What is this basic need, Arlo? Well, let's just say Daddy wants to empty his bladder. *God, I desperately need a piss.*

Fortunately, it's getting late, you and Haylee are tired, and your interest in knocking on doors is waning. So we say goodbye to Taci and her entourage of one husband and three kids, and we head back to the car.

The need to relieve myself has become desperate.

'Are you pregnant, or something?' Mummy asks me.

'Not that I'm aware of. Please walk faster.'

Fortunately, you're amenable to being picked up, enabling a brisk pace back to the car. While walking, I perform some basic calculations in my head: *five minutes to get back to the car and strapped in, then another fifteen minutes to get back home. Fuck, that's twenty minutes.* Arlo, I don't think Daddy is going to make it. Any other day of the year, I'd go and find a bush or a quiet corner to do my business, but there aren't any of those, thanks to the number of trick-or-treaters who are still out hunting sweets.

'More?' you say.

'More what? Do you want to knock at another house?'

'Yeah.'

Mummy stops short. 'Shall I see if Auntie Claire and Jon are in for a quick visit?'

'Is that a task that can be completed while walking?'

A quick call later and arrangements have been made. I am bursting at the seams. I strap you in the car, jog round to the driver's side and check how long it will take me to drive us to Auntie Claire's house. *Twenty minutes!*

'I'm in real trouble. I can't hold it for that long, and I can't go on the street.'

'What about one of Arlo's nappies?'

'Sure. D'you think they'll fit?' I say, not really appreciating what I assume to be Mummy's poor attempt at humour.

'No, you sausage, just pee into it. It will absorb it. You can do it in the front of the car. Just make sure you aim right.'

Aha! Arlo, I've said it before, and I'll say it again: your mother is a perfect creature. 'Genius, that's exactly what I should do.'

'Here you go,' Mummy says, handing me a nappy.

'OK, help me out with some light, but also keep lookout. And please stop laughing at me.'

'I'm sorry.'

'You're not. You're—' *Oh-my-God-that's-the-best-feeling-in-the-world.*

Crisis averted. Arlo, your nappies are the dog's. They've absorbed every millilitre.

Happy Halloween, son. It's been fun.

November (again)

'Parenthood is this quirky little part of the human experience that spends most of its time travelling faster than the speed of light. So you need to make every moment count. Yes, even the toddler phase.'

Tom K, the author

In Eighteen Days ...
Monday, 1 November 2021

Mummy and I wake up and the first thing she says is, 'In eighteen days, Arlo will be two.'

Talk about starting the month on a massive downer!

Hoovers
Thursday, 4 November 2021

I'm amazed that your obsession with vacuum cleaners has lasted so long. It's become quite the pinnacle of your developmental highlights for the year. I can't say for sure, but you still seem to believe that vacuum cleaners – sorry, Hoovers – are living, breathing biological beings.

You have your own toy Hoovers: one at our house and another at Nana See-See's house. You insist on getting our *actual* vacuum cleaner out all the time, and you spend an age disassembling and reassembling the components, entirely absorbed in your work.

Every morning, you ask for pens, paper and my assistance. We set up shop on the dining-table bench and draw pictures of Hoovers. I'm forbidden to draw anything else.

Nana Smurf possesses a pink Hetty Hoover, which you adore. You're always asking after Hetty's well-being. She also has a video on her phone of you playing with Hetty, and when she visits, you grab at her bag as soon as she enters our house, fish out her phone and hand it to her, saying, 'Hoover, Hoover, Hoover!' – the flow of your demands never stemmed until Nana loads the Hoover video up.

Tragically, Nana Smurf has also introduced you to an abomination of a thing called *Henry Hoover TV*. It's a channel on YouTube. I've been questioning my reality on an hourly basis since learning of this vacuum-cleaner-themed channel. I mean, how is it we live in a world where there is a YouTube channel dedicated to Henry Hoover? How, Arlo? Tell me. Tell me now. And it's not even one channel but several. These aren't under-the-radar, nicher-than-niche videos either; some of them have over a million views.

There's one where Hetty is pregnant, and Henry's assisting with the home birth, which culminates in Hetty giving birth to baby versions of Henry and Hetty. Again, how? And how do I allow you to convince me to let you watch it every night before bed? Yesterday evening, I was made to endure a fourteen-minute unboxing video of a Hetty Hoover toy, the same video we've watched every night this week.

I guess if there are YouTube channels featuring Henry and Hetty Hoover and toy versions of them, then a toddler obsession may not be that strange. It's just one of the many weird and fascinating components of early childhood.

When you're engaged in one of your favourite Hoover activities, I see a young man who never falters in maintaining presence of mind. It's amazing to watch. Though at the same time, I'm envious and a little bit saddened because one day, that ability to live in the moment and focus on one thing at a time, so natural to you now, won't come so easily. Trust me. I've spent years working to recapture this capability for myself.

That said, I find reaching that state of mind a lot easier since you came along to help me. There is nothing better to help me rescue myself from an ocean of thoughts and emotional noise than watching you play with your toys, even if your 'toys' include vacuum cleaners.

Fifteen days to go until your second birthday. Guess what Nana See-See has got you? That's right. Your very own toy Henry Hoover.

Kicking Leaves
Monday, 8 November 2021

I'm on collection duty at nursery. I've arrived a few minutes early. I'm hoping to catch a glimpse of you playing outside. However, when I peer over the wall, there's not one single toddler, preschooler or staff member in the garden.

That's a shame.

But then ... I hear a noise from up the road. I turn and behold a small group of children wearing hi-vis jackets, accompanied by two adults. They're ambling their way towards me. In the front, leading the pack, is a small young man. He's wearing a cheeky grin, and he's kicking up the fallen autumnal leaves in every direction. He's laughing. It's hard to believe that what I'm seeing is real because this same young man endured an emotionally tough time adapting to nursery. But now he's kicking leaves and laughing, and he's clearly the most confident member of the bunch.

That image of you in one of your settling-in sessions holding a cracker, crying and refusing to eat it, will never leave me. But you know what? Neither will this one. I knew you could do it. You overcame every obstacle.

Dear Arlo, Again
Tuesday, 9 November 2021

Today is 9 November, which means it's time for your annual letter, where I impart unto you the biggest lessons life has recently taught me, or in this year's case, one lesson, so that one day, if you so choose, you can leverage my words to improve your life. I am bound to this responsibility as a father, and it is one I welcome.

> *Dear Arlo,*
>
> *People will tell you that it's essential to maintain balance. You'll be encouraged to make time for yourself, friends and all the other things on your list of priorities. It's a list that I guarantee will only ever lengthen, to the point where you won't be able to see the end of it.*
>
> *Modern life presents us with many opportunities. But each requires a choice: what to watch, what to wear, what to eat, what to read, where to study, what to study, what job to apply for, when to apply for a promotion, when to go to bed, when to wake up, when to visit a friend, how much to spend on a wedding gift, what to consider important, what to dismiss as unimportant.*
>
> *It's distracting. It's hard to differentiate between what matters and what doesn't – what to say yes to and what to say no to. And that's why it's difficult*

to get anything done. Then, on top of that, you're expected to find and maintain some semblance of balance, whatever that means.

I've since come to realise that the search for balance is a fallacy. In fact, 'fallacy' is a helpful word. Let's examine the 'fallacy of balance'.

Whenever I used to think about balancing, in the traditional sense, the many priorities I have in my life, I would envision an image of a see-saw, with me standing in the middle, never moving in either direction, because to go in one direction was to sacrifice and forgo opportunities and priorities on the other side. And so, I risked remaining trapped in the middle while my head turned from side to side, paralysed by indecisiveness and by my inability to reach both ends of the see-saw at the same time.

Now, though, I approach that see-saw in a different way. On one end of it is you. I want to be a good parent: present, involved, never missing out on a single moment of your life. After all, before I know it, you'll no longer be inviting me into your 'house' at the bottom of the stairs for tea parties. I've always understood that childhood is fleeting, and that's what makes every moment of it precious. On the other end of the see-saw sits everything else: my financial responsibilities, my career, my health, my relationships, my hobbies, etc. Let's look at some examples of how we can resolve the need to attend to both ends of the see-saw while avoiding getting stuck in the middle of it.

We'll start with health. What would I rather do: chase you around the house or go for a run? Easy. Chase you around the house. But if I don't exercise, then I'm not looking after my physical self, and so I might not have the energy to chase you around the house anyway.

Next, downtime. Is taking a long soak in the bath instead of spending that time with you selfish? I don't believe it is. Say I've got a two-hour block of time. I can either devote both hours to you or devote one hour to you and one hour to having a bath. If I allocate both hours to you, then you might not get the best of me: I might be stressed, or perhaps my mind wants to wander. But say I have a bath and only give you one hour, but for that one hour you get 100 per cent of me. What would you prefer? I know what I would prefer to give.

What about money? With my current nine-to-five job, I can ensure we just about have enough to pay for all of our basic, and marginally more-than-basic, needs. But as things stand, there are two major drawbacks. One: if I lose my job, I lose our main source of income. Two: I trade a lot of hours of my life for the money I make, hours that I would much prefer to spend with you. I've been trying to do something about that with various side projects like writing and property, but these activities require an upfront investment of time. In the short term, I need to work extra hours over and above my day job in *order to get to a position in the future where I'm working fewer hours overall.*

And now we arrive at the crux of the issue: the fallacy of balance. In order for me to achieve the things I want, I need to walk from one end of the see-saw to the other, and I need to get comfortable spending large blocks of time at the other end from you. However, if I do that, I'm faced with the guilt of not being a good father and not spending enough time with you. But opting instead to do nothing about my current situation means not spending as much time as I want with you either, so I'm no better off.

I told you it was a fallacy.

I've spent all year tweaking and fiddling with my life-setting dials to try and balance my priorities, and yet that balance is something I've continually failed to achieve. That was until I realised that I was trying to solve the unsolvable. Because the word 'balance' is wrong. It's not 'balance' we need in our life – it's 'counterbalance'.

Let me repeat: counterbalance.

Counterbalance means finding within yourself the courage to throw everything you have on one side of the scale and let it sit there long enough so that you can execute your plan to achieve whatever it is you want to achieve. To get what you want – exactly what you want – you have to learn to shut everything else out, and focus on one thing; then, once you've done that one thing, you can move on to the next. If you're reading a book, then read the damn book; don't half read it while allowing your thoughts to linger on your priority list. Same if you go out for a walk. Keep your head up and observe what's in front of you instead of staring at the pavement and dwelling on what you don't have in life.

Employing counterbalance means you can achieve more because once you've invested time, effort and energy at one end of the see-saw, on 'one thing', then you can, calmly and collectedly, stand up, turn around and walk back the way you came to the other end of the see-saw, giving your attention to the moment, as I have learnt to do with you: slurping tea out of an invisible cup; playing hide-and-seek; and watching the same annoying episode of your favourite television programme.

Do you understand now? Balancing in the middle of a see-saw ensures a motionless life, but if you learn to walk from one end to the other, then the see-saw will move up and down, its motion generating the energy you require to care for, and give attention to, all aspects of your life.

Counterbalance doesn't mean I'm gone forever, or even gone for days on end, but it does require me to shut everything else out, freeing me to focus on one thing, one thing that will provide everything I, and those I hold dear, want and need.

So, while I sometimes have to ignore you banging on the door of my office while I'm concentrating on *work, it does mean that when I'm done with my thing and I answer your demands, I'm 100 per cent there, buddy, with nothing else on my mind.*

Life is a maze of choice and possibility, of opportunities and of never-ending pressure and friction. I've learnt that through counterbalance, I can navigate the maze. Counterbalance provides a map, a compass and a torch that guide me to a place of calmness and peace. Perhaps, one day, it can help you find a way through the maze as well.

Balance is out. Counterbalance is in.

I'll end by telling you that you have been beyond brilliant this year, and I remain as content as ever.

Love, Dad

The Office
Wednesday, 10 November 2021

Yesterday, I went to work in the office for the first time in twenty months. It was surreal to see my team members in person, but, aside from the obligatory IT issues we all faced, it didn't take us long to settle back into the swing of things.

When you were born, I took four months off to dedicate all my time and energy to you and Mummy. The memories I built from that four-month experience are precious, and I found having to go back to work afterwards difficult. But before I could dwell on the matter for too long, Covid-19 struck, and we were ordered to work at home. As my dadding voyage approaches the end of Year Two, I feel *almost* guilty that a global tragedy has continued to provide my small sphere of existence with so much to be grateful for, because it has meant that I've had more time with you than I would have had if you had been born any earlier.

I wonder if Covid-19 has inadvertently done a wonderful thing for families, particularly dads who earn a living from working on a computer. Do they want to spend more time at home hanging out with their children now? Previously, their mornings consisted of catching a train or driving down the motorway trapped in their thoughts. *What am I going to say in this week's progress review? How do I get that project back on track? And have I left early enough to bag a decent parking space?* Perhaps they don't think about those things now. Or at least not as much, because they've reallocated that time and invested it in their children; time that wouldn't have been available before Covid-19. Perhaps they now spend it cleaning up spilt cereal, changing nappies or watching insanity-inducing children's television.

What will those changes mean for us, for you and for the current generation of babies and toddlers? I don't know, but my gut tells me it's something positive. I hope so anyway.

Wee-Wee
Friday, 12 November 2021

'Anything?'

'No, not yet. I'm going to give him some space,' Mummy says, backing out of the downstairs toilet and into the utility room.

To bring you up to speed: I'm in the living room trying not to get too excited, Mummy is now in the utility room trying not to get too excited, and you're in the downstairs cloakroom sitting on the big-boy toilet with the aid of a baby toilet seat.

You've asked to sit on the toilet several times in the last couple of weeks, but you've not done any toileting on there. However, today when you asked, you had both hands on your nappy, which tells us we're possibly moments away from you reaching another major milestone.

But we don't want to make a big deal out of it until there's something to make a big deal out of, so that's why I'm still in the living room, and now Mummy is pottering, leaving you with some privacy to do or not do whatever it is you've come to do or not do.

'What about now?' I say.

'I'm not watching him. I can't see.'

'Mamma, down,' you say, climbing off the toilet.

She walks in to help ... 'Oh my God, Arlo! You've done a wee-wee!' Mummy starts jumping up and down in pure, joyous elation.

I sprint over to the toilet, and I can see the unmistakable colour of urine. *My boy's done his first piss in the toilet.* I am so, so, so, so, so, so fucking proud. I didn't think this milestone would set me off like this, but I'm overcome with emotion.

Well done, buddy. I can't believe you've performed your first piss in the toilet. And you did so while sitting down – a bona fide sit-down wee. *My favourite type of wee.*

Pass The Parcel
Sunday, 14 November 2021

'I'm picking up the cake on Thursday, and then I'm leaving you to sort out his Moonpig card, right?'

'Right, I'm all over it. Like a nasty ra—'

'That leaves pass the parcel.'

'Pass the parcel?'

'Yeah, I need to get some prizes for it. The main one will be a colouring book and pens.'

Oh dear! Here's the thing about pass the parcel, Arlo – it's terrible. I mean, for starters, the whole thing is a fix. Even a four-year-old knows that the stopping and starting of the music is engineered to ensure every child wins at least one round.

Then there's the physical construction of the game. The foreman (in this case Mummy, but I've never once seen the game played out any other way) finds it amusing to go hell for leather on the Sellotape application, believing this will add suspense and an extra layer of fun to the game.

Wrong. On both counts.

All it does is piss everyone off even more. The person unwrapping the layer struggles to perform the task quickly, so there is a sense of social anxiety with an 'everyone is watching me' type of thing. The onlookers are frustrated at having to watch the participant progress in such a slow manner, making the social anxiety of the child doing the unwrapping not unwarranted. A narrative runs through their heads: *If that was me, I'd have the job done by now.* But then, of course, they get a turn, and it's not as easy as they assumed, and so now they're the ones receiving the unpleasant judgemental stares from their peers.

Do you see, Arlo? There is no fun to be had with pass the parcel.

But here's the really bonkers thing about it: even though the game is total dog shit, for some inexplicable reason it psychologically manipulates the players, suckering them into a desire to win. They spend the duration of the game in a heightened state of competitive apprehension. Desperation is carved across the face of every participant, even though in their hearts they know that only disappointment lurks under the next layer of wrapping paper.

And when the music stops and one lucky child is suddenly in possession of the parcel, he or she gets a quick boost of serotonin while tearing off – or attempting to tear off – the layer of paper to find the prize.

But say you're that one who wins. You've played your part perfectly, battling rapid heartbeats, near misses and mind games with the DJ – all to finally achieve what nobody else could: to be declared the WINNER! You eagerly tear away at the final layer, like a marathon runner reaching the ribbon at the finishing line. And what's your reward? A fucking colouring book!

My Teammate
Monday, 15 November 2021

Last year, Mummy's natural talent in caring for you, coupled with her years of childcare experience, meant that I was able to enjoy my first year as a father a lot more than I was expecting. This year, she's used that same talent to make me a better parent, helping me to see the world through the eyes of a one-year-old boy and understand all the emotional and physical challenges that life throws at him. I will always be grateful to her for that. She's overseen my adjustments to new phases and taught me the right way to approach tantrums.

Parenthood might be seen by some as the process of continually climbing mountains, but with Mummy's support and guidance, I've discovered side paths and alleyways that are not only easier than steep inclines but also more fun.

Not every road needs to lead to a mountain summit.

When it comes to parenthood, Mummy and I are a great team. Each of us has things we're good at and things we're not so good at. And so we combine our skills to shoulder the weight of our individual weaknesses, ensuring that you're not only cared for but also that you're flourishing and that the environments you're placed in are secure and loving.

I'm not saying we're perfect. We're not. But I can hand on heart say that 99 per cent of the time we work *together* as parents, and not as players on a court either side of a net, in opposition to one another. Parenthood is hard, and it will still be hard when you grow up, I have no doubt about that. But it's a damn sight easier with someone by your side.

Do you remember that phase you went through at the start of the year? The one where you wouldn't let Mummy read to you? Well, I'm saddened to report that you've returned to similar territory. You don't like Mummy being the one to collect you from your cot in the morning when you wake up, and often you'll favour me over her. Mummy says you're a daddy's boy and it's hard to disagree with her. Hopefully, it will pass quickly. If not, I suspect Mummy has some tough periods ahead in the next stage of our parenting adventure. I tell her not take it personally, but of course she does, and to be fair to her I don't blame her. This isn't your fault either, so never think that! It's commendable that you're speaking up to be heard, and we're both proud of you. But understand that it's tough for Mummy because you really are her world.

I promise you, though: I'll help her through it as best I can. Because she'd do the same for me. Because she's my teammate and my partner, and I'd be lost without her. She is, and continues to be, a one-of-a-kind mummy, and we're both fortunate to have her in our lives.

Sometimes

Tuesday, 16 November 2021

Sometimes, it's getting up in the middle of the night to settle you back down to sleep using technology, soft whispers and gentle physical contact. Sometimes, it's contorting my face into unnatural and painful positions to make you laugh. Sometimes I'm the one laughing, all because of some absurd, silly thing you've chosen to do on repeat. Sometimes, it's chasing you around the house with the vacuum cleaner. Sometimes it's reading you stories, often the same story multiple times. Sometimes, you need picking up and cuddling because you've taken a tumble and given yourself an ouchie. Sometimes, a cuddle is enough. Sometimes, it's not. Sometimes, you need to go to the hospital. Sometimes, you need a special magical daddy kiss to make the hurt go away. Sometimes, it's about taking it in turns to clean each other's teeth; when this happens, it's usually with our foreheads lightly pressed together – a perfect intimate moment shared by father and son. Sometimes, Louie gets in on the teeth-cleaning action too. Sometimes, it's watching you walk up to your mother and cuddle her leg; when that happens, I experience a warm, pleasant tingle of electricity that bathes every cell in my body. Sometimes, it's trying not to overreact when you have a tantrum, even if that tantrum involves screaming, scratching and throwing objects. Sometimes, the job involves a lot of clapping and recognition of your achievements, like your amazing pieces of artwork, which I cherish. Sometimes, it's about educating you on the many dangers that reside in your environment, like a hot radiator, furniture corners or heavy objects that might hurt your little toes if dropped, like what happened last month with an unopened jar of Marmite. Sometimes, it's reading books and blogs or asking other dads for advice. Sometimes, it's sitting down with Mummy and reflecting on the day to see if we need to change our approach towards certain scenarios. Sometimes, it's about agreeing 100 per cent with Mummy. Sometimes, the percentage is lower. Sometimes, it's a lot lower. Sometimes, it's being away from you so I can work and ensure that the bills are paid and we're all provided for; when that happens, my job is to tell Mummy how amazing she is for looking after you all day and to express gratitude that we can afford childcare. Sometimes, it requires an endless supply of patience. Sometimes, the stores are exhausted and down to mere fumes. Sometimes, they're fully depleted, and then, it's about getting things wrong, and when that happens, the job is to practise forgiveness, because there will always be instances when you get it wrong as a parent. Sometimes, it's about sacrifice and compromise. Sometimes, it's about feeling more content than ever before. And sometimes, dadding is about doing nothing at all but hanging back and letting you explore your own limits and make mistakes; often, that's the hardest part of the job – doing nothing.

Sometimes, the job is impossibly hard.

Sometimes, the job is surprisingly easy.

You never know what the day will bring you when you're employed by humanity to parent another human being, but it's always something. And that something is, and will always be, the greatest accomplishment and accolade of my life.

Your Life In Motion
Wednesday, 17 November 2021

We never did get to experience that dirty protest, did we? Perhaps next year. Come to think of it, LG never emailed me back either – *fuckers!*

I'm standing in the bathroom looking at myself in the mirror. I notice a few more lines on my face and grey hairs on my head than I had a year ago. You're not to blame, although, full disclaimer: you probably don't help. No, this would have happened regardless of my fatherhood status. No one escapes the passing of time.

November (again)

I can see Louie chilling on the landing outside the bathroom. Boy, do we have a lot to thank that monkey for. He's been such a key component of your support network this year that he's well within his rights to claim Child Benefit. A child's bond with their favourite soft toy is a beautiful thing to behold. *Thank you, Louie. I still don't know why I held on to you all these years, but I'm glad I did.*

I've spent all year hating on that children's television cartoon that you like to watch, *Bing*. Bing is whiny and annoying, and he's a sulky little twat. But you know what? For the last two weeks, you've not really wanted to watch *Bing*. You've moved on. You have a new favourite show that's called *Cocomelon*, and, as laughable and pathetic as this might be, I now find myself longing for Bing Bunny and his irritating noise.

Last year, I said that being your dad felt like I had this perfect television series to watch where you were the main character. This year I've watched season two of the same television series, but it's felt like it's permanently on fast forward. I find it difficult to keep up with the central character. He keeps changing. What he did yesterday feels like a lifetime ago because, even though only twenty-four hours have passed, he is a completely new little boy, and I'm questioning whether what happened yesterday really *did* happen yesterday and not last month.

I watch you every day. I write to you, I take photos and videos of you, and I try and maintain presence of mind whenever I'm in your company. And yet, despite all of that, you are moving through life in a blur of rapid forward motion that I can't keep track of. The pace is beyond my comprehension – it's superluminal. I hate it.

Since 16 March 2019, I've often told you the benefits of learning to be present and to appreciate what you have today, right now, in this exact instant, understanding that life is fleeting and that we must value and cherish each passing second. I still stand by that. It's as worthy a goal to aim for in life as any. But just because you aim for something doesn't mean you won't miss. And I will admit that, after two years, I still struggle to deal with the speed at which you are growing, and I've come to the frightening realisation that no matter how grateful and appreciative I feel, this is one aspect of my life that I will never be able to fully accept.

Seeing you smile imbues my body with energy and vitality. Seeing your bottom lip curl up in sadness strips me of everything. Hearing you laugh elevates me higher than the homes of the gods, and hearing you cry plunges me into the lowest depths.

But there is one sound: one sound that overrides everything. And that sound is your voice when you say 'Dadda'. That word is my call to arms, my Bat-Signal in the sky, my emergency response siren, my rallying cry. When I hear that, all my other priorities are secondary. Because my little boy needs me, and to deny him is unthinkable.

A few months ago, you were with Haylee and Nana See-See. It started raining hailstones (this was before our failed trip to Dino Kingdom). I was on my own at home. I remember looking out of the window thinking, *I hope Arlo is seeing this*.

At the start of the year, I confessed that I felt unequipped going into the next phase of parenthood – mainly where your psychological development was concerned. I still feel like that, but it's a feeling I've since made peace with. How? Well, for one, we did it, didn't we? You, me and Mummy. We got to the end of Year Two. And we did it by following the same approach that we've always followed: we do the best we can with what we've got, accepting that winging it at times is unavoidable and that expecting to get every choice and decision right is a delusion.

I now understand that this feeling of uncertainty is something I'll live with forever. And that's a good thing because it means you're constantly changing and developing. As a species, we absorb unquantifiable amounts of information consciously and subconsciously every day. That information is interpreted, sorted and organised into memories. In turn those memories are used as a blueprint to upgrade our operating system so that we're more equipped to navigate the world tomorrow than we were today.

I think that's beautiful: our world view is a constantly evolving narrative. As your daddy, I can never fully predict what daily parenting tasks I will be expected to perform, because you wake up a different person every morning. Neither can I predict the consequences of my choices. Similarly, the influence of randomness can never be discounted either. After all, it was randomness that led me to you.

I am your guide, nothing more. I can point you in what I believe is the right direction, but then it's up to you to decide who you want to be. That is something I cannot control, and even if I could, I wouldn't. And neither would Mummy.

By definition, adventure is the state of not knowing.

I lack the words to convey my appreciation for what you've given me. Like the discovery of your existence or the first time I held you in my arms, words don't cut it. But I hope they give you an idea of the value I place on my role as your daddy.

Congratulations on once again reaching such a high number of milestones, each one in such pride-inducing fashion. I see in your eyes great promise and potential – someone who will grow to be better, more caring, more capable and more empathetic than I could ever hope to be. Thank you for another exceptional year. You remain the best thing to ever happen to me.

Arlo, An Almost-Two-Year-Old
Thursday, 18 November 2021

Ring ring.
  'Hel—'
  'YODA. YODAAAA!'
  'Is that a young Mr Arlo I can hear in the background?'
  'Dadda.'
  'Yes. Are you—'
  'YODAAAA!'
  'This is all I've had for the last five minutes,' Mummy says. 'I rang so you could feel my pain.'
  'Feel your pain? He's screaming for Yoda. That's brilliant!'
  'I thought you'd say that. Anyway, we'll be home in five minutes.'
  Arlo, you have no idea of the world that awaits you: *Star Wars* is awesome. You're joining at such an exciting time. You already have a significant back catalogue of content to enjoy, and dozens more projects are in development. Life is looking pretty promising for us *Star Wars* fans right now. But enough about *Star Wars* because this is your last evening as a one-year-old. Tomorrow heralds yet another new chapter as we say goodbye to one stage of your life and welcome another.
  Mummy arrives and parks the car, and you guys enter the house. You run up to me and give me a king-sized cuddle, but then you quickly break away so that you can greet the other *person* who lives here. 'Ooofer?'
  'It's getting late and it's time for your bath. Let's let the Hoover sleep, shall we?'
  You drop to the floor like a depowered robot in mid-stride and begin sobbing. I pick you up and defuse what I suppose will be the last tantrum of your second year.
  'Arlo.'
  'Yeah,' you say through uncontrollable sobs.

November (again)

'Shall we quickly say goodnight to the Hoover?'

The sobbing stops and your eyes transform from sadness to happiness in an instant. *The power is back up and running.* I open the door to the basement, where the Hoover resides, and allow you to say a quick hello and goodnight. Then I carry you upstairs with Mummy so we can begin bath time, noticing along the way the many scuff marks on the lower sections of the walls in our house.

Mummy runs the bath while I get you undressed. As soon as I unfasten your nappy, you bolt, racing around the first floor of our house, avoiding capture and shrieking the entire time. We call this 'naked-toddler running'. I allow the game to continue for a few minutes before wrestling with you on the bed and blowing raspberries on your chest.

Then it's in the bath you go. Your knees are covered in bruises. Nana Smurf says you have 'boy's knees'. When I ask you about the state of them, you react as if you've this second banged them on something and they hurt.

'Owww.'

'Owww? Are your knees sore?'

'Yeah.'

'Do you need a special magical daddy-kiss?'

'Yeah.'

'Which one?'

You lift the knee closest to me and wait for me to perform the ouchie ritual. 'Specialllll, magicallllll, daddy-kiss!' I give your knee lots of kisses in quick succession, ridding it of any ouchie-pain. 'There, is that better?'

'Yeah.'

When you turned one, your eyes had begun to include a tinge of green among an array of stunning hues of blue. But now that's gone. Your eyes are back to being blue, but they're no less striking. You have beautiful eyes. Your hair is still sandy-blond, but it's grown a shade or two darker over the course of the year. I don't believe you'll retain your blond hair for much longer. We'll see.

Once we complete bath time, I get you dry and dressed and we head downstairs. You ask to watch your new favourite show, *Cocomelon*, but instead, and I can't believe this, I insist we watch, possibly for the last time, *Bing*. After *Bing*, we do the opposite of what we should be doing as parents, which is creating a calm, relaxed ambiance to help you transition to bed. Instead, you and Mummy play-fight for ten minutes, and then you and I make up a dance to 'I Do Like to Be Beside the Seaside'. It's one that involves a lot of clapping and stomping.

At 6.45 p.m., we call it a day and begin the final bedtime routine of our second year. I clean your teeth. Then you tell us that you need a poo and that you want to sit on the toilet. I'm not sure I can handle you hitting a momentous milestone like this the night before your birthday, but if you've gotta go and you want to go on the toilet, then who am I to stop you?

You don't go, but I'm reminded that toilet-training will be one of the phases we're set to traverse in the coming year.

Next, you take my hand and lead me into your bedroom for story time. It wasn't that long ago that you were only able to hold on to my index finger. Now, it's my whole hand. Mummy lays your duvet down on the floor and invites me, you and Louie, of course, to sit. I read *On the Farm*, and then Mummy reads *Meg's Eggs*. You ask for a third, but we say no. Tomorrow, you can begin having three stories a night as you'll be two, and Mummy and I have already agreed to it. But not tonight. Tonight you're still a one-year-old.

After story time, we move on to the next stage of the bedtime ritual: pressing buttons on your clock so that it turns from orange to blue – blue signalling that it's night-time. Then, I lift you up to touch the lampshade. This is something else we've done all year. Historically, you would give it a gentle rub. But that's no longer the case. Now, you swing for it as hard as you can while laughing, and I have to move you out of the way quickly enough so that you don't connect with the lampshade.

Mummy kisses you goodnight and says the same thing she's always said to you, even when you were in her tummy. 'Night night, sweet sleeps, see you in the morning, love you lots, night night.'

Then it's into bed you go, but we allow you some soft-toy company. Louie is automatically included. The rest of the night-time gang varies each bedtime. Tonight, your selection is a poignant and fitting way to end the year because you choose Dory and your Arlo dinosaur. I lean into your cot and turn on Ewan, your white-noise-emitting sheep.

'Good night, buddy. I love you.'

'Buh-bye, Dadda.'

'See you in the morning.'

Your name is Arlo. You are 95 cm tall. You weigh 13.55 kg. Your favourite colour is purple, and your favourite animal is a 'baa baa'. You spend the majority of your life smiling. You have an obsession with vacuum cleaners, and you have a mummy and daddy who still remain utterly and hopelessly besotted with you.

Sleep well, son. Sweet dreams.

Toddler Inc.:
A Look To The Future

'If your toddler hasn't convinced you to question your grip on reality, then I'd wager you're an absent parent. Either that, or they haven't yet turned two ...'

Mr Jacobs

As the little boy Arlo drifted off to sleep, his unconscious mind wended its way to a golf course. Not a regular golf course. No. This was the most beautiful and visually astonishing golf course you could ever imagine. It was a thing of infinite splendour.

There was a lot of purple. The flag pins were purple, the balls were purple, the golf clubs were purple, the golf bags were purple and the golf tees were purple. Even the perfectly cut grass was purple; a cosmetic quirk that often caused golf commentators a headache because they didn't know whether to say the ball had landed on the green or landed on the purple.

Instead of using sand to fill the bunkers, the architects opted to lay large sheets of whole, unbroken crackers. Smiling-faced rainbows of different sizes arced across the purple-tinged sky.

The course was lined by sheep, cuddly soft toys from popular children's television programmes and red anthropomorphic vacuum cleaners, though again, the golfing commentators were always confused as to whether they should be called vacuum cleaners or Hoovers. The spectators looked on, watching the only golfer on the course, Mr Jacobs. He was about to tee off at the second.

Thwack!

'OK, it's good,' said the commentator. 'It's very good, it's better than good – whooaaa – can you believe it? Five hundred and sixteen yards! That's a new world record for Mr Jacobs. And would you look where it's landed, a few inches away from the hole, right on the green. Sorry, I mean the purple ... Or do I mean green? Oh, never mind. The point is you've never seen a finer display of golfing skill than you're seeing here today.'

Satisfied with his work, Mr Jacobs marched up the course. As he arrived on the green, or purple, he found Arlo waiting for him – looking crestfallen.

'Arlo, my boy, how are you?'

Arlo said nothing. Instead, he continued to study the vibrant blades of purple grass.

'Oh, I see,' Mr Jacobs said, somehow understanding why Arlo was in such low spirits. 'You believe you've failed the year, don't you? You believe that because you didn't break your parents' spirit and cripple their resolve that you've botched your first year at Toddler Inc.?'

Arlo nodded ever so slightly.

'Arlo my boy, you've nothing to worry about.'

Arlo lifted his eyes up, allowing a small amount of hope to pour through them.

'This is only Year One of Toddler Inc. It's the primaries, the preseason training, the preparation for the main event. No, you haven't failed at all. You've played your part to perfection. What you've done is lure Mummy and Daddy into a false sense of security. They believe they've left the toughest stage of parenthood behind. But of course they're wrong. They have no idea what's in store for them.'

Acknowledgements

I'm always humbled writing the acknowledgements section of a book. *Toddler Inc.* is no different. Because it reminds me of how many people lent their talents and contributed to making this book better than it could ever have been through my efforts alone.

To Ian McIlroy: I'm not sure how many times I've thanked you for editorial support over the last couple of years, but here's another one for your work on *Toddler Inc.*

Ross Dickinson, you make my books better. Period.

I'd also like to thank Martin Birse, Mark Jackson, Steph Kater and Marc Mason for reading an early draft of *Toddler Inc.* and providing me with feedback.

Thank you to the team at MiblArt who designed the book cover and layout. And thank you to Chandana Wanasekara for providing all the artwork – you over-deliver on every project.

And to Andrew Roberts: thanks for taking care of audiobook-production duties and for all the ideas you inject into the format.

To Stacey Dunkley, Arlo's friend: you helped him through an emotionally troubling time battling these scary things called emotions. I'm glad he had you to watch out for him when he started nursery. And to the folks at St. Matthews Nursery & Pre-School (Arlo's second placement): thank you for everything you have done for him.

To Haylee: Arlo doesn't have a brother or a sister, but he has you. And you're brilliant.

Mum, I don't know how you single-handedly raised a toddler. You're made of stern stuff. But can you please stop letting Arlo do whatever the fuck he wants? Or is this your revenge?

Charlene, if you cheated on me and our relationship ended horribly, I'd still love you forever for that comment on Gecko Decorating. You remain, as ever, a one-of-a-kind mummy.

Arlo. My pal, my buddy, my writing inspiration: you become more fascinating as each day passes. I think we've had our best adventures yet this year, with plenty more on the horizon. You cannot comprehend how loved you are.

Finally, to parents around the world: you know the drill – keep doing the best you can with what you've got. I'm sure you're doing a million times better than you think you are. And never forget to smile.

A Note From The Author

I need your help!

If you enjoyed *Toddler Inc.*, please consider heading over to Goodreads or wherever you buy your books and leaving a review. Tip: you can copy and paste the same review on more than one platform.

I cannot overstate how valuable and important reviews are to an author, so believe me when I say that your support is greatly appreciated.

And if you're planning to tell your mates about *Toddler Inc.*, they can find it on sale at all the big retailers (Amazon, Apple Books, Google Play, Barnes and Noble, Kobo and many more outlets). It's available in paperback, hardback, e-book and audio.

About Tom Kreffer

Tom Kreffer is the author of *Dear Dory: Journal of a Soon-to-be First-time Dad*, *Dear Arlo: Adventures in Dadding*, *Toddler Inc.*, and he is the creator of the *Adventures in Dadding Newsletter*. He loves *Star Wars* and Marvel movies, and he has a degree in film and television that he firmly believes to be worth less than a second-hand toothbrush.

He lives in Northampton, England with his family, whom he intends to exploit for many more story opportunities in the years to come.

Say Hello!

My website www.tomkreffer.com
email at tom@tomkreffer.com

www.goodreads.com/tomkreffer
www.twitter.com/tkreffer
www.instagram.com/tom_kreffer
www.facebook.com/officialtomkreffer

Want Free Stuff?

Free ebooks

I didn't write *Toddler Inc.* as a guidebook, but I have since created a series of e-books that focus specifically on dads during pregnancy and labour, and on dads and their newborn babies. These might be useful to you if you're a soon-to-be new parent or if you're expecting another child. If you head over to my website (www.tomkreffer.com), you can grab your free copy.

Adventures in Dadding Newsletter

I invite you to come and have a laugh at my expense: every month I send out a bite-size, scaled-down version of my dadding adventures, summarising the most recent tortures that parenting has thrown my way. Visit www.tomkreffer.com to join the fun.

More Titles From Tom Kreffer

Toddler Inc.: The Search For Sanity

Welcome to the terrible twos.

Where toddlers annihilate boundaries, convert your resolve into servitude and routinely imitate your worst qualities in public.

Join one father and his journal as he scribbles his way through this famously difficult stage of parenthood searching for a win, his keys and his sanity, while constantly fielding the question: 'Yes, but why, Dadda?'

Coming Soon

Dear Dory: Journal of a Soon-to-be First-time Dad

Partner Pregnant. Less than nine months to prepare. Holy s**t – you're going to be a daddy!

Now, a soon-to-be first-time father is charting a course through the perilous and choppy waters of living with a pregnant woman. He's dodging hormonal right hooks, evading emotional explosions, saying all the wrong things (like "Are you okay?"), and trying to figure out how the hell you install a car seat.

Written as a journal to his unborn child, *Dear Dory* is the unfiltered, irreverently funny, honest, and heartfelt account of one man's journey to fatherhood as he contemplates his new identity as a daddy and prepares for the responsibility of a lifetime.

Superb read

It's funny, it's crude, it's heartfelt – worth a read

Loved it
★★★★★

Couldn't put it down!

Dear Arlo: Adventures in Dadding

It begins immediately.

There's no transition period, no trial run, no supervised training, no e-learning module and no simulation that you can f**k up as many times as you need to until you get it right.

As soon as the midwife hands you your newborn baby, you are responsible for keeping it alive.

Picking up moments after *Dear Dory* ends, *Dear Arlo: Adventures in Dadding* continues the story of one dad and his journal as he strives to survive the first year of parenthood, blundering his way through bottle-sterilising, night feeds and some cataclysmic nappy changes – all while a pandemic sweeps across the planet.

*Absolutely brilliant –
I laughed and cried!*
★★★★★

*Fantastic –
couldn't put it down*
★★★★★

Pure Genius!
★★★★★

Excellent
★★★★★

www.ingramcontent.com/pod-product-compliance
Lightning Source LLC
Chambersburg PA
CBHW020727220426
43209CB00093B/1916/J